The Courtesan and the Gigolo

The Courtesan and the Gigolo

THE MURDERS IN THE RUE MONTAIGNE
AND THE DARK SIDE OF EMPIRE
IN NINETEENTH-CENTURY PARIS

Aaron Freundschuh

STANFORD UNIVERSITY PRESS
STANFORD, CALIFORNIA

Stanford University Press
Stanford, California

Printed in the United States of America on acid-free, archival-quality paper

Library of Congress Cataloging-In-Publication Data

Names: Freundschuh, Aaron, author.
Title: The courtesan and the gigolo : the murders in the Rue Montaigne and
    the dark side of empire in nineteenth-century Paris / Aaron Freundschuh.
Description: Stanford, California : Stanford University Press, 2016. |
    Includes bibliographical references and index.
Identifiers: LCCN 2016016070 (print) | LCCN 2016017175 (ebook) |
    ISBN 9781503600157 (cloth : alk. paper) | ISBN 9781503600829 (pbk. : alk.
    paper) | ISBN 9781503600973 (ebook)
Subjects: LCSH: Pranzini, Henri, 1856–1887. | Regnault, Marie, 1848–1887. |
    Murder—France—Paris—History—19th century. |
    Murder—Investigation—France—History—19th century. | Trials
    (Murder)—France—History—19th century. |
    Xenophobia—France—History—19th century. | France—History—Third
    Republic, 1870–1940.
Classification: LCC DC337 .F855 2016 (print) | LCC DC337 (ebook) |
    DDC 364.152/30944361—dc23
LC record available at https://lccn.loc.gov/2016016070

Typeset by Bruce Lundquist in 11/14 Adobe Garamond Pro

Contents

The Courtesan and the Gigolo

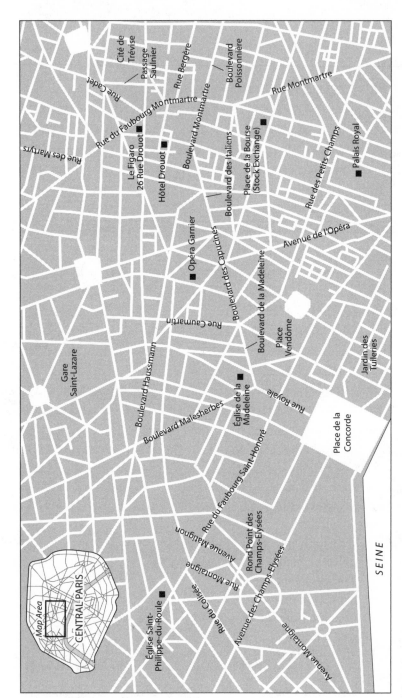

Map. The Right Bank: west-central Paris in 1887.

Introduction

Thursday, March 17, 1887

The first body was that of a woman about 40 years old. She was lying prostrate on a bloodied rug in the boudoir, her head and lower legs protruding from beneath two ends of a red satin quilt. Her neck and shoulder had been opened by a blade. She died less than a step from her canopied pediment bed, a monolith of dark wood in the style of Louis XVI that was topped with sculpted statuettes of children and aristocratic insignias. Her chestnut hair, streaked with gray, was draped over her shoulder and flowed onto the floor. According to the police report, the quilt was drawn back to reveal the victim's bloodied nightgown and, snug around her biceps, a pearl-studded arm bracelet made of gold.

The bedroom curtains were closed when they found her, the nightlight wick still burning on the chimney hearth at 11:15 a.m. on the day of Mid-Lent, a raucous street extravaganza. The houses of government were closed for the day. Outside in the streets, Paris's legion of laundry service workers prepared their parade floats, donning Rabelaisian costumes and steeling themselves against the cold with song and laughter and drink.

At the opposite end of the long corridor spanning the apartment, near the second bedroom, the police spotted another corpse in a massive pool of blood. On the bed inside that bedroom lay yet another body, that of a young girl. But to any vice squad cop with passing knowledge of the sexual underworld that flourished in nineteenth-century Paris, the apartment's sensuous surfaces, its blend of baroque and Oriental markers of status, and its location just steps from the Champs-Elysées all readily identified it as the home of an elite prostitute.

On a cabinet near the bed, investigators found a short letter, preserved today in Parisian archives, addressed to "Mme Montille, 17 rue Montaigne." This was precisely the sort of faux-aristocratic pseudonym that courtesans often used to mask their identities while nurturing sexual fantasies. The letter's breezy affection suggested that it had come from a regular client; likewise the crabbed handwriting, which veered in disregard of the stationery lines and would have made the task of deciphering it difficult for the uninitiated, to say nothing of the violet inkblots marring both sides of the sheet, which the sender creased and crammed into an envelope no wider than a fist.

The letter alludes to a deal struck recently in the French city of Nancy, a business engagement undertaken on behalf of Madame de Montille herself. The author asks for a meeting at a Parisian theater, a common rendezvous point for prostitutes and their clients. The signature reads "Gaston." Based on the postmark, the letter arrived sometime late in the day on March 16, the prior evening, when the Mid-Lenten festivities were already getting under way in some parts of the city.

The local police commissary called to the scene telegraphed word of the murders to the Paris Police Prefecture on the Île de la Cité. Then he sealed off the boudoir until investigators arrived. News of a triple homicide in this part of city was sure to spread fast. At hand were the final moments of tranquility in the brief and forgotten history of the rue Montaigne.[1]

AS INVESTIGATORS knew only too well, the rue Montaigne tragedy was the latest in a series of unsolved murders targeting women of the Parisian demimonde. In the preceding eight years the police had struggled to make any headway in solving the crimes, and Parisians, goaded by newspaper reporters, were growing anxious. The rue Montaigne case would attract far more scrutiny, not least because of Madame de Montille's status. As a courtesan, she belonged to an ethereal rank of sex workers known for fabulous prosperity. This class of "kept" women enjoyed a standing that sometimes permitted them to live every bit as luxuriously as their wealthy clients, of whom they took their pick. Attuned to market forces, the cleverest courtesans thus negotiated from a position of strength. Some amassed sizable jewelry collections and investment portfolios, including real estate holdings. In the prevailing logic of sex commerce, these material possessions in turn enhanced their desirability and drove their clients to ever greater expenditure.

Courtesans ensorcelled the general public, too: Madame de Montille's death was covered extensively by foreign correspondents who were long in the habit of keeping New Yorkers, Londoners, and Berliners apprised of the great scandals and lurid crime stories that animated Paris, the city then widely viewed as the primary node of Western culture. As the case of the murders in the rue Montaigne descended into scandal during the spring and summer of 1887, newspaper readers around the world thrilled to the implausible twists of a cause-célèbre on par with any in living memory. In Paris the investigation entered criminal lore even as it became enmeshed in a yearlong political crisis that culminated in the fall of French president Jules Grévy.

Why, then, has this string of prostitute murders faded into such obscurity that today's Parisians can recall nothing of it? Timing, in large part. The rue Montaigne investigation predates the first of the Jack the Ripper murders in East London by little more than a year. In fact, London's initial response to the Whitechapel slayings was to recall the rue Montaigne— "the only parallel to the 'East-end murders' with which the annals of crime in the French metropolis have furnished us for a long time," observed the *Daily Telegraph*[2]—and the Ripper investigation quickly took on a life of its own. Over time, Ripper lore eclipsed the Parisian cases in popular memory and scholarly interest: A steady output of fictionalizations, films, comics, and academic studies now fall under the rubric Ripperology, which has no Parisian equivalent.[3]

The murders of London and Paris bear notable points of convergence, beginning with the outsize role of the mass press, which by the late 1880s had become a blinding industrial ream, saturating the streets and boulevards with paper, much of it printed with tales of hideous criminality.[4] Both capitals were the seats of rapidly expanding global empires, and both were then experiencing major growth and social transformation brought by tides of mass immigration. In Britain the so-called foreign element competed with the working poor for jobs. Journalists found an eager readership for their investigative coverage of "Outcast London," where many immigrants were forced to settle. Rumor had it that the Ripper was a cosmopolitan infiltrator or enemy within—a Russian Jewish immigrant, some said. The cultural historian Judith Walkowitz has written eloquently about this peculiar fear of the lowly outsider in London, a capital that "epitomized the power of the empire but also its vulnerability."[5]

During the same period, comparable political dynamics and social anxieties were transforming the Parisian landscape, particularly amid the spike in immigration that occurred between the mid-1870s and the mid-1880s (Italians and Belgians being the two most represented national groups; they were joined by Jews fleeing persecution in Eastern Europe). For the first time in modern French history, immigration became a political keyword and the subject of sustained legal discussion as politicians spent the better part of the 1880s scrambling to restrict and codify French citizenship.[6]

Yet the murders of London and Paris bore as many contrasts as similarities, starting with the symbolic geography of the crimes and the social station of the victims. In a more rapid succession, the London killer (or killers) preyed on streetwalkers, who counted among the poorest and most marginalized women in the city; the victims in Paris, on the other hand, had climbed higher in the byzantine hierarchy of the local sex trade and were generally less vulnerable as a result. And whereas "Whitechapel" was shorthand for mean streets and the rugged cosmopolitanism of immigrant workers, refugees, and the poor, the Parisian demimonde was a seamy underbelly thriving about the majestic Grands Boulevards, the paragons of modern bourgeois life.

But the most glaring distinction between the two series of murders was that no one was ever seriously implicated in London. Police in France questioned suspects along the way, foreign nationals usually, but they only began to feel confident that they had found their man a few days after the discovery of the murders in the rue Montaigne. In what was immediately heralded as a major breakthrough, Enrico Pranzini, an Egyptian migrant of Italian parentage, emerged as the prime suspect in the rue Montaigne case and soon after in the other demimondaine murders. So certain of Pranzini's guilt were investigators that they also sought to tie him to a cluster of cold cases in other parts of France.

ALTHOUGH it was a spectacle to be behold, Pranzini's capture was not the stuff of crime fiction: There were no mind-bending deductions involved, no dramatic pursuits, and little in the way of a climactic confrontation. Instead, on a Sunday evening in the southern port city of Marseille, local police seized Pranzini during an intermission at the city's famed Grand Théâtre, where he was taking in a production of *The Barber of Seville*. In his narrow-brimmed hat and black overcoat, the suspect looked the part of a debonair fellow about town, and he was briskly surrounded and removed to the Marseille Police Prefecture for identification and questioning. Putting up no resistance, he provided the name of his hotel, and a search of his room was promptly conducted.

The police were merely following up on a tip they had received earlier that day from one of Marseille's ill-reputed quarters. According to witnesses, Pranzini had entered a brothel in the afternoon and paid for a threesome with two female prostitutes; afterward he offered them some jewelry, arousing the suspicions of the brothel manager. Later, officers sent to Pranzini's hotel to collect his belongings learned that he had checked in as "Dr. E. Pranzini, Swedish doctor." Asked about the alias, Pranzini shrugged and denied involvement in criminal activity. In his room were a small amount of cash, a square basket, a valise, and a satchel. Police found nothing manifestly incriminating, such as a weapon, or any other evidence that might link Pranzini to Madame de Montille. But Pranzini did have two small cuts on his fingers, which doctors in Paris would soon examine.

Far more important than the cuts, from the point of view of reporters and investigators, was the considerable stash of love letters that Pranzini kept in his satchel, tucked alongside some female garments and bespoke feminine handkerchiefs. These trifles sustained the image of Pranzini as a wily rake, an "Oriental Don Juan" whose distinguished features and worldliness enabled him to seduce well-to-do women and then to prevail upon them to part with their valuables. Investigators spent months uncovering Pranzini's history of treating his lovers' gifts as personal income and their residences as his own.[7]

In modern parlance, Enrico Pranzini was a gigolo, a term coined, fittingly enough, in nineteenth-century Paris. For his part he did not deny his colorful sexual past, yet he saw nothing sinister in his relations with women who were, as he saw it, generous and accommodating, if uncommonly so; thanks to them, stretches of his adult life had passed in a kind of genteel poverty. The pursuit of women of means or name by an aspirational young outsider was not in itself the calling card of a mass murderer,

Figure 1. A sensational rendition of Pranzini's capture at Marseille's Grand Théâtre.
La Revue Illustrée, 10 April 1887.

Pranzini objected. After all, much of the best French fiction and poetry of the nineteenth century was littered with the broken dreams of male arrivistes trying to seduce their way upward. By the mid-1880s that literary scenario had become a cliché of modern Paris, a city, insisted Europeans and Americans, that was awash in the unspeakable currencies of pornography, gutter journalism, and racy art.[8]

But the Oriental gigolo was decidedly more sexually ambiguous, hedonistic, and worldly than the social climbers of Stendhal and Balzac: Drawing on Pranzini's widely publicized adventures overseas, contemporaries infused the gigolo type with the colonial exotic. Pranzini spoke seven languages and, at age 30, cut an impressive figure. His shoulders were round, his thighs thick and muscular. He had an unblemished complexion above his beard, a faddishly trimmed growth flecked with amber. His gaze was soft, confident. In a photograph taken shortly after his arrest, we see him standing in the middle of a room, encircled by ogling members of the police staff. He stares into the distance as though to contemplate his predicament and whether it might be recognized for the case of mistaken identity he swore it to be.

Almost without delay, Pranzini—or transparent fictionalizations of him—began to appear in the pages of the great literary figures of the age. At least one artist in Montmartre said that he had seen Pranzini, or a group of his co-conspirators, in action: Vincent Van Gogh, who followed the investigation for months along with his friend Paul Gauguin, insisted that he had overheard the plotting of the rue Montaigne murders at the Café du Tambourin, a hangout where his paintings were displayed.[9] Meanwhile, New Yorkers read that Pranzini had lately seduced and deflowered a Manhattanite tourist in Paris; and Londoners grappled with the news that Enrico Pranzini had served in British imperial expeditions to Afghanistan and Sudan. In the spring of 1888 an exhibit at Madame Tussaud's museum containing a likeness of the "foreign-born" Pranzini was viewed by 28,000 spectators in a single day.[10]

Why, in a year rife with consequential news, were so many people taken in by the biography of an impecunious migrant from Egypt? In this, the first full-scale history of the murders in the rue Montaigne, I attempt to answer this question by drawing on contemporary testimonies, private letters and diaries, juridical records, press accounts, diplomatic and military correspondence, and a variety of other sources pertaining to the case.[11] The Pranzini investigation was unique in its global scale, a necessity given the suspect's itinerant life and his unwavering denials of wrongdoing, which he repeated under weeks of strenuous interrogation and in an epic courtroom trial.[12] In addition to policemen, forensics experts, and newspapermen, diplomats were drawn into the investigation, as were colonial military figures, doctors and scientific researchers, colonial entrepreneurs, and other settlers

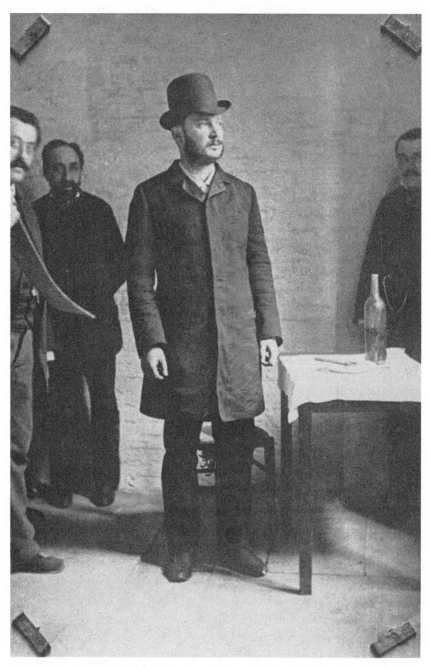

Figure 2. Pranzini, photographed with investigators following his arrest. Roger-Viollet Collection. ©The Image Works.

in the East. The ambiance was tense with rivalry: These professionals, who culled evidence from four regions of the world and, in some cases, from their own colonial knowledge, latched onto Pranzini as an opportunity to build their public reputations. I retrace their steps, giving special attention to how they made Pranzini's story their own.

Born and raised in the colonial port of Alexandria, Pranzini thought of the Islamic Ottoman Empire as his homeland. To Parisians, he was an "Arab-speaking Levantine," a hybrid of East and West who, in this era of "scientific" racism, exemplified an inferior racial constitution. Pranzini was also classified as a *rastaquouère*, a neologism that was originally a racial slur against Latin Americans and that subsequently carried the suggestion of low-life criminality, cloak-and-dagger sexual intrigue, cosmopolitan infiltration, and an alluring but seedy colonial glamour washing up on the Grands Boulevards.[13] I examine both pejoratives within the expansive sweep of stereotypes then taking root in the mass press, which fanned the flames of anti-immigrant and anti-Semitic politics.[14]

Unprecedented in the case of Pranzini was his alleged amalgamation of the two colonial types, Levantine and rastaquouère, which brings to mind the nineteenth-century myth of a "Latino-Mediterranean" race in colonial North Africa. That construct had a pro-colonial purpose, specifically because it was set in opposition to the Orientalist stereotype of the "nomadic Arab," who stood for the dregs of colonial mobility and who was effectively excluded from metropolitan France.[15] In contrast, the investigators in the Pranzini case called the public's attention to the suspect's ambition, opportunism, debauchery, and lawlessness. Consequently, in the spring of 1887 and afterward, Enrico Pranzini became a metonym of the dark side of European empire and, as such, a repository for national anxieties and undigested animus—by-products, in some measure, of republican France's hasty construction of a worldwide empire by means of military conquest and violent repression.

However, unlike the colonial caricatures of nineteenth-century Paris, where it was common to disparage marginal social groups as "Redskins" or "Apaches,"[16] the Levantine and rastaquouère types channeled prejudices related to migration, the sort that circulated within ethnically European colonial and migrant communities overseas, where settlers fretted ceaselessly about racial and social boundaries.[17] Particularly widespread in European colonies were concerns about purportedly hypersexualized colonial males and the related peril of "inappropriate intimacies" with European, or "white," women. By its transposition of these fears into the metropolitan context, the Pranzini investigation requires us to view "metropolitan and colonial histories in a conjoined analytic frame," as the historian Ann Laura Stoler has suggested.[18]

Doing so with the Pranzini case reveals, among other things, how unstable and blurry the presumed subject-object relationship between European nations and their overseas colonies could be. Pranzini's native-level fluency in French marked him as a bona fide product of France's imperial project in Egypt, but he was also manifestly the son of the Ottoman and British Empires. Moreover, the arrival of this culturally fluent foreigner in the metropole occurred as the Third Republic was taking pains to invent a homogeneous national identity and displace persistent regionalisms, especially rival dialects.[19]

"What a singular kind, this Levantine," wrote a Parisian journalist of Pranzini. "In order to have seen his likes, one needs to have traveled."[20] Pranzini's presence in the imperial capital, let alone his enactment of the privileged role of the *flâneur* who bathed in the crowds and basked in the gaslight of the Grands Boulevards, was an occurrence that Parisians invested with the direst implications. To understand why requires a brief look at the political storms that roiled Paris in the 1880s, one of the most enigmatic and transformative decades in modern European history.

THE FRENCH THIRD REPUBLIC rose feebly in 1871, the orphan of two disasters: a humiliating defeat in the Franco-Prussian War of 1870, followed by a brief but bloody civil war, the Paris Commune, in the following spring. Few gave the unloved *République* much chance for survival. Its most hard-line detractors, antirepublicans of all stripes who disdained parliamentary democracy as an execrable form of compromise, announced their intention to tear down *La Gueuse*—"The Wench"—from within.

But by the end of the 1870s, republican politicians were unexpectedly proving themselves adept at the ballot box. Led by the visionary Jules Ferry and under the stewardship of President Jules Grévy, the Opportunist republicans—liberal free-trade centrists—dominated the national government between 1879 and 1885, pushing through a series of important reforms, among them the legalization of divorce and the abolition of press censorship. They undertook massive public works projects, including a national railway system, which stimulated exchanges between the nation's disparate regions.

They also fought off fierce objections to their plans for an imperialist republic. For that reason historians have sometimes interpreted nation building and empire building as parallel, or even mutually reinforcing enterprises in which the "civilizing mission" of the "inferior races" echoes the "republic of schoolteachers" created at home. In a classic formulation, the historian Eugen Weber described the "internal colonization" of the French provinces by Paris, a metaphor that soldered republican conquest to nation making in the historical imagination of the Third Republic.[21]

It is true that the "République coloniale" sold extremely well in Paris.[22] Recent histories of French and British colonial "heroes" have shown how colonial culture flowered in Paris and London in the latter part of the nineteenth century. Imperialism trumpeted manliness just as it flattered national pride.[23] Into the modern European pantheon walked men such as the "Imperial Saint" Charles Gordon, who was memorialized at Madame Tussaud's, as well as Henry Morton Stanley and Pierre Savorgnan de Brazza. By putting a "recognizable, human face" on adventurism in Africa and Asia, writes historian Edward Berenson, these men "allowed citizens to understand overseas expansion as a series of extraordinary personal quests."[24] In short order, Britain and France, liberal democracies in name, cobbled together the two largest territorial dominions in world history.

By assembling the stories of people whose lives collided during the case of the murders in the rue Montaigne, in this book I present a darker version of the Age of Empire. The night of March 16–17, 1887, triggered the first global murder investigation. It was a substantial undertaking that ultimately cast Enrico Pranzini as a new criminal archetype: the male colonial antihero who returns unbidden to wreak havoc in the metropole, in this instance as a violent foreign parasite on the French sexual economy. By the end of the century the French *Dictionnaire Larousse* would include an entry for Pranzini, making plain his cultural significance as a shadowy doppelgänger, "an adventurer of the worst kind."[25]

It is no accident that the 1880s marked a high point for fictional antiheroes sketched in colonial hues by best-selling authors who made use of the Levantine and rastaquouère types.[26] Émile Zola's *Money* (1890–1891) traces the rise and fall of the stock market fraudster Aristide Saccard, a would-be economic imperialist with a crooked construction scheme in the eastern

Mediterranean. Guy de Maupassant's *Bel-Ami* (1885) tracks the womanizing Georges Duroy, a master manipulator who returns from a presumably deeply corrupting tour as a colonial soldier in Algeria. Then there is Jean des Esseintes of Joris-Karl Huysmans's novel *Against the Grain* (1884). Des Esseintes spurns heroism altogether, preferring to retreat into a dreamy, aestheticized domesticity in which he contemplates the decline of Rome and muses on the decadence of modern times. Each of these protagonists unveils, more or less subtly, the rotting floorboards on which trod the nation's colonial "heroes."

In the real-life drama of Enrico Pranzini we find evidence to challenge a founding myth of modern imperialism, one that recent cultural histories have left mostly intact: colonial conquest and adventurism overseas acted principally as an annealing force on the nation, a catalyst of stability and security. Undergirding this myth is the assumption, stubborn and widespread, that the conquering European nation-state, at least, stood to benefit from the colonial relationship.[27] This was an article of faith for men like Ferry, who argued in a famous 1884 speech that military conquest abroad would fortify France while promising commercial advantages.[28]

The turbulence that imperialism unleashed on the metropole, its nonmaterial cost, was left unspoken by both Ferry and his anticolonial rivals, who were led by Georges Clémenceau for the better part of the 1880s. Supporters of the colonial policy reached for upsides wherever they could be found. The social theorist Gabriel Tarde, to cite one prominent intellectual, held that a French empire would make the streets safer at home. Tarde hypothesized that colonial warfare and criminal activity came from the same well of deleterious social energies, or "criminal passions."[29] On that basis he concluded that colonial combat would serve as preventive crime policy by draining violent impulses from the metropole and channeling them toward distant locales.[30] Here was one of the grimmer undertows of the Republic's "civilizing mission."[31]

This book's microhistorical approach to empire shows how colonial expansion worked at cross purposes with the law-and-order politics that many centrist republicans shared with their upstart nationalist rivals on the right. How did it happen that the Third Republic's imperial turn coincided so neatly with a heightened sense of vulnerability in the metropole in the 1880s and 1890s? Leading historians such as Dominique Kalifa have documented the "security obsession" that took hold of the public mind and made "insécurité urbaine" (urban insecurity) a mainstay of contemporary French politics.[32] How are we to square the reassuring tales of French military triumph around the globe with Parisians' susceptibility to newspaper stories about a chimeric "army of crime" in the streets and xenophobic screeds that stirred fears of porous borders, spies, and immigrant malfeasance?[33] In the absence of statistical evidence to prove any of this, Ferry and his allies enacted some of the most draconian anticrime legislation in all of French history.[34]

By the end of 1887 the "Pranzini affair" had, to an unprecedented degree, drawn together two vibrant realms of the Parisian social imaginary: the colonial and the criminal. The case prompted Tarde to reflect on the traumas of colonial failure in an articulation of what I call imperial insecurity.[35] At bottom, the Pranzini phenomenon symbolized the erosion of the boundary between the metropole and its colonies—a social and geographic segregation, at once unrealistic and sacrosanct, that European colonial rulers strained themselves to enforce.[36] Pranzini stoked fears of the social backwash of overseas empire, a turnabout known to specialists of contemporary British literature as reverse colonization.[37] Would the Republic show itself incapable of channeling violence unilaterally toward the colonial world as Tarde and others hoped?

A report that the public prosecutor filed on the eve of Pranzini's trial contains a reflection: "The necessity [of murder] was not going to stop a man who was accustomed to the bloody spectacles of African wars."[38] The remark was meant to reinforce the prosecution's argument that Pranzini's placid demeanor was fundamentally deceptive; yet it can be read as a passing acknowledgment that the violence inherent in imperial conquest would not remain *over there* and may well return with migrants or colonial war veterans, even those like Pranzini who did not perform combat roles.

Inevitably, Pranzini became fodder in the raging immigration debate. At the time, the number of arrivals from the colonial world remained "extremely low" statistically, according to Gérard Noiriel, France's preeminent immigration historian.[39] Yet the case unearths a precocious cultural *imagining* of colonial (and postcolonial) immigration to the hexagon, including its latent associations with criminality. In the wake of the Pranzini affair the political "problem" of immigration was understood as unavoidably linked to the future of the republican empire.[40] The relation between these two issues grew only more complex in subsequent generations.

Recalling the frenetic "hunt" for Arabs living in metropolitan France during the Algerian War, Frantz Fanon diagnosed a collective psychosis that caused "even a South American man" to be "riddled with bullets because he looked North African."[41] The Pranzini case prefigured the sort of categorical confusions related by Fanon, and is best understood as a symptom of colonial transition and crisis.[42] Xenophobic sentiments aggravated these confusions while engendering ever more categorization. The Pranzini affair, a transformative episode in the history of foreignness in France, offers a case study in the ways that xenophobia racialized, classed, sexualized, and gendered its object.[43]

It bears mentioning that Enrico Pranzini was not the only border-crossing murder suspect to stand trial in the 1880s, but merely the best-known among several whom one journalist dubbed the "great lords of crime."[44] Their surnames, uniformly European, splashed across the front pages at nearly regular intervals: Gruem, Rossel, Prado, Campi, and Eyraud. Upon arrest, each man had either returned from or absconded to colonies overseas: The technologies of mobility that conduced national cohesion were the means by which they communicated and transported themselves. Each was portrayed as a virtuoso of prestidigitation, capable of unsheathing his identity at will (Campi's real name was never ascertained); of putting up a gentlemanly front and deploying novel techniques (on the telephone, Eyraud had impersonated others before his arrest in Spanish Cuba); and of slipping away by boat or rapid train (Rossel was arrested in Algeria).[45] Their misadventures, and the labor of the policemen and reporters who pursued them, belong to the history of colonial culture too. They made their mark in a world that was rapidly globalizing through imperialism; the dread and fascination they provoked were a hallmark of European life by the early twentieth century, when the *Encyclopedia Britannica* registered a "peculiar feature in modern crime," to wit, "the extensive scale on which it is carried out. The greatest frauds are now commonly perpetrated; great robberies are planned in one capital and executed in another. The whole is worked by wide associations of cosmopolitan criminals."[46]

CHAPTER ONE

Elite Cosmopolitanism and Gentrification in Western Paris

The murders in the rue Montaigne delivered a collective shock that was, at the outset at least, primarily due to the address of the crime scene. The area around the lower Champs-Elysées was a Milky Way of gorgeous limestone-fronted construction and high living. The newspaper reporter Georges Grison described the neighborhood's social character as "semi-bourgeois, semi-aristocratic," for it stood at the crossroads of modern cosmopolitan, aristocratic, and republican cultures.[1] As Grison knew better than anyone, these factors would inform the authorities' investigation just as they colored the newspaper coverage of the murders in fundamental ways. The city's last sensational multiple homicide, the Troppmann murders of 1869, were every bit as gruesome and involved even more victims. Yet the rue Montaigne case was categorically different, Grison concluded. Whereas the Troppmann tragedy had taken place in the middle of a "deserted field" on the industrial fringe to the city's northeast, the 1887 murders upended an "elegant quarter."[2]

THE NEIGHBORHOOD had not always been so pristine, to say the least. Just four decades earlier, a coalition of local businessmen and residents had banded together in a petition to brush up the neighborhood's image. At that time, and for as long as anyone could remember, the tree-lined path that intersected the lower roundabout of the Champs-Elysées had been known as Allée des Veuves (Widows' Alley). Despite the whiff of the macabre, the name's origins lie in an odd sort of euphemism, one that by the late 1840s had begun to seem coarse to the new waves of people settling there.

That was because the path's reputation was that of a notorious axis of the Parisian night, until recently embedded in an otherwise pastoral area. Back in the eighteenth century the lower Champs-Elysées was, by day, a pleasurable promenade, where fashionable members of high society removed themselves from the stench and gargoyles of central Paris. But at sundown a different crowd set upon the place to engage in unsavory commerce and revelry.

Yes, the petitioners conceded, the lower Champs-Elysées had long served as a "discreet haven for sex of a more or less delicate nature."[3] In fact, the area was neither delicate nor terribly discreet, the absence of lights notwithstanding. Generations of Parisian whores—the aforementioned "widows"—gathered along the path at night, alongside "libertines" and scofflaws who took advantage of its rustic character.

In earlier times the area had been a marshy green with a higgledy-piggledy collection of plots, plantations dotted with farmers' huts, and, farther out, a few hamlets; tree nurseries and thatched houses provided cover for the denizens' adventures in congress. At night they sneaked past the city limit just beyond the Tuileries and the place de la Concorde, where the name Champs-Elysées was bestowed upon a muddy slope with an unguessed destiny. The heterosexual and homosexual prostitution that persisted in the brothels around the Champs-Elysées well into the nineteenth century were an open secret, as the petitioners pointed out.[4] Out alone for a walk one evening in the early 1830s, the young Victor Hugo chanced upon Widows' Alley. Hugo was reciting his own poetry aloud when a lookout man, stationed on Widows' Alley to protect the homosexuals gathering, warded off the unwanted visitor.[5]

Our petitioners were adept in the jargon of development and progress, and their demand was straightforward. They wanted the prefect to scratch "Widows' Alley" from the map. In those days, Parisians thought of their city as a work in progress much more than as a historic jewel to be preserved. Like every nascent political regime, developers and neighborhood groups

saw the renaming of streets as a potent and inexpensive means of recon-
stituting the city and eliminating untoward echoes of the past, naughty or
otherwise.

The petitioners were probably aware that the terrain situated roughly
midway between the place de la Concorde and the Étoile was a perennial
target of revamping schemes, both substantial and cosmetic, that aimed
at the creation of a suburban zone of upper-crust entertainments. These
attempts often ended in comic failure, which is a little puzzling given the
desirable location. The most grandiose flop of all was Le Colisée de Paris,
a massive open-air venue designed by the famed architect Le Camus de
Mézières and wedged between Widows' Alley and the Champs-Elysées in
the 1770s. Envisioned as an answer to London's successful Vauxhall Gardens, the rotunda structure housed dance halls and shops. It attracted the
likes of Marie-Antoinette, but then languished and went bankrupt after
just a decade.[6]

Then arrived another developer with a grand vision, Marie-Antoinette's
brother-in-law, the swashbuckling, debt-ridden Count d'Artois, brother of
future King Louis XVI. He called his plan for the land Nouvelle Améri-
que. At its center would be the place Benjamin Franklin, with surrounding
streets named in honor of other American revolutionary heroes.[7] Before it
could be developed, the French Revolution of 1789 intervened: The count's
property was seized, along with a large parcel of land belonging to the Catholic Church and situated due west of Widows' Alley.

Predictably the count soured on revolutionaries of all stripes during
his long exile. Decades later, as the ultraconservative Restoration King
Charles X, he ordered the erection of a statue of Louis XV on horseback in
the middle of the Rond Point des Champs-Elysées (this time the 1830 revolution forced him to abdicate, and the statue was not completed).[8] In the
meantime, France's first roller coasters (*montagnes russes*, as they were known:
"Russian mountains") had been constructed as part of an amusement park
on an adjacent property first developed by Nicolas Beaujon, a provincial
financier who had gotten rich under the ancien régime. There were safety
issues at the park, however, and after a war commissary fractured his skull in
an accident, the police outlawed risky thrill seeking for a time. It hardly mattered. Paris's growth made speculation and further residential settlement in
the area a foregone conclusion. The city's population, which doubled twice
between 1789 and 1914, began to burst through the fortification walls. More

developers swooped in, and a cosmopolitan neighborhood grew up where Beaujon's park had entertained an international crowd (Russian soldiers had briefly camped on the Champs-Elysées after Napoleon I's defeat).[9]

The foul reputation of Widows' Alley survived nonetheless, thanks to Eugène Sue's novel about the urban underworld, *Les mystères de Paris* (1842–1843), an international sensation that is still read today. Sue used the path, almost from the first page, as the setting for underhanded conspiracies, thereby cementing Widows' Alley in popular lore.

It was then that the petitioners moved to control the damage.

To hear them tell it, the cleanup around the Rond-Point des Champs-Elysées had already been so thorough that Widows' Alley was no longer consonant with the quarter's social milieu, a gentry who, it was implied, kept their prostitutes indoors, and who were more used to reading about criminality in the press than acknowledging it in their midst. They assured the prefect in their petition that the spread of "law-abiding lifestyles has erased the memory of another age's loose morals. With the Champs-Elysées having now become, as was its mythological destiny, a retreat for pure spirits, we believe that the infamy of Widows' Alley has been buried beneath the ruins of the little houses that formerly lined it."

The petitioners proposed avenue Montaigne to replace Widows' Alley, a choice that requires some explaining, given that a small portion of Widows' Alley that shot directly off the other side of the Rond-Point des Champs-Elysées had been spruced up lately and had been renamed avenue Matignon. Logically, then, the petitioners could have requested that their portion of the old path be treated as a continuation of it. Instead, they expressed a wish to be attached, if only symbolically, to the rue Montaigne, a tiny spoke that rose in a northerly direction rather at odds with Widows' Alley.

The calculation behind their choice to connect to the rue Montaigne was limpid enough to any observer. It was because the rue Montaigne anchored the modern, prosperous neighborhood then taking form in the lower Champs-Elysées. In its salons commingled old blood and new money, high culture and hints of the elite cosmopolitanism that enticed artists and financiers from all corners of the earth. Planned back in 1795 and cut into the ground where the Colisée de Paris had been, the street stood a mere 300 meters in length, straight as a pin and just wide enough to fit two large carriages side by side. During the course of the nineteenth century it gained a reputation as a quiet residential jewel, an enviable enclave of comfort and affluence for any neighborhood association to emulate. In its modest-sized buildings, poets with their mistresses frolicked, politicians conspired, and diplomats fraternized.

The prefect approved the proposal, and the avenue Montaigne was born.

Critics recognized the name change for what it was: a whitewashing by neighborhood actors who were bent on socially rebranding the place. The disappearance of Widows' Alley augured the extinction of the underground in this part of the city, and it left the writer Paul Féval with a bout of *nostalgie de la boue* that also afflicted some of his colleagues. Féval grumbled that "self-respecting people" *would* "still call it Widows' Alley."[10] Before long, he embarked on a career as a successful crime novelist in the mold of Eugène Sue.

BY THE LATE 1840s, bankers, brokers, industrialists, lawyers, investors, and developers had amassed great wealth and were taking credit for Paris's transformation into the world's largest manufacturing city. Brimming with confidence, they changed the rules and set about building what soon would be known as the "new" Paris. It was they who had put Louis-Philippe on the throne back in 1830. As though in acknowledgment of his debt to them, the king became the *only* French monarch ever to don the three-piece suit, the bourgeois costume par excellence. It would not be enough to save him during the revolutionary upheaval of 1848, when he fled to Britain disguised as a peasant.

It was amid the bumpy and unforeseen regression from the so-called bourgeois monarchy to a Bonapartist regime that the Widows' Alley petition was published. The timing could not have been better.

Louis-Napoleon Bonaparte, Napoleon I's nephew, assumed the title Emperor Napoleon III when he revived the family name and founded the Second Empire (1852–1870).Like his uncle, Napoleon III had not spent a significant period of time in Paris before adulthood, so he was not burdened by a nostalgia that might have checked his controversial and thoroughgoing urbanism. He hired a seasoned prefect, Baron Haussmann, who liked to call himself a "demolition artist."[11]

Scrambling to absorb what was still largely an internally French migration, the duo felled enormous tracts of the built environment, annexed the city's surrounding terrains, expanded to the twenty arrondissements of today—the Champs-Elysées is the linchpin of the 8th arrondissement. The winding alleyways of medieval Paris gave way to wide corridors and attractive apartment buildings whose ornate facades glowed and smiled when looked upon by the springtime sun.

Napoleon *le petit*, as Hugo called the usurping nephew, also tried his hand at foreign invasion, but he possessed none of his uncle's military genius. Both Bonapartes made indelible marks on western Paris: Napoleon I made the Champs-Elysées into an axis of military commemoration, with the Arc de Triomphe (completed in the 1830s) built on the raised roundabout on the avenue's western end; Napoleon III had a taste for monumental construction too, but he was just as interested in the more quotidian matters of dwelling space, traffic, and parks.[12] His work around the lower Champs-Elysées made it welcoming to neighborhood children, who used it as a park for recreation. By the mid-1860s the staggering elegance of it all nearly palliated the experience of capitalist authoritarianism. Great artists, more than they had ever before, appreciated the Parisian landscape as a subject worthy of high art.[13]

The Grands Boulevards, the regime's crowning achievement, offered sight lines to the first modernist painters, the Impressionists, who chronicled the rise of the bourgeoisie in the 2nd, 8th, and 9th arrondissements. The boulevards drew these parcels together, easing the commute between the stock exchange, banks, theaters, and nightlife.[14] Understandably, elites fancied Haussmann's boulevards as their "fiefdom," as the journalist Gustave Claudin recalled. "By virtue of a selection that was contested by nobody, one was admitted only on the basis of a superiority or originality of one sort or another. It was as though there existed an invisible moral barrier that denied access to this stretch of land to the people of mediocrity, insignificance, and colorlessness."[15]

Small wonder, then, that around the same time Parisians began to speak of artistic modernism, they also coined the term *embourgeoisement*, which predates its English equivalent, gentrification, by roughly a century. *Embourgeoisement* (an overliteral translation of the term would be "bourgeoisification") referred to the perceptible segregation of the city by social class. Real estate speculation drove up prices, and rents soared. In policy terms, social homogenization was not an unintended consequence of Haussmannization but instead one of its goals; housing for the poor in the city's center came under the pickax with nothing proposed to replace it. The real estate market around the Champs-Elysées skyrocketed.[16]

By the time Madame Régine de Montille moved there in the mid-1880s from an apartment near the Grands Boulevards, such a decampment would

have demanded little adaption in social terms and no obstacles as it pertained to everyday movement about town. In the afternoon initiates of
high society, *le monde*, congregated in gilded carriages around the Champs-
Elysées and cruised together; in the evening they rolled up the rue des Martyrs and went slumming in Montmartre's bohemian taverns.[17]

Society painters who were in search of quarters unmarked by social tension gravitated to the 8th arrondissement. One thinks of two paintings
signed in the politically turbulent year of 1877, when the crisis of 16 May
nearly brought the Third Republic to an end. Gustave Caillebotte's masterwork, *Paris Street; Rainy Day*, fixes the viewer's gaze on the sheen of prim
streets, well-brushed shoes, and the small-bore dramas of the New Paris—a
crush of oversize umbrellas passing on a narrow sidewalk. The second painting, Jean Béraud's *Sunday at the Church of Saint-Philippe-du-Roule, Paris*,
lauds the city's incorporation and rapid development of the old farming
hamlet of Roule. The sociability of the lower Champs-Elysées was a favorite
subject of Béraud's, and in *Sunday* he conveys the church's well-turned-

Figure 3. Jean Béraud's *Sunday at the Church of Saint-Philippe-du-Roule, Paris*, 1877.
Oil on canvas. Gift of Mr. and Mrs. William B. Jaffe, 1955. © The Metropolitan
Museum of Art. Image Source: Art Resource, New York.

out parishioners, of whom Madame de Montille would soon became one. The parishioners are exiting the church after mass. A little girl stands closest to us in the foreground, clasping a woman's hand and preparing to cross the rue du Faubourg Saint-Honoré, where, a short walk in the other direction, Émile Hermès would soon resettle his father's award-winning harness shop, thereby signaling the brand's—and the neighborhood's—pivot toward the global market in luxury design and fashion. Behind the little girl, men's top hats stretch against a dense and distinctly modern fabric: billboard advertisements, storefronts, and a packed omnibus hurtling where regal saplings had sprouted not long before.

WHAT THE RESIDENTS of the rue Montaigne thought of the old alley's rechristening is unknown. They were content not to call much attention to themselves. In sex as in politics, the outwardly sedate street was an exemplar of discretion and normalcy, with its horse stable, post office, wine seller, and small hotels.[18] Tastefully understated, the rue Montaigne was rarely remarked on as anything other than a "peaceful" passage up from the Champs-Elysées.[19]

For that reason it was an ideal site for sexual trysts in the modern style. When the Romantic poet Alfred de Vigny, a friend of Hugo's, fell in love with the acclaimed actress Marie Dorval, he rented a flat at number 18 for their lovemaking sessions; because both were married, they relied on the building's doorman as a go-between for their erotic correspondence and for news of each other during cholera outbreaks.[20] The street was also home to child pensioners, *salonnières*, military brass, and well-heeled foreign families, including that of the German composer Giacomo Meyerbeer.

Henry James wistfully recalled his experience as a boy in that idyll where he discovered Flaubert's recently published novel, *Madame Bovary*: "the sunny little salon, the autumn day, the window ajar and the cheerful outside clatter of the Rue Montaigne are all now more or less in the story and the story more or less in them."[21] But the James family discovered that the clean air and quietude came with exorbitant rent bills. After the stock market crash of 1857, the expense grew unbearable. James called it his "long term of thrifty exile" from the rue Montaigne.[22]

The Jameses were pioneers of a sort; over the next few decades, transatlantic industrialists settled around the Champs-Elysées in great enough numbers to be called "la colonie américaine."[23] In an amusing way, the Count d'Artois's New America had thus returned, almost, in name: The city dedicated a rue Washington nearby, and in 1887, the year of the murders that shattered the rue Montaigne's arcadia, the newspaper scion Gordon Bennett found an ample readership for his Paris *Herald* (later the *Herald Tribune*).

In 1871, and in the uncertain political climate of the 1870s, the street became the informal headquarters of the fledgling republican movement. Pierre-Henri de Lacretelle, a friend of the poet Lamartine and fellow 1848 revolutionary, was the elder statesman of the illustrious republicans who settled on the street after the Commune; he still resided in the very building where the bodies were found.[24] Among the younger generation, Léon Gambetta was a star. While residing in the rue Montaigne, Gambetta sustained a long and torrid—and politically flammable—love affair with Léonie Léon, a demimondaine.[25] Down the street resided a coterie of other national leaders: Georges Clémenceau, future president Sadi Carnot, and the deputy Émile de Marcère.[26]

The murders of 1887 would scar a generation of children who lived in the rue Montaigne. The celebrated author Léon-Paul Fargue, who was then a boarder living two doors down from the crime scene, wrote vividly of the crime's aftermath in a manner reflecting a child's experience of trauma. Fargue recounted that he got in the habit of peering down at the "fantastic silhouettes of passersby" in the street, wondering who would be the next victims. "Shadows on the walls slipped past like ominous birds," he remembered. "We sensed coming catastrophes."[27]

Meanwhile, on the other side of the roundabout, the upstart avenue Montaigne had far surpassed its namesake and had established itself on the world stage. The reversal of fortune was completed by the tragedy of March 1887. The avenue Montaigne, widened immensely and erected in grand style under the Second Empire, was charting its course in haute couture, even as it maintained something of its sexual past (Napoleon III himself kept a favorite mistress in the avenue Montaigne).[28]

Fargue lived long enough into the twentieth century to witness a proposal to erase the rue Montaigne from the map. No one stepped forth to object, and in 1937 the rue Montaigne became the rue Jean-Mermoz, which is still its name today.

CHAPTER TWO

The Crime Scene

At that age, one girl might fuss over her *toilette*,
While another'd go to hell for a *tartelette*.
In her breast she held but one modest goal:
To ride on the wash house's parade float.

—"The Little Laundress" (1887), popular song[1]

The telegraphed message announcing the three murders was bungled at Security,[2] so Chief Ernest Taylor and Deputy Chief François Goron were delayed in leaving their offices on the Île de la Cité. The two leaders of Security, the Police Prefecture's criminal investigative branch, were going to be scooped by Georges Grison and other reporters who were already knocking on doors in the rue Montaigne and launching their own investigations. Taylor and Goron hustled out onto the Quai de l'Horloge, and as they made their way to a fiacre, a parade float carrying a group of laundresses slid past. The music was loud. One of the women tossed a bouquet of withered flowers toward them. Goron reached up and caught the bouquet and boarded the fiacre with it. Traffic was slow, and the route toward the Champs-Elysées was snarled and icy.[3]

THE FESTIVAL of the Laundresses was an annual Parisian gala featuring festooned chariots. It coincided with Mid-Lent and celebrated the city's laundry workers, an almost entirely female workforce that by 1887 numbered 18,000.[4] Like Carnaval, which preceded the Catholic season of Lent, the laundresses' parade was notorious for exhibitionism, drunken gropers, and playful reversals of social and gender hierarchies. The laundresses, dressed up as royals, cupids, and deities, tossed sweets and charms to onlookers, many of whom wore costumes of their own. There were Japanese jockeys, jesters, "chic Indians," and celebrities. Men and women could be seen in garters and lace ruffles.[5]

Elites made preparations for more exclusive feasts, which were usually followed by masked balls along the boulevards. The newspapers carried menu advertisements and soirée announcements proposed by the city's finest restaurants. The opulent Garnier Opera, another of Napoleon III's signature projects, was the most sought-after venue. In 1887 the Grand Hôtel, which faced the Opera, was offering a regal multiple-course dinner—filet de boeuf, pain de lapereau à la Montmiral, poularde de la Bresse truffée à la Périgourdine, and so on—which would be accompanied by a concert conducted by Eusèbe Lucas of the Monte Carlo Philharmonic Orchestra.

Patricians who preferred more intellectual or edgier fare could find it easily. "The most curious, the strangest, and most provocative will be neither at the Opera nor at the wash houses," predicted a writer for *Le Gaulois* that week; the place to be, he added, was the city's best-known insane asylum, where doctors put the patients on display at a *bal des folles*, a theater and dance show billed as a mix of edification and entertainment. "For those who would like to see a production of Poe's short story 'The System of Doctor Tarr and Professor Fether,' the Salpêtrière [Hospital] offers the 'Dance of the Insane.'"[6] It was a hot ticket, thanks to the stardom of Dr. Jean-Martin Charcot, lately a mentor of Sigmund Freud. Society's upper crust arrived at the hospital, nibbled on buffet food, sat along the periphery of a hall that was 15 meters long, and watched costumed hysterics, epileptics, and hypnotics dance and writhe, yank each other's hair, and throw punches at one another.[7] This spectacle, accompanied by a droning piano quartet, gave attendees cause for earnest self-congratulation.[8]

The day's festivities would at first appear to have suited Georges Grison's reporting beat perfectly. Grison wrote daily tidbits, known as a *fait-divers* column, for *Le Figaro* under the byline Jean de Paris. His was a page that readers could rely on for profiles of the most eccentric and obscure characters to be found in the capital: prostitutes and provocateurs, underworld toughs, street urchins, deadbeat cops, and crooks of all kinds. Their stories, but especially crime-related news, were the stuff of the *fait-divers* genre. Grison knew of the secrets that the laundresses kept: the compromising biological events, the lipstick traces, an entire medical archive stained into linen.[9] The laundresses might even have made good sources for him; he was a consummate gossiper who monetized rumors and soiled reputations for a living: Grison revealed in a figurative sense what the laundresses' knuckles, washboards, and chemicals effaced in a material one.

Yet, as though in unspoken protest, Grison made an annual tradition of paying the laundresses no mind.[10] He spent that third week of March 1887 prowling about for the violent and the hideous. News was slow, but he managed to break stories about the suicide of a widowed aristocrat, the mugging of a plainclothes cop by some pimps at a dance hall, the jacking of a fiacre in the Faubourg St. Denis that left one horse with multiple stab wounds, the poisoning of an Oberkampf butcher by an underling, and the combustion of mailboxes in separate Paris neighborhoods. "The resemblance of these two *accidents* does seem strange," Grison wrote, ever wont to gin up a criminal conspiracy.[11]

Grison radiated the image of the intrepid crime reporter, but he was a traditionalist working for a center-right newspaper that took a jaded view of the working class. His commentary on Mid-Lent skewed to church teachings, if he mentioned the holiday at all.[12] His fellow conservatives, more fervent in their rejection of the laundresses' celebration, suggested that the spiritual significance of Mid-Lent was being displaced by a tribute to urban labor, and *female* labor at that. Couching their grievances in religious and nationalist language, they bemoaned the festival's commercialization, disenchantment, and what they saw as its contrived escapism.[13] True joy had been a casualty of "Prussia's bullets" during the war of 1870, moralized one such critic.[14] Monarchists dismissed the parading laundresses as pawnlike advertisements for laundry business owners.[15]

All agreed that the 1887 edition of the festival was a catastrophe. Parisians woke that March morning to find the city's rooftops carpeted in white. Heavy snow had begun to fall in the small hours, and the temperature dipped a few degrees below the freezing point. The celebratory music was muted, the hats of the newspaper barkers dampened, and the blizzard devoured the gray winter light like Balzac's fog, so thick it was liable to "throw the most punctual people out in their calculations as to the time."[16] Municipal policemen, fully deployed across the city to keep the laundresses in check, were called on to fix traffic jams as the horse-drawn omnibuses contended with the deep snow and ice.[17] There were reports of entire teams of service horses losing their footing and collapsing to the ground. Turnout for the parade suffered badly. Onlookers huddled to keep dry beneath awnings and arcades; preferring to stay out of the arctic wind, others just peered through carriage-door slats.[18] Naysayers pointed to the rue Montaigne tragedy as further evidence that Gay Paris was a thing of the past. "There are singular dramas in this sad city, which forces itself to have fun," commented a writer for *La Croix*. "Historians of the future will be able to write many novels [*sic*] with these horrors."[19]

WHEN TAYLOR AND GORON finally arrived at 17 rue Montaigne, they confronted a bevy of reporters cramming the staircase and knocking on doors. They climbed to the third floor and stepped into a large and well-appointed space.

The public prosecutor stood in the middle of the apartment, displeased by the tardiness and sloppy oversight of the crime scene. A truism of crime scenes is that they are fertile ground for professional rivalries. Complicating matters, the collection of big names who made the trip to the rue Montaigne that afternoon were there, at least in part, because this was going to be a major news item; the entire investigation would take place in the public eye. Magistrates, rival branches of the Paris police force, detectives, doctors, and forensics specialists all asserted their authority from the start.[20]

The public prosecutor upbraided the commissary of the Roule Precinct, Mr. Crénau, who had been the first policeman on the scene, for the slowness of his response. Then he turned to correct Taylor and Goron, who were idling obliviously in pools of blood deep enough to stain Goron's lower pant leg. Although second in command at Security, Goron stood out in the apartment as a rookie investigator surrounded by illustrious figures, among them the police prefect, to whom Taylor reported directly.

The police had learned of the murders from Madame Toulouse, a round-cheeked woman with droopy eyes who lived with her husband on the sixth floor. Toulouse identified the victims as Marie Regnault, a.k.a. Régine de Montille, the mistress of the house; her house servant, Annette Gremeret; and Gremeret's young daughter, who was Regnault's namesake, Marie. Toulouse had been employed as Regnault's personal chef for the past dozen years.

LE CRIME DE LA RUE MONTAIGNE
Portrait de Marie Regnault, dite Régine de Montille
Dessin de Henri Meyer (photographie Nadar). — Gravure de Méaulle. — Voir l'article, page 106.

Figure 4. Marie Regnault, alias Régine de Montille. *La Revue Illustrée*, 10 April 1887.

In different rooms of the apartment the men went about their work, taking measurements and samples, sketching the scene, and taking statements. Two pugs had been discovered. They were a nuisance now, yapping and refusing all entreaties to come out from behind the sofa in the salon. Glum neighbors and newspapermen filed in and out of the apartment's entrance while bursts of merriment and clanging music seeped through the windowpanes. Masked revelers were spilling en masse into the 8th arrondissement, chanting the traditional "Ohé! Ohé! Ohé!"[21]

Someone spotted a bloody stain in the shape of a toe print on the living room rug. Had the killer been barefoot?

Deputy Chief Goron took in the carnage, recording all that struck him in his case notes, which were published a decade later in his memoirs. Nigh on 40, Goron was a short, loquacious man with gray eyes. Beneath his nose, a silver-tinged hank of hair furled like a baby fox. Undeterred by the downwardly mobile path of his life thus far—a fate that his parents, *petits bourgeois de province*, had tried to forestall by forcing him to study pharmacology—he admired the ostentatious luxury of the place zestfully and acknowledged the house mistress's fine taste: Louis XV furniture in the dining room, Louis XVI in the salon, walls hung with Salon paintings, the sculptures of celebrated academics. Furniture pieces and silverware were of sophisticated craftsmanship; fashionable Japanese trinkets were set atop decorative ebony tables, the props of a courtesan's everyday life. The *cabinet de toilette*, which connected to the salon, was padded with black satin and had room enough for large divans on either side, plus a chaise longue and a *table de toilette*. The bidet, pitcher, pail, wash basins, and other bathroom items were made of silver and together were worth a small fortune.

Goron walked down the long corridor to the boudoir, which opened onto a small courtyard. The room looked like a stage flared with red satin wallpaper, thick curtains, and lavish furnishings.

Some minutes later, in a fleeting moment of self-awareness, the deputy chief noticed that he was still grasping the bouquet of flowers he had caught in the parade. Trying to fling it away furtively, he watched it sail instead into a puddle of blood on the floor near the entrance to the dining room, where it was certain to be remarked.

That blood belonged to the second victim, Annette Gremeret, a heavyset woman in her early 40s whose nightcap had fallen to the floor. She was found on her back, her right arm extended outward and her left arm bent slightly at the elbow, such that her hand rested on her stomach. Her blood had spurted as far as the bedroom door leafs. On the floor nearby was a stray cufflink. There was also a bronze candlestick with a candle of red wax, almost entirely burnt; there appeared to be flecks of dried blood on the wick. It had come from the master bedroom and surely had guided the murderer through the corridor and the antechamber that separated the two bedrooms. Further back in the bedroom lay the third victim, Marie Gremeret. She was on the bed, entangled in the covers and pillows, her body folded inward. She wore a small medallion. Her head was cut almost entirely from her torso; a thin patch of flesh was all that kept it attached.

Goron submitted a bloodied pillowcase, initialed "R.M.," for laboratory analysis, to be done under the guidance of Dr. Paul Brouardel, dean of the prestigious Medical School of Paris and a pioneering forensics scientist of international reputation. Brouardel would prepare the bodies for transport to the morgue and try to determine the nature of the weapon used, the circumstances of the struggle, and the precise causes of death. By the time he arrived in the rue Montaigne, it was 4 p.m., and the bodies had thoroughly

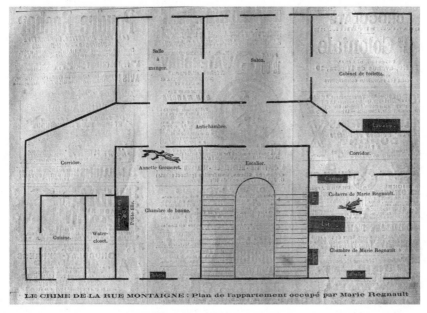

Figure 5. A police drawing of the crime scene: Marie Regnault's third-floor apartment. *La Revue Illustrée,* 10 April 1887.

stiffened. Forensics was in its modern infancy: One of Brouardel's first tasks was to interpret the facial expressions worn by the victims as he found them, from which he would extrapolate something of their emotional state at the moment of death. Of Marie Regnault he wrote, "The contracted muscles of the face have preserved the most vivid expression of terror."[22]

One of the other heavyweights at the scene was the investigating magistrate, Adolphe Guillot, a legal theorist and author of several volumes. He sat at the large dining room table with his clerk and questioned people with intimate knowledge of the household. Guillot's job as the investigating magistrate (*juge d'instruction* in French) was to spearhead the investigation, collate evidence from all sources, and file an official report that would be the basis of an eventual indictment. The French criminal justice system invested great authority in the investigating magistrate. He was empowered to detain and question suspects and to issue orders to the leaders of Security.

Goron toured the apartment, which had a salon, kitchen, dining room, and two bedrooms. The place appeared in order but for the bodies. Nothing was overturned or out of place. The furniture and books were neatly arranged, the paintings hooked into the wall, the shelves intact. The apartment had been found sealed. On first impression at least, it fit the mold of the classic locked-room mystery, in which a murder has taken place but there is no evidence of broken entry.

Certain clues were obvious enough. Regnault's bedsheets bore the distinct imprints of two bodies: The killer had known her intimately. Her throat had been sliced by a large, perhaps artisanal blade that was both sharp and wide. Goron surmised that Regnault had died of what street thugs called a *coup de cornet*: The assailant pulled the victim's head back so that the neck was exposed; then he plunged the blade's edge into it, turned it from side to side, and drew it back toward himself until the weapon met the vertebrae. There had been a brief struggle. Goron noted that Regnault's golden necklace, adorned with a cross of diamonds, was sinking into the slits in her neck. On the parquet floor, near her shoulder, another stray cufflink sat in plain view; like the one found in the other bedroom, it bore the initials G.G. Near the bed were bloody markings near a cord connected to an electronic bell. The cord had been pulled with enough force to rip it half out of the wall.

There were scores of books on the nightstand and in the salon. The century's greatest writers were represented. The victim was bookish. There was pulpy reading too. Near the bedside was *The Gambler*, a popular novel released several months earlier by an author called Paul Dumas (since utterly forgotten). The deputy chief noticed that the novel was marked at the penultimate page.

Elsewhere in the boudoir the investigators picked up a journal in which they found some of Marie Regnault's personal notes. One striking passage, which the dates confirm she had written recently, hints at the tumult her life had become. Police noted that it also contained references to a sexual affair with another woman.

> My sister died on 28 February 1886.
> D—— broke my heart on 3 February 1887.
> I want to die!
> I am going to try to forget. Otherwise I am liable to kill myself.
> Met with Henriette today, Wednesday the 23rd. She must have suffered as well not to see me: I was naive about the ache that love can cause. I saw her at the Mirlitons, where she had sent a message to implore me to come. She is still very pretty. At least with her my heart is not in danger: it is only about sensuality. I should not have left her: I would not have given myself so completely to him and I would not be suffering so atrociously as I am now. . . .
> D—— left this morning at 9. I had a crying, nervous fit for an hour and a half after his departure. I don't want him to see how much I suffer: he doesn't love me enough, and he wouldn't understand me. For him to have the strength to love another woman, he must no longer love me.
> What will happen to me on his wedding day? How will I spend that night, feeling that he is in the arms of another! . . . If I am alone, what will I do?
> I always mocked people who were in love: I am now punished enough for it! I never believed myself capable of loving that way.[23]

Regnault's pained journal entry contains a scenario that was not at all uncommon to a woman of the demimonde: the melodramatic moment when a regular client, one to whom she had become emotionally attached, declared his intention to end the relationship and move on, possibly because he was at an age to retire from the military and hence could at last afford to marry properly and, because he would no longer suffer transfers, settle down. It would be best to end their arrangement to avoid "embarrassment," the client would tell her.[24]

Yet Goron's case notes suggest that the police began quite early to rule out client involvement in the triple homicide. As society men, the clients could be prodded in private for information, but their names were rigorously shielded in police documents and in newspaper accounts, blotted out or simply replaced by the conventional "Mr. X."

MADAME TOULOUSE, the last witness to see the victims alive, recounted the morning's events. As was her habit, she descended the building's service staircase at 7 and, arriving on the third floor, took a wooden baton and rapped it against the wall outside the second bedroom to awaken Gremeret and her daughter. This was done to avoid disturbing Regnault, who often worked well into the night and slept late in the morning. On a typical day the girl would rise immediately to open the service door located at the back of the kitchen. Toulouse would then prepare breakfast for everyone.

When she heard no response to her rapping, Toulouse tried to use her own two keys, one for the door lock and the other for the bolt. A security chain had been added, however, and she was stuck in the service staircase. Rather than knocking at the main entrance, she went out to run errands.

In the hours before the murders, Madame Toulouse had cooked dinner for Regnault and a client, who had an early start to the Mid-Lent celebration. She cleaned up in the kitchen a half-hour after the client's departure and then returned to her apartment upstairs. It was not yet midnight. Young Marie had already gone to sleep. Regnault did not mention any plans for the rest of the evening. Toulouse found her behavior ordinary. Then again, Regnault was not an expressive woman, and she did not share information unnecessarily.

Still receiving no reply to her knocking a while later, Toulouse went downstairs to ask the concierge, Zacharie Lacarrière, for assistance. He had the keys to Regnault's front entrance, but he was stymied by the door locks. Lacarrière knew about Regnault's hushed business, of course, which demanded tight security and a wariness of the police. They waited as long as they could to act because involving the police would have been risky and advisable only under drastic circumstances for an unregistered, or clandestine, prostitute like Regnault. Finally they agreed to walk together to the commissary in the rue Berryer, Mr. Crénau, who contacted a locksmith and a local doctor named Pietri. When the four of them entered the apartment, Regnault's two dogs, Dick and Lily, immediately recognized Toulouse.

Under questioning, Toulouse elaborated on the operations of the household, which depended on loyalty and discretion. In addition to a live-in

Figure 6. The discovery of Marie Regnault's body. *La Revue Illustrée*, 10 April 1887.

servant and chef, Marie Regnault kept a seamstress and a personal stylist, each of whom had been with her for the better part of two decades. To avoid risk, she had employed the same private laundress for eighteen years.[25] The police quizzed Lacarrière and also Mrs. Lacarrière. Who had Regnault been seeing before the murders?

The house of a courtesan depended on dissimulation for its survival, so consistent answers remained elusive to even this basic question. The people on Regnault's payroll shared their recollections, although these were, they hastened to add, jumbled by the horror of the scene. Lacarrière remembered leaving his loge downstairs to shut off the building's gas main at 11:15 or 11:30 p.m. He said that while he was doing this, a man in a roomy overcoat walked past him, his collar pulled up high, practically over his face. Without pausing, the man mumbled something about Madame de Montille and breezed up the staircase without asking on what floor he would find her. Lacarrière could not remember what color the large overcoat had been, and he was unable to describe the visitor in much detail. All he could say was that the man in the corridor was of "forte corpulence" and that he was wearing a top hat, along with—perhaps—a foulard or a gray *cache-nez*. He may have had a moustache. All these trappings of bourgeois dress were barely useful as clues; virtually every gentleman in the neighborhood wore them.

There was nothing noteworthy about a gentleman showing up at that advanced hour to see Regnault, so Lacarrière went to bed and did not open his door again until sometime between 1 and 2 a.m., when Welhumeau, a restaurant chef living on the sixth floor, rang to be let in and went up the service staircase. During the night the concierge heard nothing. If someone else pulled the cord lock to open the door—this was the only way to be let out of the building after hours—Lacarrière did not recall it, but nor could he be certain either way because such things happened any night with a courtesan in the building. The front entrance remained locked until between 6 and 6:15 a.m., the hour at which suppliers arrived with daily deliveries. The delivery men had their own keys to the building.

Dr. Lepetit lived on the second floor. His bedroom was directly beneath the one shared by Annette Gremeret and little Marie. His servant, Madame Leblond, lay half-asleep at around 5 or 6 a.m. when the short cry of a child rang out, she said, followed by the sound of something dropping to the floor; 15 minutes later, Leblond heard someone descending the staircase. Dr. Lepetit also heard footsteps, as his bedroom was separated from the main staircase merely by a sealed door. The footsteps seemed unhurried. Madame Jean, the concierge in the adjacent building (at no. 15), heard "hideous" cries around the same time, as did Mr. Morel, an employee at the Ministry of the Interior who lived in a building at the back of the courtyard. Morel was feeling unwell that night and blew out his candle at 5 a.m. Minutes later, he heard a voice and then the cries of a child. Thinking that his own son had awoken, he went to check on him but found him fast asleep. Finally, Mrs. Hillecamp, who lived in the adjacent building, said that she heard the dogs barking at short intervals, but she was unable to recall precisely at what hour.

Based on these accounts, the Prefecture put out a police bulletin.

Did the killer live on the premises or possibly in the neighborhood? Was he a client? Madame Toulouse and Madame Lacarrière had their own hypotheses. Both women had noticed an unfamiliar visitor coming to call on Marie Regnault in recent weeks, a man they found unsavory and vaguely suspicious. He was evidently not a high-society gentleman, and the two women had secretly nicknamed him *le gringalet*, "the little runt." He was, they said, a "petit homme brun," a short man with brown hair. He came around more than once, discreetly. "I wouldn't be able to recognize him," Toulouse added.

In the boudoir investigators found an emptied wallet on the mantel with bloody handprints and a broken piggy bank near the bed. Traces of blood could be seen near the combination lock on a large safe tucked away in the bedroom. This safe was a "veritable gem" in itself, wrote Grison in his case notes. It was encased in solid ivory and delicately sculpted; its lock had the capacity of 20,000 possible combinations that would have taken an experienced locksmith 24 hours to open. Fortunately, the correct combination was hit in a couple of hours. Inside the safe "a perfect order reigned," with letters, jewelry, cash, and investment papers carefully labeled and inventoried, valued at the staggering sum of 200,000 francs all told.[26]

Investigators retraced the killer's steps: After committing the murders, he attempted to crack the safe but gave up; he grabbed the cash he could find; then he washed his hands, leaving fingerprints on the silver kettle and reddish water in the toilet pan, got dressed, and absconded. The hypothesis, which did not significantly change in the months to come, was that Regnault had known and welcomed her murderer, or murderers, into the apartment late in the evening.

Investigators rifled through a small box in the boudoir containing numerous calling cards; orders were given to officers to track down all the men whose names and addresses appeared on them. One name not found on any of the calling cards was that of Gaston Geissler. Yet all the material evidence at the scene pointed to him: the initialed cufflinks, the Gaston letter, and a leather belt bearing his name that was found under a fauteuil. Police noted that the cufflinks were of fine quality, adorned with small blue buttons and the brand insignia of an artisanal shirtmaker in the city of Nancy, the city also mentioned in the Gaston letter. Taylor dispatched one of his best brigadiers to the train station.

These promising clues perhaps encouraged Goron to take only a cursory glance at the client who had dined with Regnault on the eve of her death. The deputy chief made quick inquiries and found out that the gentleman was "known in the neighborhood and [was] of an honorability that precluded suspicion of this kind."[27] The lead was shelved.

The Police Prefecture sent out a second, more detailed bulletin to police departments across France by the end of the first day. It described a suspect with a "shifty" countenance, a "swarthy complexion," and a black moustache. The suspect was of thin build, was perhaps a painter or photographer, and carried himself with the "air of a déclassé." The name Geissler rang foreign. The bulletin was careful to allude to the suspect's foreignness without mentioning Geissler's name or specifying any of the incriminating items found at the scene.[28]

Investigators felt acutely the hesitations of Madame Toulouse and the botched telegraphic communications of earlier that morning, which had allowed the crime scene to go cold. An unhappy political reality also hung over the apartment. Five quite similar murders targeting demimondaines on the Right Bank going back to 1879 remained unsolved. The press was certain to recite their names again: Marie Fellerath, Marie Jouin, Hélène Stein, Lucie Alhiaume, Marie Aguétant.[29]

There was no more adamant critic of Security than Le Figaro's Grison. In his published notes on the rue Montaigne case, Grison wrote, "We were convinced in advance" that Chief Taylor, who was "so notorious for his incapacities, would produce another of the flops which are his specialty."[30] As the chief stepped out of Regnault's apartment, the reporters called him on it. The enmity and mutual disdain are palpable in Grison's retelling of what happened at the end of the afternoon, when the assembled reporters provoked the chief of Security by asking him whether he had any hope of catching the culprit this time.

"Another matter involving a hooker?" replied Taylor, in a feint of sarcasm. "Once again, we will arrest nobody!"

"Oh, how Parisians must be proud to have such a policeman," answered Grison.[31]

Goron and Taylor left 17 rue Montaigne and returned to the Quai de l'Horloge. It was dark, and Mid-Lenten roisterers were still standing outside. It looked like a lugubrious vigil, the crowd waiting until a hearse arrived to deliver the bodies to the public morgue on the Île de la Cité, where they were placed in a sealed room.

For once, Chief Taylor had some solid leads. But behind the closed doors of his office, his mood was dour. "Another case that's going nowhere," he predicted, "for which I'll be ridiculed in the papers."[32] On the latter score, Taylor was soon proved correct. The outcry that followed the official announcement of the murders in the rue Montaigne was intense. Decades later, Parisians would remember it as a "violent campaign" with Taylor as its target.[33]

IT WOULD BE no exaggeration to say that Taylor and Goron swam against the tide of history when, just months before, the two men assumed their respective posts atop the Security bureaucracy. For generations, Security, the only major agency dedicated solely to criminal investigation in all of France in the nineteenth century, had struggled to live down its own checkered past. Created in 1800 as Napoleon was consolidating executive power, Security was staffed largely with ex-convicts, on the theory that outlaws were best suited to apprehend their own likes. The agency's reputation was made—and forever tainted—by one of these men, Eugène-François Vidocq, who has gone down as one of Europe's most notorious police leaders. Vidocq's controversial reign at Security ended amid a political cleanup in the 1830s, but he refused to go quietly into the night. From the embittered margins of public life, he joined the agency's many critics. Security survived, but as a measure against corruption it was placed under the thumb of the Paris Municipal Police, where it remained for a half-century—that is, until Ernest Taylor took the helm in the mid-1880s. By then, Vidocq's crew of 30 men had grown to 300.[34]

Before Taylor, several chiefs of Security had decried their inferior position relative to the Municipal Police, which had, in fact, done nothing to alter Parisians' abiding belief that the agency was peopled by crooks,

a conviction historians have dubbed "le syndrome Vidocq."[35] Other, related public relations problems hobbled the Parisian police apparatus
more broadly, for example the institution's much-deserved reputation for
arbitrary and antirevolutionary violence. As France drifted into liberal democracy, Security's long litany of abuses of power and shadow operations
became, if not entirely unacceptable, then at least awkward.

A fundamentally political issue arose: How was Security to carve out
a new professional identity that was in tune with the liberal-democratic
tenets enshrined in the Third Republic's constitution? In response, republican politicians undertook a makeover of Parisian cops, a professionalization, which included massive structural reforms, the advent of more
rigorous screening and training of newly hired policemen, and a great deal
of image making.[36] Having assumed their positions at Security in a time of
transition, Taylor and Goron had the opportunity to construct a new vision
for the refreshed agency.

A slight man with small brown eyes, Taylor had spent years as the local
commissary in the Chaussée d'Antin, which practically abutted the vibrant
quartier de la presse along the boulevards. Known as a humble and decent
man, he emphasized the importance of efficiency at a time when the mass
press demanded charisma. "The discretion of the policeman is a duty; the
indiscretion of the reporter is mere commerce," professed Taylor's predeces-
sor, Antoine Claude.[37] The quaintness of Claude's statement was already
becoming apparent.

And in reality, Taylor was far more discreet than Claude or arguably any
other Security chief going back to Vidocq. He carried himself like a genial
functionary. He was the courteous and conscientious sort for whom Parisians of the period reserved the adjective *precise*. To his way of thinking, an
investigation was foremost an accumulation of facts. Unlike Goron, a brash
former soldier and self-described hothead who had shot up the ranks at Security in just a handful of years, the chief exhibited a jadedness about police
work. The men under his command appreciated him, as did his superiors,
who perhaps saw in him a man who was happy to leave well enough alone:
It was public knowledge that the police prefect had needed to cajole Taylor
into accepting his promotion to chief back in late 1885.[38] The new configu-
ration at the Police Prefecture, which theoretically empowered Security by
separating it from the Municipal Police, meant that Taylor would be under
the microscope.

By unfortunate coincidence, Taylor's accession was greeted with a spate of violent crimes in the city. Although the crimes were nothing out of the ordinary statistically, the enraged response of journalists may have contributed to the Prefecture's decision to create a new post, deputy chief, which Goron filled in October 1886. It was insinuated that Goron had been brought in merely to shore up the incompetent chief. This, anyway, was the position taken by Georges Grison, a muckraker before the letter, who ridiculed Taylor as an "umbrella inspector." Grison believed that Taylor had been named chief in the first place because the prefect of police, himself a political appointee, had viewed him as harmless and malleable. As for the more obscure deputy chief, Goron, Grison had seen enough of him within a few months to ask mischievously whether the relationship between Taylor and him would suffer from "competition" and "jealousy."[39]

How well did the two men get along? Given the agency's importance and its continuing expansion, the question is not without consequence. Taylor's name comes up on numerous occasions in Goron's memoirs, as we would expect, and usually in a positive light. At times, though Goron's expressions of respect come across as desultory or tepidly formal—Taylor was "an excellent man despite the appearance of coldness," he wrote.

Within his first hours on the job, Goron had gotten a good idea of Taylor's style, particularly the secrecy in which he sought to conduct police affairs, a legacy of authoritarian regimes like the Second Empire. It had been the eve of an execution; because Security oversaw guillotinings, which were then semipublic, Taylor initiated Goron in their arcane protocols. But in Goron's telling, the chief seemed more concerned with neutralizing his enemies in the press by depriving them of valuable information. "Above all," Taylor said, "we have to prevent any slip of the tongue so that *Le Soir* doesn't publish news of the execution."[40]

CHIEF TAYLOR'S PESSIMISM turned to elation during the investigation's first weekend. On Saturday, the Security brigade in charge of monitoring hotel registration rolls—transients and migrants were viewed with suspicion and carefully tracked[41]—sent Taylor a message from northeastern Paris. A guest named Geissler had registered in a flophouse near the Gare du Nord, it read. Within an hour Taylor and Goron and a team of inspectors were questioning the owner of the Hôtel Cailleux in the rue de Dunkurque. On Wednesday, March 16, the eve of Mid-Lent, he had con-

fronted a young foreigner whose tab had run to eleven days without payment. When asked to settle the bill, the guest demurred and a bit later he
trudged out into the cold, never to return.

Investigators went up to inspect the abandoned room. Rummaging
through the belongings left behind, the first objects they spotted were a
yellow valise, a paper bag that had contained cigars, and a medallion locket
that was old and weathered. They flipped open the locket; inside was a
woman's picture.

Goron bent over to pick up a bound document and fingered through the
pages. It was written in German; the papers in it were ragged and stained by
the grease of the charcuteries that they had been used to wrap. The inspectors
understood that it was a campaign pamphlet supporting a socialist candidate
in an upcoming election in Breslau, one of the German empire's largest cities.[42] Clothing and linens were strewn about the floor. Goron turned over
a shirt emblazoned with the initials G.G., and the room erupted: "Gaston
Geissler!"[43]

Fancy bespoke shirts like this were a little out of place in a flophouse
in northeastern Paris, but they were nothing extraordinary. The locket,
however, stumped everyone present. If the suspect had intended to leave
the room permanently, he likely would not have purposely left a possession of sentimental value. He might have forgotten it, but could he
have forgotten the shirts too? Perhaps he was planning to *return* to the
room. Perhaps he was simply waiting for the public uproar to subside, at
which point he could come back to plot another strike. It would be a bold
calculation, but if this was the same man responsible for the mystifying
deaths of the other prostitutes, those earlier successes could have inflated
his confidence. Hubris might also account for the general sloppiness in
the room and the carelessness of leaving an upaid bill at a shoddy hotel
such as this one. Taylor and Goron sped back to the Île de la Cité to alert
the magistrate Guillot and set a trap back at the hotel before the suspect
learned that he was being sought.

But the city's newspaper reporters had other ideas. As the police devised
a stakeout of the hotel the next day, a handful of reporters, including *Le
Figaro*'s Grison, began publishing highly sensitive information regarding the
principal leads in the case, such as details about the evidence found at the
crime scene in the rue Montaigne and the neighbors' statements and descriptions of the suspect. Most jarringly, the newspapers printed Geissler's

name, that of the Hôtel Cailleux, and even the investigators' hunch that the suspect, if he was not still in Paris, had left for Brussels.

How had the press obtained information that was closely guarded by the Police Prefecture? Taylor and Goron, as they came to realize, were being followed.

CHAPTER THREE

A Reporter's Ambition

Georges Grison and the Rise of Investigative Crime Reporting in Paris

> As you know, I'm just a poor devil with no money, trying to find my place. But I've got willpower and some intelligence, I think, and I'm moving forward on the right path.
>
> —Georges Duroy, ersatz journalist and antihero of Guy de Maupassant's *Bel-Ami* (1886)[1]

> As soon as there is one of these strange crimes, rumors of which the police can't manage to keep from the crowds, Grison goes to the crime scene, only to return once he's loaded with documents and larded with notes—with the age of the victim and the menu of the last meal she ate. All of it is interesting to know. And it is fun to read. But rest assured, it's even more curious to see.
>
> —Pierre Giffard, Parisian newspaperman, on the crime reporter Georges Grison (1880)[2]

It was an astonishing assertion of journalistic prerogative: Hungry reporters trawling on the Quai de l'Horloge, tailing cops, gleaning their findings, and then publishing them—all without any official interaction with the Police Prefecture. Goron later discovered how they had done it. When Taylor and he jumped out of their taxi after the visit to the Hôtel Cailleux, the reporters hailed that same taxi before it could pull away, and to cover their ruse, they led the coachman to believe that they were government officials; they demanded to be taken to the address where the chief had begun his fare.

Once there, the reporters inspected Geissler's room. They interviewed the hotel staff, who recalled the departed suspect as "rather puny, swarthy, and wearing a dark moustache." The description, of course, matched that provided by Marie Regnault's neighbors. The reporters would try to break the case open on their own.[3]

With years of hindsight, Goron would argue that his copious case notes were "historical documents" because they attested to the "battles between the investigating magistrates, the police, and the press."[4] In his oafish manner, he conveyed the bafflement and exasperation of investigating officials as crime reporters encroached in radically new ways on police work. "Monsieur Guillot shot me a frigid look," Goron recalled after he had accidentally tipped off the newspapers about the hotel, "like he was about to accuse me of handing my taxi over to the journalists to help them."[5] Catching murderers was difficult enough without the added requirement of round-the-clock stealth, which was what meddling crime reporters were effectively imposing if they intended to publicize every police maneuver. As Goron put it, "Go ahead and try, after that, to speak of the confidentiality of a criminal investigation and the ability of the Chief of Security to conceal his operations!"[6]

Are these the words of a retired cop who is seeking to absolve the police of their failures, or did the rue Montaigne case bring to light something qualitatively new in Parisian media culture?

Historians have produced a raft of studies on the press during the latter half of the nineteenth century, but they do not agree on what was transformative about the crime-oriented *fait-divers* columns that multiplied during this formative period of the mass press.[7] The stakes of this lively field of research are evident when one considers the durability and centrality of the *fait-divers* content, especially local crime reports and freak occurrences, to the modern Western news media.

The proliferation of *fait-divers* crime stories during the nineteenth century, as measured in newspaper column inches, has been well established in the Parisian case by Dominique Kalifa, who linked their irresistibility to, among other things, formal changes in storytelling: Rather than focusing all their attention on the criminal act, modern newspaper writers emphasized the gradual unfolding of the investigation; like serialized fiction, the titillating and episodic hunt for clues and new developments was an ideal mechanism for getting readers to purchase the same newspaper day after day. And because daily production demanded a constant replenishing of information, investigative leads, whether fructuous or not, were well suited to sustaining a real-life crime story in tiny increments. Before the daily newspaper, the traditional popular news genre known as the *canard*, or broadsheet, had not peddled this idea of news as inherently breaking.[8]

In sharp contrast to Kalifa's findings, the U.S. historian Thomas Cragin has argued that continuity was the general rule in nineteenth-century crime news. He claims that the old *canard*'s principal themes and headlines, notably its focus on sensational murders, survived the industrialization of the press more or less intact. For Cragin, the crime stories of the newspaper *fait-divers* columns were really more of an elite imitation of the *canard* than an innovation. Yes, industrialization made the press more voluminous, but the survival of the *canard* well beyond the inception of the mass press offered proof of the Parisian "news media's remarkable resistance to change."[9]

The conflicts that arose between the press and the investigating officials during the rue Montaigne case speak to this historical debate and demand a closer look at the obscure figures who actually generated the crime stories in question. By unearthing the career of *Le Figaro*'s Georges Grison, a key player in the rise of investigative reporting in general and in the rue Montaigne case in particular, in this chapter I bring the small-time reporter to the fore, yielding a picture of piecemeal evolution in investigative reporting.

In fact, we know little about the individuals who made up the first generation of *fait-divers* reporters, those drudges who actually remade the information industry between 1870 and 1900. The main reason for this lacuna is that *petit-reporters* were generally not allowed to sign their articles unless they did it pseudonymously.[10]

That Grison's storied career could have eluded attention until now—not a single article has been written about him in any language—merely illustrates this point. Grison's name likewise goes unmentioned in popular and scholarly accounts of the rue Montaigne case, despite his crucial part in it from beginning to end.[11] Through the lens of Grison's career, the rue Montaigne investigation can be viewed as the culmination of a years-long effort to pierce the state's monopoly on legitimate criminal investigation.

It is true that, as Cragin's argument would have it, Grison's career in journalism, which began at the dawn of the popular press, was built on a self-consciously elitist, right-wing, and conservative bourgeois co-opting of the popular demand for urban grit. Yet Grison's ambition—acted out in a crucible of technological change, the morphing urban landscape, the estab-lishment of liberal democracy, and the intense competition in crime report-ing, as documented by Kalifa—created novel opportunities and substantial innovations in the attainment and circulation of information. For several years—going back at least to the demimondaine Marie Fellerath's 1879 mur-der—Grison had been laying the groundwork for his clash with Guillot over the rue Montaigne evidence. Grison's trajectory shows that the lowly crime reporter required not only new reporting techniques but also networking savvy and panache.

It is instructive, I think, that where Cragin refers to the "makers" of the *canard* in the general terms of social class, the modern investigative crime reporter, thanks in part to Grison, became a recognizably individual urban type during the 1870s and 1880s. The *canard* tended to depict Parisian police and magistrates as intelligent and capable; the modern newspaper reporter, on the other hand, would have quickly succumbed to his competitors if he had followed the same course.

As the shadowing of Taylor and Goron gave way to outright spying later in the spring, Parisian reporters kept pushing their boundaries further and further beyond the subdued beginnings of *fait-divers* crime reporting in the 1860s, when there was no questioning the institutional deference to the po-lice and magistrates of the Second Empire. Back then the police were under no obligation, nor did they face much pressure to provide updates on a given investigation. The state controlled the news, and it dispatched it as it saw fit. Although journalists did not pretend to much in the way of inde-pendent information gathering, during the Troppmann investigation they at least made an effort to verify police statements, venture out to visit the crime scene in northeastern Paris, and question witnesses, if tentatively and unsystematically.[12]

Less than two decades later, the deference had thoroughly eroded. The venerable Adolphe Guillot, "furious" at the Hôtel Cailleux incident and the precedents it set, launched into a rare public tirade attacking the report-ers. The magistrate scolded the reporters for their disclosures—"imprudent indiscretions"—which, he asserted, forewarned and enabled a murderer still on the loose. The identity of the rue Montaigne suspect was "known from the first instant," and the police were well positioned to nab him when he returned to the hotel to recover his valise; but now, thanks to the press, there was no hope for a swift arrest.[13]

It was a matter of course that Grison would be the one to step forward to defend himself and his colleagues. With customary irreverence he shot back in a column-long manifesto, "If it were not about something as mournful as the murder of three people, this statement could pass for a masterwork of buffoonery." The press corps was being frozen out of the investigation, he added, distanced "like wild animals."[14] Grison offered a point-by-point critique of Guillot's investigation. The rue Montaigne killer was certainly aware that he had left his belt and cufflinks at Regnault's apartment, said Grison. There were traces of candle wax on the rug where he had tried to find them in the dark. Likewise the personal effects at the Hôtel Cailleux: "It would take a handsome dose of naïveté to believe that he would've risked his head to go recover a valise—even one of yellow leather. He would sooner leave that to Monsieur Taylor as a consolation prize." Reporters will "relay, and *have the right to relay*, all that they can uncover."[15]

As a matter of law, Grison was correct: Press censorship had been abolished several years before, in 1881 (though it lingered in other domains, such as theater).[16] This flung open the door onto a new world in which personal privacy and government secrecy were at once endangered: "From now on, all houses are made of glass," complained one society journalist. And the reporters held the stones: "Given the rights that reportage is assuming, any person of notoriety in Paris will soon be unable to drink, eat, walk around, sit, love, or hate without" the threat of publicity.[17]

In a society animated by the free flow of information, obscure young provincials could turn up in the capital and begin selling bits of information to newspaper editors. That is how Grison himself had slashed his way through the journalistic underbrush back in the 1870s. The democratization of the spotlight provided a weapon to the first generation of investigative reporters, but it was a weapon completely divorced from fortune and prestige. The deep ambivalence that Grison's ilk inspired in literary elites is well-known and can be found, for example, in the flummery-filled journal of Edmond de Goncourt, a forerunner to the contemporary tell-all. Although Goncourt grasped the commercial appeal of indiscreet nonfiction as well as anyone then alive, he also objected to the freewheeling culture of the *petit-reporters* who profited from it. Their presence was an "exasperating aspect" of celebrity funerals, he groused after his friend Gustave Flaubert's burial, where reporters had swarmed "with little pieces of paper in the hollow of their hands, on which they write down the names of people and places, which they mishear."[18]

Even Grison's more highbrow colleagues at *Le Figaro* resented the expanding role of the reporters in the modern newspaper business, which they rightly perceived as a threat. Reportage, declared the political journalist Albert Millaud, was "the last word in the literary decadence of an era; the man of letters replaced by the concierge." Reporters were "killing journalism" by lowering writing standards and barriers to entry. "While it is difficult to be a writer or a journalist," Millaud charged, reporting is accessible because "one need not know how to write a single line."[19]

Of course, Grison disagreed. The *fait-divers* was "the work of pure imagination," he believed: Newswriting was a literary genre. In a letter written midway through his career, he argued:

> The facts, such as I write them, demand more time and work than any article for which copyright protections are granted. One must first do research, gather the right information, and do an investigation, using all the ingenuity at one's disposal. One has to give form to the information, shape it into a small drama or a little novel. It is thus a work of imagination and a literary work that merits, like all others, to be treated as the property of the author; it should bear his signature.[20]

One reads clearly in these lines the assumed superiority of fiction, its place at the top of the cultural hierarchy. Grison would spend decades trying to raise the reporter's profile, with measurable results.

Few descriptions of Grison have survived. The famed playwright and novelist Gustave Guiches, who recalled spotting Grison breezing by in the street, described a face that was "furtive and somber"; his demeanor was tense, his posture purposeful, as though he was "preparing himself to commit a nighttime assault."[21] With time, these became commonplace descriptors of Parisian *fait-divers* reporters, whose professional frustration and embitterment were said to be the outgrowth of unrealized literary success.[22] Grison breathed life into these and other contemporary clichés of the investigative crime reporter: the clever provincial gadfly; the irritating and audacious arriviste whose work always straddles the line between public service and the profit motive, the latter best captured by the commercial demand for the "exclusive news report," or scoop.[23]

GEORGES GRISON was a brisk 80 when he ended his career in the late 1920s. Born in Saintes, capital of the old province of Saintonge in southwestern France, he told colleagues he was quitting Paris for the Pyrenées, jesting on his way out the door that he had "consented" to an early retirement and planned on writing his memoirs.[24] For nearly six decades, including a half-century at *Le Figaro*, Grison had done a young man's job.

To initiates, Grison was a fixture in his gray overcoat, a white scarf around his neck. He outlived two wives (or three, if we count his undocumented marriage to the starlet Lucy Léo) and survived two catastrophic wars with Germany. He published thousands of newspaper columns, dozens of novels, several volumes of investigative nonfiction, and numerous plays—so many titles that they could not be squeezed onto the handwritten list card that was inserted into his file at the French National Archives.[25]

Grison expired after only a few months in the southwest, not having reserved enough time to pen his memoirs or even draw up a will. His royalties would not have been worth much to his children; his oeuvre had already begun its slide into oblivion. To this day, only one of Grison's books, the quotable *Paris horrible*, has seen a reprinting.

A scant few obituaries appeared, kind professional tributes that nonetheless betrayed a view of Grison as having outlived his time by a few years. He was eulogized as a "connoisseur of the Parisian underbelly" and the "macabre spectacles" of everyday Parisian life.[26] The Association des journalistes parisiens, an important organization of newspapermen that had been slow to admit Grison as a member decades before, called him one of the "deans" of the Parisian press.[27] A more prestigious literary association, the Société des gens de lettres, which had made Grison a full member only once he was past the age of 40, counted him among its decorated alumni: Grison had won the Prix Taylor, the Prix Petit Bourg, and the Prix Jacob de la Cottière. He was once a runner-up for the Prix Balzac.[28] This professional recognition can be appreciated only in light of Grison's lifelong struggle in the meat grinder of Parisian newspapers; he managed to survive the depths of freelancing anonymity and the abject poverty it entailed.

Grison's early career coincides with the entry of the terms *reportage* and *detective* into French usage in the latter third of the nineteenth century, and indeed, the two professions were intertwined.[29] Long seen as an "illegitimate" Anglo-American import, the first reporters were likened by the elite journalist Aurélien Scholl to a marginal "floating company," the "dregs of the press."[30] The culture of the Parisian newspaper business remained attached to an old hierarchy that placed fiction writing, ponderous

chroniques, political journalism, and society fluff at the top, leaving reporters to toil in a pseudonymous (or anonymous) netherworld.

They arrived in droves, were ill-paid, and, though treated as unschooled
interlopers, were ordered to spin urban miscellany into tiny three-line anecdotes. It was both simpler and more harrowing than it sounds. For those
who, like Grison, chose criminality as their muse, social respectability was
out of the question; the more pressing problem was paying for food. Those
who managed to earn a living could expect to face the backlash of an array
of critics. Foremost among those condescending to the reporters were the
moralizers—the theorists and other intellectuals who worried about the social
consequences of crime reporting, which they decried as a corrupting spigot
that never shut off. Does the consuming of violent crime stories inspire copy-
cats, or "contagion," as contemporaries preferred to call it? Countless medical
and psychological metaphors pointed to the corrosiveness of *fait-divers* crime
reports, which for one observer conjured the sight of a "foreign body that
contaminates a healthy organ."[31]

Consequently, the notion of a heroic crime reporter would have seemed
an oxymoron in the 1870s, a fantasy from science fiction: The novelist Jules
Verne featured the first fictional globetrotting reporters in his novels of that
decade, but his characters are less in the mold of the investigator à la Grison
than they are global adventurers and explorers.[32]

Not until the 1880s did investigative crime reporters belatedly begin to
appear in a warmer light, largely because of Grison's inspiration. In the
spring of 1887, just in time for Grison's disagreements with Guillot, Fortuné du Boisgobey, an author of international following and a part-time *Le
Figaro* fiction contributor, released the crime novel *Cornaline la dompteuse*.
One subplot of the book involves a character that historians have identified
as one of the earliest sympathetic portrayals of an investigative reporter in
French fiction (it would be another two decades or so before the reporter
was made a heroic character in a French novel).[33] Press insiders would easily have fingered Grison as the model for du Boisgobey's fictional reporter
Saintonge, whom the author named after Grison's beloved *pays*. Saintonge is
described as the "king of reporters," a middle-aged man with the "intuition
of a professional policeman" and "a rough look, wearing a face as tired as
his overcoat, but intelligent and fine."[34] Like his real-life alter ego, Saintonge constantly pushes the limits of what can be printed; and like Grison,
Saintonge struggles with the quid pro quo that was a requirement of close

dealings with the police. One of the novel's virtues lies in its revelation of the informal deals that Parisian police and reporters struck routinely with each other. We learn that Saintonge spotted clues that "would have gone unnoticed" and that he "knew how to be discreet," which gained him the trust of the police. In exchange, investigators fed him information that "was kept hidden from other journalists."[35]

GRISON EARNED the notice of high-profile writers through the primary means available to him. He wrote himself into the story, became a character in his news reports. He instinctively grasped the performative element of the investigation, and he mastered the art of making a virtue of necessity. He labored to embody the ideal of a reporter as an omniscient sage of the boulevard, a citizen whose ostensible craving for renown was, deep down, really just the voice of a middle-class type whose public duty as a reporter had been thrust on him by government and police incompetence, and the moral burden of knowledge acquired through overachieving.[36]

Grison found a way to shape the public's perceptions of all the landmark crime stories of the early Third Republic. His reporting made waves in the early stages of the case against the Jewish army Captain Alfred Dreyfus. Later in the 1890s, when the Dreyfus affair was engulfing the nation, an anti-Dreyfusard play that Grison co-authored was censored, nearly causing a public riot.[37] In the next great case to roil France, involving Henriette Caillaux—a politician's wife who in 1914 gunned down Gaston Calmette, a prominent editor at Le Figaro—Grison provided witness testimony that sharply contradicted Caillaux's claim that she had acted in a fit of passion and thus deserved leniency. Grison had been working a few steps down the hall at Le Figaro's headquarters; he said he heard Caillaux pause as she emptied her revolver and, seeing her stand over Calmette's body, Grison judged that she had killed his boss in cold blood, with the demeanor of a "dame who is waiting for theater tickets."[38]

Grison could have felt existentially threatened by Calmette's murder: Caillaux attacked the editor for publishing embarrassing correspondence and intimate information from her past. Grison and his sort (long-forgotten reporters such as Georges Mensy at L'Intransigeant) trafficked in precisely this sort of society gossip. For scandal mongers, information was a business in which secrecy did not remunerate; on the flip side, being subpoenaed to testify in well-publicized cases involving family matters such as adultery and extortion only enhanced Grison's stature as an information clearinghouse.[39]

Ostentatious risk taking was another practice in Grison's repertoire. He got into the habit of combing the streets at all hours in search of dreadful tales, which sometimes leapt at him from the darkness. On one occasion rival newspapers reported that Grison had been mugged by three men as he returned home at 2 a.m. He was well past 70 years old at the time; the police heard him crying out and opened fire on the assailants.[40]

A more sophisticated way for a reporter to make himself the star in a competitor's *fait-divers* reporting was to go looking for conflict with men of name. To this end, Grison aimed searing censures at public figures of all walks. When he savaged the staff at the Hôpital Saint-Louis for patient mistreatment, one of his targets, Dr. E. de Bourgade La Dardye, felt that his honor had been besmirched and challenged Grison to a duel. The two men met on an island in the Seine beyond city limits, where the doctor wounded Grison on the right forearm (he was treated on the spot).[41] Grison lost the duel, but what mattered was that an aristocrat had dignified a small-beer hack with his seconds.

NOTORIETY is a relative notion, but it is safe to say that Grison's career took him far from his 1841 birth to a tax collector. How did a young Catholic conservative on the straight road to a career in public administration wind up as one of Paris's most prolific purveyors of scandal and sleaze?

During the 1840s and 1850s, one of the most widely reprinted guides to career development in France was that of Édouard Charton, a hugely successful editor of popular journals and a fervent republican. Taking the pulse of his era, Charton concluded that, despite there being less pressure to follow in one's father's footsteps than there had been in the past, doing so remained the "most simple and natural course" for a young man.[42] Grison began his training, such as it was, for a fiscal career and a life of practicality: The junior high school in his hometown had two mathematics teachers, one physics teacher, and a history teacher.[43] He finished and took a job in the local tax administration.

But Grison, like countless other provincial Frenchmen of his generation, real and fictional, came to embrace his own ambition unabashedly. This meant overcoming the prevailing view of climbing as a shameful passion. Contemporary doctors warned against ambition's influence in terms otherwise reserved for tuberculosis or cholera. Classified as a mental illness, some argued that ambition led to crass longings for social betterment and materialism. Ambition's power could riddle a healthy body with cancers and other mortal illnesses, even heart attacks.[44]

Grison may have dutifully taken the administrative job for which he was destined, but at age 19 he seems to have grown bored with it. From his remote corner of France he began to cast about for new opportunities elsewhere. Ambition was an urban disease—"all young ambition" goes to the big cities, wrote Charton[45]—and doctors, who were often of conservative inclinations, tried to stanch its spread with prescriptions to avoid cities altogether. (To alleviate the symptoms of ambition, doctors prescribed warm baths, walks, hunting, and other pastoral activities.)[46] Historians have interpreted these views as expressions of anxiety about increasing social fluidity and the specter of "representative government." The French and Industrial Revolutions had, it was feared, stoked the pride of society's lower orders.[47]

Grison began to send off pieces of writing to other parts of France and managed to get a couple of them published, including one about the ocean dunes on the Atlantic coast. The newspaper business, forever altered by the dual revolutions, at that time constituted the future of mass culture in Europe; not surprisingly, historians have identified early newspapermen as exemplars of galloping ambition.[48] They joined the entrepreneurs, salesmen, shopkeepers, and other small proprietors who made up the *nouvelles couches sociales*, all striving to find their place in the professional classes.[49]

These nouveaux riches made easy targets. Arguably no novel of the decade was more lacerating in its depiction of the newspaper business than *Bel-Ami* (1885), written by the part-time *Le Figaro* contributor and editor Guy de Maupassant. This classic satire of Parisian society unspools the schemes of Georges Duroy from his early days as a freelance reporter with little money through the ranks of the press and up to the very top. "Everything is only egotism," Duroy tells himself. "Egotism as regards ambition and fortune is better than egotism as regards woman and love."[50] The book was an enormous success, propelled by hilarious sequences that skewered newspaper backrooms, which were awash in feckless scroungers like Duroy, only less handsome.

THE FIRST recorded recognition of Grison's writing appeared in a prominent monarchist literary journal in Lyon. The journal had an essay contest in which the entrants were asked whether one should, if given a choice, be a genius or a model of virtue. Grison's entry concluded on a rather liberal note—genius would be his choice, because virtue "can be acquired"—that did not sit well with the editor, Adrien Peladan, a widely read journalist with monarchist affinities. "We applaud [this] intelligent essay, even as we remark that the concluding reflection, itself debatable, does not rigorously follow that which precedes it."[51]

In 1862, at age 21, Grison found some work at a local newspaper, *L'Indépendence de Saintes*, and found time to launch a satirical rag, *Le Moustique* (The Mosquito), which led to conflicts with local notables. Having established himself as a gadfly, he moved, in 1865, to the nearby town of Jonzac, where he met Émile Gaboriau, who would soon be the internationally recognized father of the crime novel. Like Grison, Gaboriau was the son of a government functionary and a native of the southwest who had only recently begun to write professionally. Before long both men were in Paris, though charting markedly different courses.[52]

In addition to cultural deficiencies, an outsider such as Grison faced a survival-of-the-fittest ambiance among would-be journalists and writers, who swamped the labor market in the latter half of the nineteenth century: Paris had less than 500 professional journalists in the 1860s; by 1885 they numbered 1,000, but these figures do not reflect the countless freelancers who further cheapened the price and esteem of the labor involved.[53] A reporter's chances of making it out of this inferno and establishing a name for himself were infinitesimal.[54]

Although writing anonymous columns as a freelancer had surely not been his dream, Grison looked back on his first years in Paris as an invigorating time: "I had just arrived in Paris, my heart was gay and my wallet light—I was eating leftover bread more often than truffles."[55] Precariousness was the price of admission and, suffering a shortfall, Grison was forced to take a job as an administrator in the Lyon railway company. It beat the alternatives. Many reporters worked without contracts; known as *passants*, these men roamed the streets like organ grinders, knocking at news bureau after news bureau, selling whatever scraps of information they could gather along the way.[56] Their fabrication of news stories in back offices was common. In that sense, reporters were in part responsible for their reputation as unscrupulous blabberers.[57]

Grison's debut in Paris took place against the backdrop of a radical transformation in newspapers. Editors were working with a new business model of cheap papers, beginning in the mid-1860s with the overnight success of *Le Petit Journal*, the first "penny press" newspaper in France. The first reportages then appeared, mainly in the dabbling of a few noted writers in the *fait-divers*. Jules Vallès, one such writer, announced the ethos of investigative writing: "look closely and tell everything," but in a spare prose style that could combine the ordinary and the sensational.[58] He and others implemented a mode of urban observation that was familiar to readers of Eugène Sue's gritty prose, which was part of a tradition that stretched back to Louis-Sébastien Mercier's eighteenth-century classic *Tableau de Paris*.[59]

The success of *Le Petit Journal* spawned several imitators, and Grison gained his first exposure to a mass readership through one of these, *La Petite Presse*, a one-sou sheet run by the newspaper mogul Paul Dalloz.[60] He signed a few articles in the popular press, notably in flourishing papers such as *Le Journal pour Tous*, a cheap popular magazine. What survives of these pieces indicates that Grison was either more interested in writing about provincial life or simply had not yet gained a purchase on the capital. Nothing in these early publications—a paltry list of signed articles—suggests an engagement with urban subjects. But pastoral anecdotes about the Saintonge could only carry him so far.[61] Grison would need to make major thematic changes and develop a professional network. The more regular freelancing work that *Le Figaro* offered him in the early 1870s gave him a chance to make necessary changes.

GRISON'S two most important friends in Parisian letters were Gaboriau and du Boisgobey. (Du Boisgobey had also grown bored in a financial administration job in the southwest, and, like Grison, he had published in *Le Petit Moniteur* upon arriving in Paris in the mid-1860s.)[62] If they did not prod Grison to produce more salable material, they at least demonstrated how to carve out a space in Parisian publishing.

Literary stardom came to Gaboriau somewhat late in life, but it was immense. He pulled detective fiction out from Poe's long shadow by placing the criminal investigation at the center of his novels and in the process taught Parisian newspaper crime reporters how to string along a criminal investigation to maintain reader interest; rather than the traditional focus on the criminal and his act, Gaboriau shifted the focus to the search for clues and for suspects.[63] Friendship went a long way: In 1872 Gaboriau agreed to sponsor Grison's application for provisional membership in the Société des gens de lettres—a mark of legitimacy that traditionally eased admittance into professional networks—even though Grison had published nothing of note and his first book was still a decade off.[64] Grison's other sponsor that year was the journalist Charles Monselet, a chronicler of urban life in the lineage of Mercier and Rétif de la Bretonne. A decade later, in 1883, Grison applied for full membership to the Société. By then Gaboriau had died, so du Boisgobey served as his sponsor, calling him a "friend" in his warm letter of endorsement. Du Boisgobey's support was not a given; a powerful figure behind the scenes, he was not above dooming an application to the Société.[65] By then the author of several successful books, including *Les mystères du nouveau Paris* (1876), Du Boisgobey had written fiction for *Le Figaro* in the late 1870s, so he already appreciated Grison's driving investigative style as a nonfictional extension of the burgeoning crime novel.[66]

Du Boisgobey was well connected in the social world of letters, which in those days organized itself socially around clubs and food, the so-called literary dinners. "It is just as impossible for a Parisian of any social standing not to belong to a '*diner*,' as it is for a 'Boulevardier' not to belong to a '*cercle*,'" wrote a foreign observer.[67] Du Boisgobey was a regular at the Taylor Dinner, which began in 1866 and ran for almost two decades. Sponsored by the playwright and philanthropist Baron Taylor (no relation to the chief of Security), this group met every week at Notta, a restaurant popular among writers and newspapermen at the corner of the rue Rougemont and the boulevard Bonne-Nouvelle. In the hierarchy of Parisian letters, the Taylor Dinner had neither the intellectual clout nor the cachet of more prominent dinners; it was less "academic" than the Bixio Dinner, a group that included Alexandre Dumas *fils*, and it could not compare to the monthly *Boeuf nature* Dinner, which from the mid-1870s hosted heavyweights of Zola's Naturalist camp, including Maupassant and Huysmans.[68]

What they lacked in stature, Taylor Dinner authors repaid in page counts and sales. Along with du Boisgobey, there were fellow crime novelists Elie Berthet and Pierre Zaccone, as well as Hector Malot, Ferdinand Fabre, Adolphe Belot, Paul de Musset, and Paul Féval (he who had resented the loss of Widows' Alley).[69] This collection churned out popular crime and adventure novels with numbing speed. Berthet fired off half a dozen novels in a single year; in all, he published more than 100 volumes. The Taylor Dinner authors were generally published by Édouard Dentu, a quasi-official publisher of authors in the Société des gens de lettres who frequented these gatherings and was known for being "as welcoming to unknown writers as to those who already had a reputation, or at least commercial success."[70] In 1880, after Baron Taylor's death, the party was renamed the Dentu Dinner. Whether Grison met Dentu at the Taylor Dinner is unknown; as a reporter, his name would not, and does not, appear on published short lists of regular attendees. But Gaboriau or du Boisgobey could have introduced Grison to the publisher, who wound up offering the reporter his first book contract in the early 1880s (followed by several more).[71]

In Grison's crime reporting, which was the basis for his first book, *Paris horrible*, he confronted the same challenges that his Taylor Dinner mentors were facing, namely, tapping into the reading public's passion for the underworld of Sue's *Les mystères de Paris*, when, in fact, Haussmann had destroyed many of the medieval alleyways and other hangouts that had been Sue's inspiration. "If the hammer of the demolishers has annihilated some vestiges of the past that one would have liked to preserve," wrote an approving observer in 1864, "it destroys even more haunts of thieves and places of debauchery."[72]

Beyond the glaring problem of anachronism lay the related question of politics. Sue, Parisian born and bred, famously showed sympathy for the lower classes and was in turn adored by them; he ultimately agitated for the Left. Likewise had Jules Vallès, in his early reporting, brought his own social concerns to bear on his subjects.[73] On the other hand, Sue's descendants among the Taylor Dinner crowd, notably du Boisgobey and Zaccone, had distinctly conservative and provincial backgrounds. For these crime writers, Sue's Paris was more literary than lived; undeterred by Haussmannization, they clung to Sue's geography but dispensed with the empathy and political proclivities. They took it upon themselves to convince readers that the swank, gentrified Grands Boulevards were, somewhere behind their facades, criminal badlands.[74]

This required a concerted effort to douse reader skepticism. Zaccone wrote in his 1879 novel *Les nuits du boulevard*, "Great thoroughfares have opened up; air and light are now profuse," an observation that could mislead some into believing that it was safe to go outside alone. "This is incorrect. The night is still the night! The danger has modified, but it has not completely disappeared."[75] One finds similar passages in the crime novels published in the 1870s and 1880s, which set crime around the Garnier Opera, the Champs-Elysées, the business district along the Chaussée d'Antin, and even in the rue de la Paix.[76]

Critics charged that the novelistic conceit of thieves descending on the gentrified neighborhoods of Paris was an "enormous joke"; and for their part, historians of Paris have affirmed that a hypothetical contemporary reader who was well informed would have found the "archaic" attempt to portray the inner arrondissements as crime zones risible.[77] But the murder of Marie Fellerath—the same year that Zaccone's novel appeared—and the subsequent unsolved killings around the Grands Boulevards, legitimized the school of popular crime writers who were Grison's mentors.

IT WAS IN 1879 that Grison, now with a secure position and his Jean de Paris byline at *Le Figaro*, began to earn public accolades as a crime reporter who, according to one press observer, "digs into a crime with the instincts of a police officer and writes an execution with the greatest mastery."[78] The idea that Grison and his fellow reporters longed to mimic policemen was already becoming a point of contention.

Marie Fellerath's death was the first to unite the combative threesome of Grison, Ernest Taylor, and Adolphe Guillot. Fellerath was found dead on July 23, 1879, in the passage Saulnier near the Grands Boulevards. The murder weapon had been found. It was a Japanese knife, which Grison judged to be that "of a native, gotten over there and brought back here as is."[79] Grison cultivated the ambient xenophobia at every turn, for this was a narrative that would gain broad appeal in the coming years: Immigrants were attacking the women kept by the elites around the boulevards, the center of the theater world where many sought-after demimondaines resided.

Little was known about Fellerath herself. She was 22 years old; in addition to her patrons, she was said to have a lover, a Polish immigrant, who was immediately arrested but later released for lack of evidence. This was before the liberalization of the press, but Grison had begun to use republican rhetoric to strengthen his defense of the reporter's participation in the pursuit of criminal suspects. A few months before Fellerath's death, he published an article arguing that "it is the act of a bad citizen not to reveal facts that could lead to the discovery of the truth."[80]

But far more compelling was the genius Grison exhibited for nosing around and doing the kind of menial labor that official investigators either did not think of doing or, more likely, believed to be beneath the dignity of their professions. Shortly after Fellerath's death, Grison went down to the Police Prefecture to sift through the objects in the lost and found, as

he did from time to time anyway. Like the best *fait-divers* writers, he was
a ragpicker at heart who figured out how to play on the public's insatiable
appetite for the unseemly in their midst.

Grison's spadework posed a predicament to police, magistrates, and editors alike. What made his work inglorious also made it extremely valuable
and entertaining to readers. Brevity was the soul of the *fait-divers*, and Grison understood that reader curiosity was not a fixed set of desires to be
satisfied but instead a formless, renewable resource. The energy that readers
would devote to little nothings was untapped, and it might even govern
their reading habits as it pertained to the news. A reader could get through
a *fait-divers* column on a noisy omnibus trip across the city, after all; he
could remember its anecdotes without trouble and recapitulate a favorite
one upon arrival at the office.[81]

Ultimately, however, Grison's columns derived gravitas from the realization
that the apparently inane could turn out, in fact, to have urgent application,
such as in the pursuit of a murder suspect. Amid the detritus in the Police
Prefecture's lost and found bins in the summer of 1879, Grison found the
matching sheath to the Japanese knife. It had been turned in just a day after
Fellerath's body had been found. After some more digging, the reporter confirmed that police investigators themselves had found the sheath among other
objects in the staircase of an apartment building near the crime scene. Eager
to highlight an embarrassing investigative oversight, Grison wrote in his next
column: "The neighborhood police commissary, Monsieur Taylor, didn't realize what this sheath shaped like a hand fan could be. Thinking nothing of it,
he forwarded it to the Prefecture with a package containing other objects."[82]

Grison applied some pressure to Guillot too, by demanding that the
magistrate share information about other suspects and by taking it upon
himself to tail *potential* suspects. There were rumors that a server in a local
café had a part in Fellerath's death. In his column Grison reported on the
suspect's movements, identifying the man only as "C." Grison wrote that
he had seen C. "last night at Valentino, dancing very gaily and not in the
least carrying himself as if 'burdened by the weight of remorse.'"[83] The
reporter also went to interview witnesses to find out if C. had an alibi on
the night of Fellerath's murder. While Guillot was conducting the official
investigation, Grison broke the news that he had found 200 people who
could testify that C. worked his usual shift at the café that night from
7 p.m. to 1 a.m.[84]

In July 1885, the month when Hélène Stein and Marie Jouin, the second and third demimondaine victims, were found dead, members of the press corps grew weary.[85] Paris had some experience with serial killers, most recently in the 1860s on the Left Bank, when Louis-Joseph Philippe confessed to murdering seven common prostitutes.[86] Guillotined in 1866, Philippe set the mold of the "public-women killer" (*assassin de filles publiques*) in modern Paris. Following Fellerath's death and particularly after those of Stein and Jouin, that term was revived and again became common in the press.[87]

IN THE INTERIM, Grison published his breakthrough book, *Paris horrible* (1882), much of which was recycled material from his *Le Figaro* columns.[88] The book, released when Grison was 41, bridged the styles of popular crime fiction and newspaper reporting without ever fully distinguishing between the two. More important, Grison used the book to explicitly vector the *fait-divers* toward a conservative discourse on crime and morality. *Paris horrible* opens with a paragraph about Haussmannization that could have come from the pen of Zaccone or du Boisgobey.

> Each day, Paris expands and gets more beautiful. . . . One could no longer write a work like *Les mystères de Paris* in our time. The Cité, the hideous Cité, fell under the demolition worker's pick-axe, erasing the web of ignominious alleys in which . . . a vile population had stirred. . . . Of all the strange and dangerous places described in the novels of thirty and forty years past, none have survived. Okay, but did you imagine that in tearing down a dilapidated hovel, you could at once rid yourself of all that was revolting within it? . . . All of that migrated, but where? You don't know? Well somewhere, after all.[89]

Despite Haussmann's laudable efforts, in other words, the old *classes dangereuses* were alive and well in the Third Republic. For the reporter the investigation of criminality aimed to locate "*that* population" which, supposedly displaced by gentrification, has shown that it can "appear suddenly, furious and avid with demands and vengeance during the dark days of rioting and revolution."[90]

From Grison's standpoint, revolution and criminality went hand in hand, and social purification and harsh criminal punishment were the antidotes: Haussmannization merited completion. Grison won favor from hard-liners on crime for his defense of harsh penalties, including the death penalty for murderers and, for recidivists, banishment to the hellholes that were

France's expanding penal colonies overseas. Parisian recidivists dispatched to the penal colony "wouldn't be so bad off," he told readers. The horrors of Guyana, a penal colony known as "Europe's Tomb," were overblown. It was no more dangerous in Guyana than in Paris, according to Grison, and at least the experience developed prisoners' taste for work.[91]

When Grison ventured out to eastern Paris and detailed the awful conditions of the housing stock or the lives of prostitutes, there was never a pretense of compassion. He believed that the police were wrong to regulate the lucrative prostitution industry in a corporatist fashion when it should have been treating prostitutes as criminals. Grison rejected the cliché of the hooker with the heart of gold, and in *Paris horrible* he took issue with the sentimentality that characterized some of the more accomplished authors of the day. Naming names—Zola, Dumas *fils*, and so forth—Grison charged, "People have tried to render prostitution poetic. They have turned it into something gracious and playful, interesting and moving. *La Dame aux Camélias*, *Manon Lescaut*, *Nana*: so many conventional tales that real life brutally negates."[92]

Grison was aware that his opinions could make for strange bedfellows. In *Paris horrible* he tells of his encounter with Josephine Butler, leader of the British feminist movement, who came to Paris to propose the full-scale abolition of prostitution. "Upon hearing that I wrote for *Le Figaro*, she couldn't conceal her stunned smile. In effect, surrounded by radical personalities, the presence of a representative of a conservative newspaper was surprising."[93] Of course, the two arrived at abolition from different perspectives. Butler saw herself as defending women against exploitation. In Grison's view the prostitute was, whatever her grade or appearance, a "rogue."[94] He spared the poorest prostitutes nothing in his biting description; debauchery was "imprinted" on their skin, which was "dry and wrinkled like witches on the Sabbath; most of them are big-boned and thick-lipped, fattened, pimpled, and bearded."[95]

The hard line that Grison took was self-consciously aimed at distinguishing himself from his rivals and predecessors, whom he thought of as soft or "naïve." The reporter was not braving the harder edges of the city to socialize, make friends, or play the part of the bohemian. Grison carried a revolver and asked direct questions of his subjects. "I went to their houses, always in an overcoat and a top hat, without disguising myself, without hiding, and I told them straightforwardly what I wanted to do." That, averred Grison in a reprise of Vallès's injunction, is "how I went everywhere, saw everything, learned everything."[96]

Grison's posturing gave some critics cause for mockery. Here was the reporter in an overcoat and top-hat—the middle-aged envoy of an *haut-bourgeois* literary newspaper, no less—out accosting whores and scribbling their colloquialisms. "To complete the education of young women of the upper classes who read *Le Figaro* aloud to their mothers every evening," cracked one journalist, "Monsieur Georges Grison, in the edition of November 24, began to instruct his joyful newspaper's audience in the delicate language of pimps and hookers."[97]

In general, though, *Paris horrible* garnered approving reviews, even in rival newspapers.[98] The book was praised as a primer on professional crime reporting, and it introduced the most elaborate account yet of journalistic embedding within police units.[99] An incessant networker, Grison persuaded members of the police to contact him when a manhunt was under way, no matter the hour. He took readers along on sting operations aimed at notorious gang members on the lam. There were dramatic arrests, great escapes, and so on.[100]

THE JULY 1883 murder of Marie Jouin, a 24-year-old kept woman whose body was found in her rue Condorcet apartment, was another milestone in Grison's self-promotional siege on the state's investigative apparatus. Jouin's death was discovered by reporters and broke in *Le Figaro*, a source of pride for Grison, who boasted that the magistrate Guillot and the police "knew nothing of it as yet."[101] To get the scoop, Grison had wrangled with the concierge to gain access to Jouin's apartment and was soon followed by his rivals at other papers.

A native of Auvergne, Jouin was described in the press as "very pretty, blonde, svelte, deliciously built."[102] Her story was similar to that of countless young women of the era: Pregnant at 14, she moved to Paris and put her newborn in a pension in the suburbs; "launched" as a prostitute, she worked her way toward a comfortable life, which she had finally attained around age 20, when she moved to 50 rue Condorcet, an apartment signed for by her "protector," on the record as Mr. X, an older gentleman whom she had pretended to have married and who, despite a falling out some months before, still "came from time to time to visit." When Mr. X was not present, she kept a low profile: "She never went out late and always returned before midnight."[103]

More recently, it was rumored, Jouin had been returning home at night with a different gentleman. One Saturday night the concierge saw her go upstairs to her apartment with him. No one had thought anything of her absence over the next several days. It was early July and the weather was hot; kept women could afford to take a few days to relax in the countryside or at the seaside. Then neighbors remarked on an odor emanating from her apartment, and when they entered, Jouin's body was in a state of advanced decomposition, rolled up in a quilt, her face covered by three pillows and a chair.[104] She had been strangled with a silk necktie, which was found fastened around her neck. There were holes in her forehead, as though she had been struck with brass knuckles. Her drawers were emptied, indicating robbery as the motive. Her killer slipped out in the morning, after the front door was unlocked.[105] Dr. Brouardel estimated that she had been dead for about a week.[106]

Jouin frequented the Folies-Bergère and hung around in a milieu of show business types (she was a close friend of the gifted actress and Sarah Bernhardt look-alike, Madame Dosais of the Théâtre de l'Ambigu-Comique).[107] "As with all the crimes of this genre," regretted a journalist, "the lover [*amant de coeur*, as distinguished from a regular paying client] of the victim was arrested, but then released several days later."[108] In fact, in Jouin's case one foreigner and one neighborhood man of ill repute were arrested, but Guillot's investigation stalled for lack of strong evidence, and both men were released.[109]

Each unsolved case invited its own power struggle and dynamics of information. Once a murder was discovered and the police began to seal off the crime scene, put pressure on witnesses, interview neighbors and patrons, and make arrests, newspaper reporters could either cooperate or attempt a parallel inquiry based on spare (or redundant) discoveries. In the Jouin case, Grison and his fellow reporters made a show of their restraint and deference, apparently in exchange for information from the police. "In order not to hinder the ongoing investigation, we did not report that Marie Jouin . . . owned valuables that disappeared from her apartment" and were found in the possession of Jouin's close friend, Mademoiselle D., reported *La Justice*.[110] Grison followed suit a few days later: "We are authorized to say" that the investigation has taken "a step backwards," namely by suspecting Mademoiselle D. for her possession of investment stock titles in Jouin's name, for Jouin had merely sponsored their purchase by a third party, an "intermediary" whose "honorability was not in doubt for a moment."[111] That gentleman stock buyer, like others of the elite with ties to murdered prostitutes such as Jouin, went unnamed.

THERE WERE a few professional obstacles that Grison's tireless reporting could not overcome. Accustomed to taking the offensive in print, Grison received his share of poison darts, tossed at him by better educated colleagues, who were always ready to pounce when the reporter's mask slipped to reveal the son of the provincial tax collector. In the nineteenth century, Greek and Latin bons mots were the province of sophisticates; Grison was taken down a notch when he botched them. "It seems that Mr. Grison never did find himself a Latin instructor," wrote a journalist at another paper, content to flag the reporter's errors. "Mr. Grison confuses Augias with Hercules" jeered another. "It's regrettable!"[112] That Grison was the most important *fait-divers* columnist of the era is another way to interpret the slights he attracted, which were meant to check the reporter's zeal and cast the whole lot of news peddlers as ersatz journalists powered not by culture but by unrefined "instinct," as one newspaperman alleged.[113]

The growing appeal of the *fait divers* complicated Grison's relations at the office. A number of his prestigious colleagues at *Le Figaro* sought to close ranks by joining exclusive professional organizations in the mid-1880s, notably the important Association des journalistes parisiens; but Grison was shut out of them. So he worked independently to develop his own professional networks and organized his fellow outcast reporters at the other major dailies. He founded and headed the Association amicale et professionnelle des reporters, which met at the Café Hollandais in the Palais Royal.[114] He presented his new organization as a public and professional service whose aim would be to uphold "the most severe guarantees of *probité profession-nelle* and private morality."[115] As president, he lobbied the Police Prefecture to institute a system of credential cards that would be granted to vetted reporters—a transparent attempt to create an air of exclusivity and credibility. This initiative fell on deaf ears, but Grison's confrères acclaimed him when he stepped down from his leadership position so that he could tend to "his numerous occupations."[116]

The list of these ventures was growing impressive indeed, and they signal Grison's most important strategy for earning the plaudits he desperately craved. The surest way for the *fait-divers* reporter to enjoy broad respect was to prove that he could publish in other genres. Around 1886, Grison got involved with Lucy Léo, an actress and revue dancer known as "the best legs of the era," who performed on all the great stages of Paris.[117] At first blush Léo might appear inaccessible to the likes of Grison, but by all accounts Grison was likable, if not a dream match for someone in show business. Léo was a minor celebrity but of international reputation, the sort of actress whose personal affairs were reported in the back pages.[118] She was also the daughter of a police commissary.[119]

Seizing the opportunity, Grison cowrote a piece that could capitalize on Léo's sex appeal by having her appear in risqué costume, a coup that he boasted about to the famed critic Georges Montorgueil.[120] Léo agreed to appear in *Place au jeune!* at the Folies-Bergère. The show, which featured scenes from the Parisian underworld (the rats who lived underground and the construction of the *métropolitain* train lines figured into it), was well received by critics, who credited the authors with inventing a "new genre of revue: the *revue dansée.*"[121] It was the beginning of a long and successful collaboration between Grison and Léo, who were known in society as a married couple.[122]

The production had the salutary effect of elevating the Jean de Paris byline to new heights of respectability. One editor observed that Grison, "initiated by his profession to all the mysteries of the new Paris," was now rather suddenly "known in the press as the most skilled and well-read of the reporters at *Le Figaro.*"[123] Granted, this was not a ticket out of the *fait-divers*—note the restrictive qualifier of a single newspaper—but it was major progress. "I willingly recognize," wrote the editor Édouard Cavail-hon, "that among Parisian reporters, there are men of talent," and Georges Grison stood out among them for his "incessant spirit of observation."[124] The disdain and disapproval of elite journalists was not going to disappear, but by 1887 it was clear that Grison's reporting represented the future. Citing Grison's "steadfast method of research," Pierre Giffard, a prominent press critic and colleague at *Le Figaro*, told his colleagues that the reading public of 1886 "must be given news, because there are 100 means of obtaining it—from Paris, from Rome, from Peking . . . —because the telegraph throws them hot on the cobblestones."[125]

Even Grison's archrival, the magistrate Guillot, occasionally acknowledged the reporter's labor, that is, when he was not at daggers with him. The magistrate called the reporter "one of the great masters of Parisian reportage," an "agile and ingenious explorer of the Parisian underworld."[126]

Indeed, in Guillot's influential law treatises, which later helped him secure nomination to France's illustrious Académie des sciences morales et politiques, one finds extensive quotations of Grison's work. Loftier praise would have been hard for any reporter to come by. It was the truest indicator of how far Grison had come.

STILL, it was the friction between Grison and Guillot during the first weekend of the triple-murder investigation that inspired the reporter's most inventive, boundary-pushing work yet, *L'affaire de la rue Montaigne*. Tellingly, he did not put his name on the title page, preferring to sign it simply "by a reporter."

The volume marked a variety of departures from the *canard*, which delivered news of extraordinary events without precisely dating them, as though the timing of the story in question bore only a loose relation to its conveyance. Modern reporting, as practiced by Grison, was moving away from this model, namely by giving primacy to the currency of information—the newness of the news.[127] In *L'affaire de la rue Montaigne*, Grison carried the trend fully into the 1880s by time-stamping updates to the story such that the reporter's work was understood by readers as a round-the-clock endeavor. The result was a mimicking of the continuous circulation of bits of information in real time. Narratively, the sensationalism derived less from exclamation points than from the sense that readers were peering into a dynamic newsroom, with access to a barrage of unedited bulletins written in the present tense. The news here was not presented as a certainty but rather as a frank hodgepodge of speculation, dead-ends, and breakthroughs. As such, the volume was a visionary anticipation of the hourly news report and its successor, the 24-hour news feed.

In *L'affaire de la rue Montaigne*, rushed to publication in the summer before the case was finished, Grison harmonized form and function and threw down the gauntlet to Guillot and the police. Befitting the heyday of the pointillist painters, who aestheticized the microdot by bringing it into the foreground, Grison staked this investigative account on, as he put it, "the smallest detail, the seemingly insignificant anecdote, and things that pass unnoticed and go forgotten until, one fine day, as a result of further discoveries, they assume capital importance."[128]

Suffice it to say that Grison's method did not meet with universal approval. His focus on minutiae disagreed with Deputy Chief Goron, who liked to dismiss as irrelevant all the "stupid details written about in old-fashioned crime novels."[129] A newspaper review of *L'affaire de la rue Montaigne* voiced a similar opinion. If the broad lines of the rue Montaigne case were clear enough, why unsettle the waters? "We believe that we have already spoken too much of this affair," concluded the reviewer; "we must admit that the utility of this publication escapes us."[130]

CHAPTER FOUR

The Courtesan's Objects
Sexual Danger and the High Life of the Demimonde

The funeral mass for the rue Montaigne victims was scheduled for Monday morning at 9 at the Église Saint-Philippe-du-Roule. The patriarch of the Gremeret family, Annette's father and little Marie's grandfather, arrived the prior evening from Burgundy despite the falling snow. Amid press reports of two potential breakthroughs in the hunt for the killer, the church filled to capacity. Outlets in Brussels declared that a man fitting Geissler's description had been spotted reading French newspapers in a café; the same man was seen again later while visiting a hair stylist, presumably to alter his appearance. French authorities increased their vigilance at the Belgian border in response.[1]

Deputy Chief Goron, occupied with the search for Geissler, was examining the valise from the Hôtel Cailleux in his office when a reporter was escorted in, demanding to see him regarding a matter of "extreme urgency." The reporter handed him fresh news from the wire: A man called Pranzini was being held in a jail in the Mediterranean port of Marseille; local police were waiting for Paris to advise them as to how to proceed. The name Pranzini meant nothing to Goron. "I was stupefied. Here was a newspaper

bringing word" of the arrest. "Oh, the disorganization of the police bureaucracy!" Goron put down the valise and hastened to Chief Taylor's office. The
two men were apprised that mention of the Marseille arrest was already in
"every newspaper in the country." Taylor was "more indignant than me,"
recalls Goron, "if such was possible." The deputy chief tapped a few colleagues, and within hours they boarded the rapid train to Marseille.[2]

GAWKERS AND REPORTERS insinuated themselves into the crowd
of mourners at the Église Saint-Philippe-du-Roule. Grison stood near the
entrance, and with a clinician's eye he scanned the attendees as they wobbled
up the snow-packed stairs. It was not unheard of to order a police detail to
keep order at funerals like this. The general public could not resist the rare
peek at a demimondaine's life. Coverage of Regnault's death and investigations into her past, the life she lived in Paris, and her possessions had only
just begun.

Common prostitutes, in contrast to courtesans, were highly visible on
Parisian streets in the nineteenth century, and sexual violence perpetrated
against them was regularly reported in the press. Yet when a streetwalker was
found murdered in the 1880s, as several were, the newspapers dedicated significantly less column space to her death than they did to a woman of Marie
Regnault's stature. After the 1889 murder of a common prostitute named
Marguerite Dubois, for example, one Parisian paper drew a sharp distinction between her career and that of Marie Regnault: Dubois "was a girl in
the registries of the prefecture of police who had few resources beyond the
random encounters of the pavement or the repeated calls to passersby from
behind a set of green blinds and a red curtain."[3] There the investigation of
Dubois's homicide effectively ended, a day or two after her death.

The courtesan, who sat atop the demimonde, was a near mythological
figure who recalled eras of splendor and sensuality going back to the Old
Regime, though the modern courtesan's place in society had evolved since
then.[4] Courtesans were inaccessible to most men, and partly for this reason
they were the subject of countless portrayals in the work of artists and writers, from Delacroix and Balzac to Zola, but most famously in the novel *The
Lady of the Camellias* by Alexandre Dumas *fils*, which the author based on
his lover, Marie Duplessis. (The novel spawned countless representations
and inspired Verdi's opera *La Traviata*.) It was Dumas *fils* who first coined
the term *demimonde*, literally the "half-world" that paralleled and inter-

sected polite society. He knew it too well: His passion for Duplessis brought him to the brink of bankruptcy, a hazard that commonly befell men whose desire outpaced their income. Duplessis, who passionately loved the composer Franz Liszt, flamed out at 23 years of age, her material existence having set the standard by which all demimondaines would be measured. Charles Dickens, staying in Paris as a tourist at the time of her death, could hardly believe the public's raptness at the announcement. The demimonde was a Parisian phenomenon; so baffled was the British visitor at the sight of high society coming to a standstill over the passing of a provincial commoner that he promptly rearranged his schedule to attend the auction of Duplessis's personal belongings, which netted tens of thousands of francs.[5] The sale of Marie Regnault's possessions would produce a similar scene at the Hôtel Drouot, the city's preeminent auction house.

A courtesan never so much entered the public eye as in her untimely death, an event, particularly if it was the result of foul play, that raised uncomfortable questions because of the symbiotic and abundantly problematic relation that Parisian society maintained with sex work. From the moment the news of the rue Montaigne tragedy spread across the city, the public set about assigning meaning to it. The consensus was that little Marie Gremeret, and to a lesser extent her mother, Annette, were innocents whose deaths justice must avenge.

What about Marie Regnault? Did the murder of a courtesan count as a mournful occasion? On this Parisians were in dispute. The debate was inevitably colored by the language used. Words that signified prostitute—"lost girl" and "fallen woman" to cite common synonyms in French and English—were laden with moral judgment and spite for a life gone to perdition. That courtesans were known for material pursuits, disease and dissipation made their sins all the more troubling for having occurred needlessly. Police and journalistic investigations into Marie Regnault's life never completely broke from the notion that Regnault had gotten her just deserts in the end.

Still, the press corps was not entirely devoid of sympathy for the decade's ill-fated demimondaines. For example, the prominent journalist Edmond Roland of *Le Radical* bristled at the callousness of the coverage of their deaths. Murdered prostitutes, he complained, were too often referred to as the "girl-named-such-and-such" or, worse, "that prostitute." Roland made the same point about the justice system, which did not investigate or punish violence against prostitutes as exhaustively as it should have, he opined; in the rare case when a suspect was identified and found guilty, he was sentenced more leniently than was called for, particularly if he had served in the military and had a record as a "good soldier."[6]

Roland did not mention Georges Grison by name, but he may as well have. In his antipathy toward prostitutes, Grison's accounts of their funerals were characterized by cool detachment and traces of a faint-hearted schadenfreude. In his pen, scenes of bereavement became matter-of-fact gossip and salacious details. The funerals presented him with low-hanging fruit: acquaintances, family, neighbors, and friends, all gathered under one roof, bereft and vulnerable, with no abiding incentive to go on protecting the departed's secrets.

Following the July 1885 funeral of Hélène Stein, a demimondaine who had come to Paris from eastern France six years before she was found mutilated in her apartment near the Grands Boulevards, Grison wrote, "Slated for 3 o'clock, the funeral of Hélène Stein, the girl killed at number 24 rue Bergère, did not actually begin yesterday until a few minutes before 4." His article went on to quote the cost of the funeral and burial and provided the initials of the official lover (*amant de titre*) who footed the bill for them.[7] Grison could, with some evidence, claim that putting such information in circulation might ring bells in the minds of acquaintances, possibly producing leads. After all, a tipster responded to the publicity surrounding Stein's funeral with a plausible scenario: "The killer of the Stein girl could well be the same person who killed the Jouin girl," he said. "I call your attention to a man named V——, 40 years of age, and his mistress, both regulars at the house in the rue Condorcet. The man goes by different names; he says he works in insurance and lives in Montmartre, as does his mistress."[8]

Stein had been found covered, on her bed, "unrecognizable." She had been strangled and simultaneously stabbed in the chest with a stylet. Some jewelry was missing; the materials that allowed a common prostitute to reach an upper level of the hierarchy of sex commerce also made her more vulnerable.[9] As in the earlier cases, the first suspect was a man imagined to have come westward to Paris. The police presumed that Stein's killer was from the contentious borderland of Lorraine, recently annexed by the Germans, and an inspector was sent to a small town near the Moselle River to look for him.[10] Then, on the door of Stein's stylish apartment, which was located just steps from the Grands Boulevards, someone posted a note that

Grison reproduced in print: "Madame Hélène had a lover, a businessman, who was said to be generous. She had—as according to custom—a second [lover] who didn't pay. But these two lovers didn't suffice, and between their visits she ran around the so-called places of pleasure where the *femmes galantes* gather. When it was necessary, she wasn't above streetwalking. Her name was inscribed on the plaque outside her door. It was also on the special registries of the Prefecture, where she had a number and a dossier."[11]

Police believed that they had a good lead. On the night of the crime, reported *Le XIXᵉ Siècle*, Hélène Stein, wearing a green moire dress, had appeared with a gentleman at a café in the rue du Faubourg-Montmartre. The man was "tall and bulky, and dressed like a well-off country gentleman," and was "très brun." The pair stayed for about an hour. Ultimately, investigators came away empty-handed.[12]

In his call for a more compassionate tone, Roland batted away the self-justifications of voyeuristic crime reporters like Grison. "We've read the story of the murder of the unfortunate woman in the rue Bergère in all the newspapers," he wrote. "Everywhere we have enacted the details of the crime, the habits of the victim, but nowhere has there been a word of pity for her." When a woman leading an "irregular life" is murdered, he continued, the newspapers always focus on the sordid aspects of the case, omitting all "regret or even one of the standard phrases like, 'We cannot begin to describe the despair felt by the parents and friends of the victim.'"[13]

Roland's criticisms would have no discernible effect on the tenor of the public's discussion in the rue Montaigne case. To the contrary, within a few weeks of the triple homicide, awful reproductions of morgue photographs taken of the three victims by Dr. Brouardel's team were leaked and began circulating in Parisian broadsheets (and soon after in London's equivalents).[14]

GUILLOT'S ORDER that the burial take place Monday morning had allotted Dr. Brouardel and his team only three days to perform three complex autopsies over the weekend. Numerous objects and other materials brought from the apartment complicated the job. Brouardel's report, running to dozens of pages in minuscule print, begins with the usual fare in autopsies involving criminal charges, anodyne observations such as the fact that Regnault's laundress had recently washed the linens. It specified that one of Annette Gremeret's front teeth was freshly fractured, probably because she

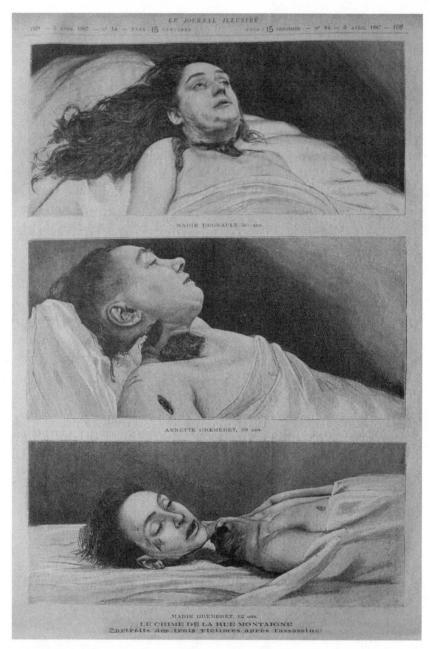

Figure 7. The three victims of the murders in the rue Montaigne, from top to bottom: Marie Regnault, Annette Gremeret, and Marie Gremeret. These images, based on photographs taken at the Paris Morgue, circulated internationally. *La Revue Illustrée,* 10 April 1887.

was dropped to the parquet floor from a standing position after her throat and shoulder were sliced. The wounds on the bodies varied in depth, number, and size. But Brouardel conjectured that they all were produced by the same weapon, "operated with a vigorous and very determined hand," perhaps a Nontron, a traditional wood-handled knife of the Dordogne region of southwestern France.

Brouardel also opened up the bodies. His findings corroborated the hypotheses based on forensics evidence at the crime scene. The massacre was finished in a few minutes. The empty stomachs meant that the previous evening's dinner had been fully digested, and the full bladders indicated several hours of nighttime sleep. Brouardel established that the victims had died around 5 or 6 a.m. Placed under a microscope, tissue drawn from the interior of Regnault's vagina showed a "great number of spermatozoids," but science was not yet advanced enough to determine whose they were.[15] She was menstruating when she died. Brouardel imagined that she had had sex with her killer, then fell asleep with him for some time, perhaps several hours. Finally, Brouardel discovered a voluminous cyst on her left ovary, a condition that could have caused pelvic and back pain as well as discomfort during menstruation and sexual intercourse.

Guillot made one more demand of Brouardel, a particularly onerous one. Supplemental to the inquest, Brouardel was to determine the precise order of the three deaths. Investigators had good evidence that Regnault was the first to be struck, but this did not mean that she was the first, technically speaking, to die. As chief medical examiner in the case, Brouardel replied enthusiastically to Guillot's request by devising a scientific experiment that involved letting the blood of three live dogs through wounds made to approximate those found on the three victims. Brouardel simulated the near decapitation of the child by guillotining the first dog; the slashing of Regnault's throat and the combination of stabs and cuts inflicted on Annette Gremeret were replicated in two proportionally larger dogs.

Brouardel's results would not bring them any closer to the culprit. The experiment would, however, permit officials to determine the fate of Regnault's fortune, a sum greater than the lifetime earnings of an ordinary Frenchman. In question was Regnault's will, which investigators found in the safe near her bed. She had made a change to it just one month before her death, when she named little Marie Gremeret the sole heir. Investigators hoped that Brouardel's findings would settle the issue in accordance with French law, which stated that when potential heirs died roughly in the same moment, those who were under the age of 15 would be presumed to have perished first. In other words, if Brouardel showed that young Marie Gremeret died after Marie Regnault, then the Gremeret family would have a strong claim to the fortune. But if not, Regnault's fortune would fall into the hands of the state, because no one came forth with a credible claim of family relation to her.[16]

All of this came to light well after the funeral at Église Saint-Philippe-du-Roule, at which an abbé officiated and which Grison described as "highly moving."[17] But this, Grison hastened to clarify, was due to the presence of the 11-year-old girl's casket, which was set between the two others at the front of the church. The small casket was adorned with rose bouquets and wreaths with blue and white pearls. One card read, "To Marie Gremeret, from her friends at school." Another was dedicated "To my dear little friend."[18] Officially, Regnault was the girl's godmother, and she took a special interest in her by all accounts, providing for the girl in a maternal way. There were rumors that little Marie might have been Marie Regnault's daughter. Others speculated that she was born of a liaison between Gremeret and a domestic servant in a neighboring apartment, back when Gremeret worked for Regnault's sister, Louise, who was also a demimondaine.

According to Madame Toulouse, the child was reared in a nest of secrets: Gremeret and Regnault kept her innocent of any knowledge of the business and did everything to ensure that the girl's life set itself on a path markedly different from their own. Little Marie went to school in the rue du Faubourg Saint-Honoré, where her teachers called her an "excellent student, full of good intentions." In this neighborhood she would have imbibed the manners of privileged children until they became her own. She was preparing for the sacrament of First Communion that spring; her catechism notebooks, issued by the Église Saint-Philippe-du-Roule, were found at the foot of her bed.[19] After the funerary mass the elder Gremeret led a procession of seven carriages on an hour-long journey to the cemetery at Saint-Ouen, beyond the city's fortification walls.[20]

Officials and reporters began to piece together the circuitous life of Marie Regnault, laying bare the biography of a successful entrepreneur. Described as a "pretty" or "passably pretty" woman as she entered middle age, Regnault was tall and curvy, with pale and fleshy arms. She had a small, downward-sloping nose, full lips, and eyes that were round and lively. In a damaged archived photo she can be seen in a corset, her bust heaving forward and her wide hips accentuated; she is wearing a trademark piece of jewelry: an arm bracelet, connected to another bracelet on her wrist by a long chainlet. Her teeth, it was reported, were "white and healthy." In short, she was known as a "very desirable woman" in the demimonde, according to Grison's sources, both for her looks and her "good manners."[21]

As investigators probed into Regnault's life, the line between investigation and prurience grew indistinct. From Deputy Chief Goron's case notes, for example, we learn that the police found in Regnault's nightstand drawer "objects whose public sale is illegal and that are used by the priestesses of Sappho."[22] All told, early findings shed little light on who may have wanted to kill Marie Regnault. Stories of jealousy there were not. Jilted lovers, if there had been any, did not materialize as a result of witness accounts. Police could find no enemies or rivalries anywhere in her past; she carried no debt and had no addictions.

"Despite her lifestyle" as a prostitute, reported police investigators in bewilderment, "one finds only excellent things said about her everywhere." As an established courtesan, she had a stable routine. "Her existence was quite peaceful; she did not go out much and hardly received anyone outside of her *amis attitrés*," that is, her exclusive clients. Her "bourgeois habits" were supported by the "generosity of her lovers, which granted her a comfortable, even luxurious lifestyle," concluded one police report.[23]

At the pinnacle of the sex trade, Regnault saw whom she wanted. She had navigated the social world of the Grands Boulevards, narrowly avoided the police, and in her more cautious 30s, had the distinct privilege of a stunning apartment in the rue Montaigne. How, police wondered, could a woman of sober self-discipline, known to be reclusive and fussy about her security, have so badly misjudged the circumstances of March 16?

MARIE REGNAULT was born in the revolutionary month of February 1848, in Chalon-sur-Saône, Burgundy. What began that month as a patchwork of grievances against King Louis-Philippe soon ignited all of France and cities across Europe. It was a great republican moment, one that saw the abolition of slavery in French lands, even if the republicans themselves would have to wait another generation to establish a regime based on their principles.

Taylor and Goron learned that, when the revolution broke out, Regnault's father was working as a *huissier*, a low-level employee in the judiciary something like a bailiff. After the revolution he lost his job. And he drank. The family hit financial straits, and its public reputation suffered. The record of Regnault's youth is full of holes and is slanted by the reprobation of the police investigation and its local sources, who examined the lives of Marie and her sister, Louise, through the prism of March 1887.

According to those who knew the Regnaults, Marie's mother was neglectful and spent her days reading novels, a habit most famously pilloried in Flaubert's *Madame Bovary*, where it exuded bad maternal instinct. Others said that Mrs. Regnault suffered frail health. Relations in the Regnault couple soured, culminating in Mr. Regnault's epic departure. Before storming out of the family residence, he sawed the matrimonial bed in two. He lugged away his half, plus a portion of the couple's furniture. Mrs. Regnault slept thereafter on a thin straw mattress. She fell gravely ill when Marie was 16 years old and died three days after Christmas, in 1864.

Interviews with acquaintances yielded the tragic arc of the fallen woman common in this period: Two beautiful sisters, intelligent, charming, and hard-working, were forced by circumstances into prostitution by the misdeeds of their parents. Marie "would have made an excellent worker if her maternal example had not caused her to lose her work ethic. In her sad family milieu, exacerbated by poverty, her fall was likely—and was not long in arriving." In the simple formulations of the police, Marie wound up in the Parisian demimonde because the city offered a "refuge" from her broken reputation; in Paris, at least, she could "hide her mistake."

Louise was a person of "peaceable character and honest nature" and she dreamt of a career as a schoolteacher but lacked the funding then required for training. Locals said that she grew embittered as a result, adding that Marie "had a happier disposition." At age 15, Marie completed her studies and left her boarding school. Her passion was embroidery, and she found an apprenticeship in an embroidering atelier; her supervisor there described her as "lively, happy, affectionate, and hard-working."[24]

A comparable story had circulated in the wake of Stein's murder. According to Grison, Stein was working in a clothing atelier in Mulhouse in 1879. One day she met a young man on the street, and soon he promised to marry her. "Confident, the young woman, having given herself to him, was waiting for the promises of her lover to come true, when something happened to change her future." An older woman came into Stein's atelier and inquired about a dress order for her daughter, who was to be married. The groom-to-be, Stein learned, was the young man to whom she had given herself. It was shame, in Grison's telling, that drove Stein to the big city.[25]

The Regnault sisters first fell into debauchery at local balls and soirées that continued late into the night, witnesses recalled. Men made advances; the local public prosecutor seduced Louise. Following her mother's death, Marie began the first of two serious sexual intrigues with local notables. At age 17 she became the mistress of Albert G., scion of one of Chalon's largest merchant families. The affair lasted a few years and overlapped with another relationship she had with the Count de Montille, whose chateau and vineyards were situated in the Côte d'Or region of Burgundy. The count became enamored of Marie during a business trip to Chalon and took her as a lover. (It was his name that Marie used upon her arrival in Paris, refashioning herself as Régine de Montille.)

The year that she turned 20, Regnault mastered the vital entrepreneurial skill of shuttling between wealthy lovers, even traveling abroad with them for extended periods. Albert G. brought her to Koblenz and Leipzig, where they spent two years, from 1868 to 1870. During her absence, Marie's father, homeless, fell from a parapet on a train station staircase in his sleep and died. The outbreak of war with Prussia in 1870 forced the couple back to France; Albert G. was badly depleted by financial setbacks, it was said, and he and Marie were soon finished. After the Paris Commune, Marie and Louise moved to Paris. They were joined by Annette Gremeret, an old friend from Chalon. Louise found an apartment at 4 rue de Rome; Marie moved in up the street, at number 48, practically across from the Gare Saint-Lazare.[26]

THE REGNAULT SISTERS joined the tens of thousands of prostitutes at work in Paris in the early 1870s; the timing of their arrival was unfortunate. The protracted economic crisis caused by civil war and revolution brought a definitive end to the frothy days of the Second Empire, which had been prosperous for the demimonde. Gone was the easy money generated by real estate speculation during Haussmann's tenure, for instance. Having endured starvation in 1870–1871, the French population now owed billions in reparations to the Germans. Crippling deflation would be the general trend in the 1870s; following a rush of hope, the stock market crashed in 1882.[27]

The Regnault sisters held a few advantages over their competition. First, they remained close, which allowed them to pool their risk and resources. They were young and attractive and had some education. They were experienced and relatively polished; their exposure to society men, even if only provincial notables thus far, distinguished them from the laundresses or other service industry workers who prostituted themselves occasionally to make ends meet. Marie dedicated herself to the profession knowing full well what it entailed.

Nonetheless, the risks were considerable and there were few true allies. There would always be the unpredictability of demand and the deplorable threat of infection, violent johns, exploitative pimps, and corrupt cops. Self-defense was truly the only weapon the women had. In nineteenth-century Paris the toxic mix of contempt and fascination that society heaped on prostitutes was reiterated in the work of novelists, the state, administrators, journalists, and painters.[28] A visit from the police was an unsettling, sometimes dangerous event. That was because of the fundamental paradox of Parisian prostitution, bound up in a regulatory regime that put policing power outside the rule of law.

No consideration of violence or murder perpetrated on Parisian prostitutes can proceed without considering this regime. The material problems presented by prostitution, in the view of an influential administrator, were akin to those associated with public sewage: Both were receptacles for excess bodily fluid that demanded a pragmatic and hygienic intervention.[29] Honorable men would always visit "girls," and although this was not to be condoned, the greater good would be served by registering the prostitutes and keeping tabs on them, the better to protect respectable families from infection. Prostitution was hence tolerated and controlled by an extralegal bureaucracy outside the French penal code and court system. The vice squad, which in 1887 fell under the control of Security's Chief Taylor and Deputy Chief Goron, was tasked with its day-to-day regulation.

The vice squad's reputation was dismal and deserved, and Marie Regnault was fortunate to avoid the horrors of regulation, a legal netherworld of invasive medical checks and looming imprisonment. In effect, the state granted "quasi-absolute power" to a brigade of low-ranking, poorly trained male officers to manage the situation. Unsurprisingly, abuses of power were endemic and always tinged with considerations of social class; officers on the vice squad knew that some sought-after prostitutes earned as much in a single trick—100 francs for 20 to 30 minutes of work—as a rank-and-file cop cleared in a month.[30] Vice squad officers acted in effect as investigators and judges; then, as political alignments broke down and new allegiances were set in the first years of the Third Republic, the police announced a "sustained war" on the clandestine prostitutes, or *insoumises*, with the vice squad promising to beef up its ranks.[31] The Regnault sisters would confront harsh administrative circumstances.

The police also took care of punishing prostitutes who got caught without registration cards, which corresponded to files containing information on their regular medical checks. There were roundups and brutal quarantines plus imprisonment. There were sexual assaults and exploitation by officers against the prostitutes they were regulating. As a vice squad leader put it, officers were liable to "succumb quickly to the temptations" that came with the job.[32]

An unquantifiable cost was the relative isolation that the threat of arrest imposed on those attempting to evade detection. It is telling that when Stein vanished, many simply assumed that she had gotten "pinched in one of the police roundups that occur from time to time," as Grison put it, and perhaps gotten lost in the hellacious administrative labyrinth that inevitably followed.[33]

BECAUSE of the vice squad's extensive recordkeeping, historians know something of the lives of the city's registered prostitutes, or *inscrites*, if only from an administrative perspective. But clandestine prostitutes, who constituted the majority of sex workers, have mostly been lost to the historical record.[34] There are exceptions to this general rule, however, because of a parallel, secretive surveillance program that the vice squad undertook to track women it believed to be tricking clandestinely.

By chance, Marie Regnault was one of the clandestine prostitutes whose records have survived in the "secret archives," an invaluable resource for historians of the demimonde in the early Third Republic. Several years ago the French historian Gabrielle Houbre oversaw the publication of these files in an extensive volume, *Le livre des courtisanes*. Regnault's secret file may be spotty, but it allows us to draw some conclusions about her life during her first years in Paris and to situate her fairly precisely within the demimonde and its clientele.

Why did these secret files need to exist in the first place? Why weren't suspected prostitutes such as Regnault simply forced into the vice squad's regulatory regime? Many of the women whom the vice squad placed under surveillance were celebrated demimondaines, the "stars of elite prostitution." No less than Sarah Bernhardt, the immense stage talent, had a secret file that detailed the astronomical fees she charged clients for a single pass. Even women of polite society had secret files. Yet often they remained "clandestine" because they had found *protecteurs*—government officials or bankers or crooked cops—who could prevent their arrest.[35] This was in part the legacy of more favorable times, when the courtesan's reputation for education and love of culture made her indistinguishable, from the perspective of policing, from society women. During the July Monarchy, for example, administrators spared courtesans the numbered registration cards that burdened common prostitutes. Over time, though, the perceived health threat that the courtesan posed to bourgeois families held sway.[36] As the secret archives make clear, there were no bedrock guarantees against arbitrary police or administrative action, and at least 2,000 prostitutes were arrested every year.[37] Thus were Marie Regnault and the women of her generation forced to navigate a republican model in which the rules of the game were hazy.

The police had more sinister reasons for maintaining their secret files: The dirt they contained could come in handy politically. The program doubled as targeted spying on scores of rich and powerful men and of the odd prominent newspaperman, such as *Le Figaro*'s Albert Millaud. As Houbre points out, the early years of the Third Republic saw a disproportionate amount of data collection on the lives of men hostile to the regime.[38]

This is the first clue we have about the clientele with whom Marie Regnault got her start in Paris; after her death, it was observed that she had received help from notable *protecteurs*, "among whom, distinguished politicians," which involved long-term relationships and far more than sexual intercourse.[39] Likewise did Louise Regnault settle into a comfortable arrangement with an aristocrat identified in the press only as "C. d'A.," who later served as Marie Gremeret's godfather.[40]

Marie Regnault began by selling her services through a number of contractors in what were called *maisons de rendez-vous*. In these establishments, clients explained to the madame what they sought; she showed them photos or described the women in detail. Specific sex acts were not often mentioned in the police files, but we get a clear idea of what was on offer from contemporary sex guides. Houbre observes that voyeurs did try to bring boudoir experiences into polite society, for example, by exhorting respectable ladies to engage in homosexual stimulation.[41]

At this stage in her career, Regnault needed to earn money and market herself by doing some high-end brothel work while at the same time cultivating an air of exclusivity, which would permit her, in principle, to charge higher fees. By early 1873 the prices she was charging caught the attention of the vice squad, who opened file 292 under the name "Régina Regnault, aka Mentel, aka de Montille." The first notation in the file contained the kind of basic biographical information that was readily obtained from a loquacious concierge, such as the sorry tale of her family and her level of success: "She is a rather pretty blonde who debuted early in the *vie galante*," notes the entry, and "it seems that she possesses a certain fortune." Within three years Marie had built a large enough cushion to move to 11 rue Caumartin, which was closer to the theaters around the Grands Boulevards.

Although peaceful, Regnault's climb in the demimonde was not without its bungles and humiliations. The file contains a story about an assignment that Regnault got through one of her intermediaries. She was to service the Peruvian consul in Paris, Alvarés Calderon.[42] Calderon was well-known in the sex industry for his rabid pursuit of virgins and for his fetishization of women who appeared Dutch. He was an extravagantly wealthy man—an "amateur of the demimonde," in a favored expression of the vice squad, who meant by it a man of experience and willingness to pay for the most desired women.

People in the business viewed Calderon as a sucker easily parted from his money. In exchange for colossal sums, Parisian whoremongers arranged meetings between him and would-be virgins—actresses, essentially, which dovetailed well with his appetite for stage performers. With cash and diamonds, Calderon believed, or simply wanted to believe, that he had bought the virginity of the Belgian soprano Marie Heilbron, who would go down as one of the most recognized names of the era at the Théâtre des Variétés; for the obscene sum of 10,000 francs he also bought the virginity of Thé Rose, later known for her stint at the Théâtre des Folies-Dramatiques.[43]

Regnault had not been in Paris long when she was sent to meet Calderon. She was not an aspiring actress, yet she found herself tasked with impersonating one in what quickly turned into an embarrassing encounter. Calderon had, in fact, requested a pass with the Parisian actress Antonine, a mistress of the playwright Victorien Sardou. Regnault was chosen for the trick because she bore a passing resemblance to Antonine, and as Calderon was a known dupe, the plan was for Regnault to play the actress. What Regnault did not know was that Calderon knew Antonine personally. He had even traveled with her and Sardou. Regnault stood no chance. Calderon's objective may have been to bed the actress behind his friend's back.[44]

The first half of the 1870s was a transitional phase in which Regnault received support from an unnamed "aged" patron. "These days," wrote a vice squad snoop, "she still frequents the *maisons de rendez-vous*, but she does not sell her favors for less than 200 francs." Her new apartment in the rue Caumartin was an impressive space. A luxury two-bedroom flat with two fireplaces, a salon, a dining room, and indoor toilets, it rented for 2,500 francs annually—and Regnault, not a client, was the signed lessee.[45] Regnault found her way into one of the toniest of the *maisons de rendez-vous*, managed by Louise Couteux, alias the Widow Rondy. A former chambermaid and industry veteran turned entrepreneur, Rondy had several scrapes with the law during the 1860s and 1870s, including accusations of child prostitution. She ran her business on the mezzanine floor of an expensive bourgeois apartment in the rue de Surène, and by the end of the 1870s everyone had heard of her. For women like Regnault, establishments like Rondy's were a common means of staying off the registration rolls.[46]

At Rondy's place, Regnault would have encountered some of the city's most sophisticated and storied women in the demimonde, including the future feminist luminary Marguerite Durand (*nom de demimondaine*: Marguerite de Laurency) and Lucie Lévy, the inspiration for Zola's novel *Nana*.[47] In exchange for providing protection, the whoremonger collected 50% of the fees paid by the client.[48] Still, getting into the Widow Rondy's black book was worth the fees because of the exposure to wealthy clients—until, that is, Rondy's ring was brought down by police and her black book, seized in the bust, became a source of endless public fascination.[49] It is possible that the black book helped lead the vice squad to Marie Regnault in the first place: Surveillance of her activity began at around the same time as Rondy's highly publicized arrest.

"THE REAL *COCOTTE* is the provincial, and above all the foreigner," commented Grison on the internationalism of the capital's high-end prostitutes.[50] Coming from the reporter, this was a rebuff, but as historians of prostitution have shown, client demand for racial variety made difference a prized commodity. Courtesans and other demimondaines likewise formed a cosmopolitan corps with origins across France, Europe, and overseas colonies. A fair number of the era's most celebrated courtesans—La Paiva and Cora Pearl, to cite just two—traded some on their foreignness. The Parisian demimonde's sale of Eastern bodies was matched with satiny decors that played up the exotic: The congress of East and West was a leitmotif in boudoirs, where one could smoke Egyptian cigarettes or enjoy trendy Turkish coffee.[51] At the same time, foreign prostitutes carried extra burdens. Goron reported that, much to his irritation, society men often used the police as a tool to put pressure on their uncooperative mistresses. If the woman in question was a foreigner and found herself in conflict with a Parisian man, her situation was even more precarious: "We drove them to the border."[52] Following a public scandal with an obsessive society man, it was Cora Pearl, not the man in question, whom the police interrogated. Having already been tailed by the police, who were working at the behest of a client, she was shocked to be ordered to leave the country.[53]

An indication of the internationalization of demand and supply that distinguished the milieu of elite prostitution in the latter half of the nineteenth century can be gathered from a perusal of the notorious sex guide *The Pretty Women of Paris*, an anonymously published critical rating of scores of upscale Parisian prostitutes in the early 1880s aimed at Anglophone tourists and expatriates. In it we learn of Blanche Pierson, a widely acclaimed actress who was also a sought-after demimondaine: "This lovely, blonde, Creole woman was born in the French colonies, in 1842, and is still a most enjoyable companion on the couch." And we are introduced to the Countess Pegère, "a handsome negress from the French colonies, [who] comes of a well-known noble family." There was Léa D'Asco, who "has just returned from a tour in South America, and has brought back a little negro boy, who she takes about with her to theatres . . . as an advertisement. Her house is full of animals of all kinds, her latest acquisition being a tame bear." Desire and racism were of course not mutually exclusive. There is an approving review of the services of Mab de Folligny, an Arab Jew from Algeria possessing "dwarf-like charms" who has brought back to Paris "all the indolent ways of the Orientals."[54]

Entrepreneurs and traffickers ferried whores between Paris and cities in Latin America, Russia, Egypt, and the Ottoman Empire. In Paris, demand for the exotic was high enough to merit the funding of prostitution-specific supply networks based in ports on the western and southern coasts, which imported women of mixed race from overseas.[55]

THE POLICE FILES also show how deeply integrated the sex industry was in elite male sociability. Far from the solitary passes arranged in darkened streets, the demimonde was, for the chaps who patronized it, a shared endeavor.

Regnault serviced Hubert Delamarre, a society figure "well known at the Parisian racetrack." Delamarre then introduced her to his friend, the Count de Vogué, who paid Regnault 10 louis d'or (about 200 francs) for sex.[56] Reading through other files, we gain a sense of Regnault's talent as a negotiator. Actresses such as Berthe Dulac, a regular performer at the Folies-Bergère, were typically the most coveted among clandestine prostitutes and hence the best paid. But Regnault's fees rivaled or surpassed those charged by Dulac and other celebrities. For a pass, Delamarre paid Dulac half of what de Vogué paid Regnault.[57]

What this also tells us is that Marie Regnault made early inroads into a deeply conservative political milieu: Delamarre and de Vogué were both high-level military figures and men of illustrious families who were hostile to the Third Republic (de Vogué was an unreconstructed monarchist). Both Delamarre and de Vogué were also members of the Jockey Club de Paris, the most exclusive *cercle* in Paris, owing to its nepotistic admittance policies and steep cost. The *cercles* were important nodes in the social geography of the demimonde that developed around the central and western parts of the Grands Boulevards. As centers of masculine sociability typically organized around professions or political inclinations, they provided a space for retired army officers, renters, and businessmen to gather and idle, read, drink, play billiards, laze about in smoking rooms, and listen to music.[58] They also furnished a vehicle of collective whoring. "To 'protect' a dancer was seen as a good thing to do at the time," recalled a contemporary. "A young man debuting in high society earned himself a serious reputation that way."[59]

WITHIN a few months of the 1883 murder of Marie Jouin, Regnault left her rue Caumartin apartment for western Paris, a magnificent property formerly occupied by an admiral in the French navy. The murder of Marie Aguétant, a kept woman and dancer at the Éden-Théâtre who was found dead in her rue Caumartin apartment in 1886, made Regnault's move to the rue Montaigne look prescient.

The last years of Regnault's life, though materially comfortable, were painful. Her sister Louise died after a long unspecified illness in 1886; perhaps her decline had begun in 1883, for it was then that Gremeret came to work for Marie Regnault.[60] Marie probably supported Louise financially during those years—there is no information on Louise's final months, not even whether she ever moved from the rue de Rome. Regardless, it would have been a significant financial burden from the moment Louise ceased to work. Thanks to Marie's business acumen, the challenge was met easily.

"She hated debts," recalled a friend of Marie's. She was meticulously organized and every day made sure to tally up all revenues and expenses. Because she was discreet, she could be trusted, a rarity in the loud and often gaudily eccentric demimonde. After 1874 the police file on Régine de Montille goes silent. This limiting of her exposure was the first, and perhaps greatest, advantage of life in the rue Montaigne. Henceforth she was able to manage her staff carefully and to restrict herself to a small group of men with whom she could deepen personal relationships, providing each with a simulation of eroticized domesticity, down to the two little dogs she kept in the salon. It involved considerable labor. Perpetually clean linens and professionally prepared meals were just the beginning of it.

The staff insulated Regnault from dangerous encounters while ensuring that her clients never bumped into each other or otherwise discovered that she was maintaining, in 1887, no less than three "official" *protecteurs*. Two of these men, reached by police investigators after her death, swore that they believed themselves to be paying for exclusivity. This fudge on Regnault's part, while by no means an anomaly in the demimonde, worked like an insurance policy against sudden shortfalls, such as an unforeseen departure, arrest, or death of a *protecteur*. On the other hand, juggling several "exclusive" clients could be dangerous. Marie Moret, a kept woman who lived comfortably on the payouts of an employee of the Banque de France, was summarily cut off and abandoned by him because, according to a police snoop, "when he arrived at her place, he found a competitor."[61]

Regnault invested in interest-generating vehicles and was a saver. Her *protecteurs* picked up her expenses and paid at different rates to reflect the specific services they demanded. Mr. X., who lived on the Champs-Elysées and who saw Marie Regnault on the eve of her murder, paid her 3,000 francs per month to see her on a weekly basis, with the occasional large dinner given in her apartment for his friends.[62] Another client, Mr. L., the businessman who paid for Regnault's funeral, gave her numerous gifts, though he was above all a friend who took her to the theater and managed her investments and diverse acquisitions. The two had grown close over the course of several years. When Mr. L.'s mother died, Regnault wore black to show solidarity in mourning for several months.[63] The third known client was an army captain said to be from a well-known family; he paid Regnault 1,000 francs per month.[64]

How had Regnault managed to attract and retain these generous *protecteurs*, and possibly others whose names were kept secret? According to a friend, Regnault's breakthrough occurred when word spread in the *monde galant* that she had refined tastes in art and that she herself had become a patron. From that day forward, she was "overwhelmed by courtiers."[65] She acquired the work of respected painters and treasures and furniture from the East that a *New York Times* correspondent knew his readers would appreciate.[66]

In response to the interest she was generating among gentleman callers, the friend recalled, Regnault made the smart play: She rejected all offers ostentatiously.[67] The self-fashioning of Regnault as a courtesan was the result not of celebrity but instead a brilliant sleight of hand. She triangulated her suitors' desires and, as a result, she could name her price. Money flowed in, and with it, the collection of fine art and the exquisite jewelry that were the coin of the realm, in the demimonde as in polite society. Leveraging market forces, she put her buying power and taste on public display. She seemed never to wear the same dress twice. Her jewelry collection expanded and became a source of personal pride. She spoke often of her collection and was particularly fond of a bejeweled aigrette worth more than 25,000 francs.[68] This single piece of jewelry, to put the figure into perspective, was valued at more than what the average French worker could earn in over a decade. In the late nineteenth century, only 10–20% of households in France earned 2,500 francs annually from employment, and an annual salary of 5,000 francs placed a man among the highest earning 5% of the nation. As the auction of her belongings would later confirm, Regnault's income and assets put her on par with high-ranking public officeholders, liberal professionals, and businessmen.[69]

Provided such wealth, it is fair to ask what a woman in Regnault's position might have hoped to accomplish, socially speaking, in marriage. A page from her diary mentions a love story that had recently ended as a result of her lover's decision to marry someone else. Was a courtesan marriageable? Realistically, the prospect of a life as a respectable woman—and acceptance in polite society—was a long shot, as marriages between demimondaines and society men remained uncommon. There were exceptions, such as the Countess de Chabrillan, who as a girl of 16 registered with the police as a common prostitute—with her mother's blessing. She became a streetwalker and then broke into the demimonde under the alias La Mogador. Later, as a courtesan, she stunned polite society by reeling in the elderly Count de Chabrillan in 1854 and setting off for Australia with him. She inherited the count's fortune after his death.[70]

More typically, the path to a stable, relatively conventional life in the demimonde involved so many obstacles and indignities that women who did eventually find success often flamed out in addiction or debt. The secret police files supplement the standard rags-to-riches-to-rags biographies that attest to the difficulty of softening the conditions of sex work. File 9, which belongs to a certain Adèle Bataille, tells of a relationship with an American gambling cheat who, in trouble and on the run, holed up in one of the rooms of her apartment. Separately, Bataille was herself arrested for theft and served six months in prison. From the depths of debt she caught on later with a high-ranking state functionary who unburdened her of financial obligations and agreed to pay her a modest salary. Using that money, Bataille became a whoremonger in her own right.[71]

PARISIANS knew well where to go to witness the booms and busts of elite sex workers play out at convenient hours: the Hôtel Drouot, the city's most prestigious auction house and an address known to art historians for its role in the making of the taste for modern art. After its opening in the early 1850s in the heart of Haussmannian Paris—steps from the stock market, the *cercles*, and the theaters—the Hôtel Drouot fascinated Parisians as an extension of finance capitalism, a den of collectors steeped in speculation, a spectacle of "popular capitalism" where money talked loudest and prices for art tracked stock prices and broader market sentiments.[72]

Preserved auction catalogues, observed the society journalist Jules Claretie after Sarah Bernhardt was forced to liquidate a trove of valuables in the early 1880s, could serve as a "document de la vie" for future historians to pick through. The objects that passed through the auction house were believed to contain something of the essence of the events that had brought them there. Not all "documents" were equal, of course. Claretie contrasted Bernhardt's presence at the Hôtel Drouot, for her sale of diamonds, jewelry, and silver, with the superficial reasons behind the recent auction of her fellow performer and demimondaine Hortense Schneider's valuables: Bernhardt's was the story of a "courageously braved debacle" stemming from the economic crash of January 1882.[73]

Demimondaines exercised considerable buying power at the Hôtel Drouot. In the chatty eight-volume chronicles of the auction house that the art critic Paul Eudel published during this period, the demimondaines' presence at the Hôtel Drouot was a much remarked on commonplace. Eudel's auction reporting, much of which first appeared in *Le Figaro* before publication in bound form, offers a wealth of information about the auction house within the urban geography of sex commerce around the Grands Boulevards and serves as a compendium of the noteworthy choices made by the buyers seeking to put their discernment on display. Reporting on an 1881 auction of modernist paintings, Eudel mentioned them by name much in the manner of a tabloid: "The demimondaines and theater women also made great use of the ivory gavel; their favorite was [the neo-Impressionist painter Edgard] Pillet: Mesdames Anna Deslions, Adèle Courtois, Alice Regnault, Cora Pearl, Laure Hayman, Constance Reysuche." At the auction house, these women circulated freely among their well-off clients—and the clients' spouses. One can imagine awkward encounters as veteran collectors such as the Baron Gustave de Rothschild sat alongside all "the pretty demimondaines, Mademoiselles Mangin, Angelo, Marie Lannoye, and Alice Regnault, the actress who now possesses the most houses in Paris."[74] As it happens, nearly every one of these names appears in the secret police surveillance files.

The great auction house functioned as an extension of the demimonde and in key respects operated as its analog. At the Hôtel Drouot buyers and sellers traded in innumerable types of objects, the value of which was assessed by individuals; cultural fetishes had free reign because prices were determined through a collective process of bidding. Like the demimonde, with its aristocratic pseudonyms and alternative domesticity, the Hôtel Drouot suffered a reputation in the 1880s for counterfeit pieces—art forgeries that sold at high prices.[75] Finally, both the demimonde and the auction house were marketplaces in which networks of supply and demand were global and sustained in significant measure by expatriates and tourists.

From its beginning, the Drouot auction house fostered modernist styles and permitted artists to circumvent the salon system, the monolithic, state-sanctioned arbiter of taste that remained attached to a conservative notion of art as separate from commerce and that frowned on ambitious formal experimentation at the time.[76] The young Vincent van Gogh, as a tourist visiting Paris in 1875, stood awestruck in its display rooms. "I don't know whether I have already written to you about it or not," he wrote to his brother Theo, "but there has been a sale here of drawings by Millet. When I entered the hall of the Hôtel Drouot, where they were exhibited, I felt like saying, 'Take off your shoes, for the place where you are standing is Holy Ground.'"[77] Millet's work counted among the most expensive of the nineteenth century, and a virtual monopoly on it was amassed by a Drouot-attached dealer in the early 1870s.[78] By the mid-1870s, Renoir, Manet, Monet, Caillebotte, Pisarro, and Sisley were all promoting their work in foreign markets and to foreign buyers at the Hôtel Drouot, overtly embracing commercialism.[79]

Just as the auction house's price points were bound to market forces, so were the demimondaine's fortunes. As a result of the stock market crash of the early 1880s, the bidding power of demimondaines dropped markedly.[80] The names of the demimondaines who came to sell off their significant collections amid rumors of financial duress, insolvency, or death were hardly obscure. And when a courtesan died without an heir, the international press reported the scene at the auction with the same cool tone of the local newspapers. "This week the idlers of the Hôtel Drouot saw the very end of Cora Pearl," reported the *New York Times* after the famed courtesan's death in mid-1886. "None of her old admirers came in a hurry to buy souvenirs."[81]

In Eudel's reporting, the Hôtel Drouot was a gossipy social space in which strategies of bidding and selling could seem secondary to the spectacle of the objects. The auctioning of domestic decoration effectively turned the privacy of notable apartments and mansions inside out. When the courtesan Gabrielle Elluini announced the sale of artwork and objects in the mid-1880s—the decorations of her chateau on the western outskirts of Paris—amateur sleuths and rumor mongers revisited her "loud and dazzling life" and conjectured as to whether this was another story of a demimondaine who had squandered enormous sums despite the fact that she was still "young and pretty" and able to work. Moralizing envy stained the proceedings. "Aren't the 900,000 francs from the sale of her mansion sufficient to arrange her life more modestly?" asked an attendee at the liquidation of Hortense Schneider's belongings.[82]

The demimonde, wrote Dumas *fils*, "picks up where the legal spouse leaves off, and finishes where the venal spouse begins."[83] The auction house was like a window between the two domains. Demimondaines occasionally scheduled viewings of the objects going up for auction directly at their residences. Oscillating between voyeuristic pleasure and detailed inventory, Eudel published virtual walk-throughs of these properties. At the courtesan Elluini's chateau, he perused and judged the items on offer and described the "modern style" of her salon.[84] It is a safe assumption that Eudel counted among his readers the housewives of polite society who likewise assumed the twin tasks of fashioning domestic space and bejeweling themselves. To them, Eudel's walk-throughs (and the subsequent auction sessions) were an approximation of the uncanny domesticity experienced by their spouses. But as the straight-laced Eudel would not quite acknowledge, the rank commercialism and conspicuous consumption of the Drouot auction house undid the normative separation of the *monde* and the demimonde. Eudel presented his publication as the work of a historian documenting, as he put it in an exposé of a large residence in 1882, the "underbelly of *la vie élégante*" and specifically the "high-society interior [*intérieur mondain*] in the year of the stock-market crash."[85] As a state-operated forum, the auction house was a rare daytime space where high-society women—whose presence at Drouot became common in the latter decades of the nineteenth century[86]— and high-class prostitutes could at last observe each other buying and selling valuables from all over the world.

Why would it have mattered to respectable women how demimondaines decorated their apartments? The auctions of the 1880s took place against the backdrop of revolutionary sexual changes that not only called attention to female pleasure but also acknowledged female autonomy (signaled by the legalization of divorce) and prompted a radical rethinking of fetishism as a psychosexual concept to treat sexual desire and its objects.[87] The auction house was a unique showcase of the demimondaine's sex life in objects, one that, because of its interactive format, required a public visibility. Elite women saw courtesans in the role of serious bidders, as tastemakers whose choices were filtered through Eudel's discernment: The journalist sat in judgment, claiming to draw the line between "vrai chic" and "faux chic."[88]

Society women also were confronted with the collision of the Oriental exoticism of the demimonde and the residence of bluebloods such as the Vicomte de la Panouse, who married the demimondaine Marie Heilbron in 1878. Eudel's investigation of the smoking room shared by the Vicomte de la Panouse and Ms. Heilbron dwells on the bordello chic of the space, the touchstone of the apartment's East-West blend at a time when Parisians remained steeped in Greek and Roman antiques.[89] Arranged like an "Arab encampment tent," it was filled with Japanese and Persian stylings that sent Eudel into raptures of fantasy. There was a divan with a Japanese silk screen "to isolate oneself, if need be, in delicious pleasure." Of the precious stones on display in another part of the apartment, Eudel overheard one female visitor remark, "What use are diamonds if not to tempt thieves!"[90]

MARIE REGNAULT'S move from the Grands Boulevards to the rue Montaigne and the decorations with which she filled her apartment were of a piece with the accounts of her life, widely published in the press, as "almost bourgeois" and "almost retired"—that is, a picture of a house mistress who had left behind the glitzy Grands Boulevards in favor of an outwardly conventional family life. The demimondaine was foremost an illusionist; Regnault remade herself as a bourgeois housewife and continued to prosper as she kept in step with the rapprochement between the *monde* and the demimonde.

The bland-sounding "almost bourgeois" turn of Regnault's life in the 1880s carried risks that she saw with clear eyes. The extraordinarily valuable objects with which the courtesan decorated her home and body were, banal as the point may seem, kept in her boudoir and salon. They were worthless if out of sight, and anyway there was no one else she could trust to safeguard them. She installed extra locks on her doors and set up an electrical security system of sorts, which allowed her to contact Annette Gremeret at the other end of the apartment at a moment's notice. It consisted of a switch, mounted on the wall above her headboard and connected to a wire that ran the length of the corridor to a bell in Gremeret's room. Months after all of this had become public knowledge, the denizens of the Hôtel Drouot were at last permitted to ogle her belongings.

The event felt long in coming. Countless articles had been written; a theater production from the summer of 1887 had supposedly used some of Regnault's impressive collections of art and jewelry as a stage set, raising the level of anticipation.[91] "There's no need to rehearse the history of the triple and horrific murders in the rue Montaigne," commented Eudel. "Public memory has sufficiently conserved the memory of the entire variety of episodes of the drama."[92] Because Dr. Brouardel had been unable to make a determination of the precise order of the three deaths, by default Regnault's estate fell into the hands of the state. As the three-day auction approached—officials scheduled it to correspond with the one-year anniversary of the crime—there was no need for advertisements or announcements to alert the public that her jewelry, bibelots, clothing, furniture, books, and art collections were to be liquidated. All necessary steps had been taken to ensure that the sale would proceed as it would for "just any demimondaine," wrote Eudel.[93]

But this was not "just any demimondaine," as Eudel admitted. In a coy aside, auctioneers assured buyers that they had removed the valuable stones from Regnault's jewelry temporarily to wash away the flecks of dried blood before putting them on display; they also scrubbed the stains from her furniture and the rug. Three showrooms were made available. This was insufficient, as the international press corps was quick to point out. As soon as the doors opened, "the crowd was great, the crush terrible, and the assistance of many policemen was necessary to keep order and render the sale at all possible," reported a British journalist.[94]

It was a "riotous exhibition," Eudel said, and the halls were "taken by assault." Eudel assessed the collections with approval.[95] His proclivities tended toward the conservative. The auction documents reveal that Regnault had a taste for martial and hunting motifs. In painting and sculpture, she preferred traditional styles. The militarist-nationalist painter Édouard Detaille counted among the academic salon artists in her collection (the drawing *Soldats du premier empire*). A salon piece that had hung in the boudoir, the 1880 painting *La pluie d'or* by Horace de Callias, had received critical mention years before.[96] Regnault was an avid and eclectic reader, and her collection of 230 volumes included works by Belot, Zola, Claretie, Richard O'Monroy, Erckmann-Chatrian, Sainte-Beuve, Ulbach, Balzac, Richepin, and Musset. Her luxury edition of *La dame aux Camélias* sold for 475 francs.[97]

Regnault's jewelry attracted the most attention. A neck pendant of black pearl framed in fourteen *gros brilliants* and twelve *petits brillants* sold for a whopping 14,020 francs.[98] Furniture pieces and items directly tied to the murder were also of great interest to bidders. The cheap novel found at her bedside, *The Gambler*, worth 3 francs on the street, fetched 95. A common hot-water bottle was bid to 77 francs because "the killer boiled the water with which he washed his hands after committing the crime" in it. The ivory-paneled iron safe in which Regnault stored her valuables went for 420 francs.[99] Unfortunately, Eudel makes no mention of Regnault's personal diary in connection with the volumes sold at the auction. Perhaps someone connected to the investigation kept it as a souvenir.

CHAPTER FIVE

Colonial Picaresque

The Trans-Mediterranean Investigation of a Migrant

The colonial press of Alexandria picked up the news of Enrico Pranzini's arrest in time for Antonietta Pranzini, the suspect's mother, to prepare herself for the summons to appear before the French consul. Still, one can imagine the stir caused by the arrival of the consul's subpoena at her daughter's Cairo home, where the 68-year-old former florist, whom everyone knew as Zunta, had resided since her son's departure for France. Newspapers everywhere between New York and Calcutta had been talking about Mrs. Pranzini's wayward son for several days. He had made quite a mess of his life on the road, the stories repeated. In Paris the consensus taking form was that the Parisian prostitutes' elusive murderer had at last been caught.

On the day of Mrs. Pranzini's scheduled appointment at the consulate, a francophone colonial newspaper printed a letter to the editor denouncing Enrico Pranzini as "a real rascal" who was still "notorious in Egypt." The letter's author went further, suggesting that Pranzini's minor scrapes with the law years ago in Alexandria presaged his recent "exploits" as the "clever and audacious killer" in Paris.[1]

But based on the consul's findings, this hypothesis was an outlier. To be sure, no one interviewed thus far had characterized Pranzini as a man of high integrity. Pranzini's own brother-in-law attested to his "passion for gambling and for money," and he had little to say that was positive. Pranzini's acquaintances and employers came forward to tell stories and settle old scores. A schoolmate remembered him as "lazy and rebellious." Others told of having been duped by Pranzini's schemes and petty thievery. The consul's impressive reach permitted his office to verify these and other accounts of the suspect's youthful indiscretions.

Witnesses, given an opportunity to recall violent incidents involving Pranzini—or simply to invent them, for these were likely not friends— could think of nothing to say. Some expressed surprise at the murder charges. Pranzini was gentle, pretty, and extravagantly gifted when it came to learning languages. He was warm, sweet, and engaging. He had friends. His old adversaries balked at the notion that he had a violent streak. If anything, it was his vanity that caused problems. Pranzini was a scamp who often succumbed to garish impulses. Big-boned and muscular and cultivating a dandy's panache, he could have followed in his father's footsteps and led a respectable, middling lifestyle. But he badly misplayed a decent hand. He was restless, and yes, he liked to gamble.

Consul Alfred Kleczkowski's summons shouted across the chasms of class and ethnicity that divided the local European community, his signature unwinding in an impossibly long train of scribbles and loops; the consul was, as the bold typeface announced, a Chevalier de la Légion d'Honneur, an honor of distinction awarded in Paris. Mrs. Pranzini's face-to-face meeting with him would have been an exceedingly rare event for people of her station. His missive took for granted a level of French-language proficiency of which Mrs. Pranzini was not possessed. She probably asked her son-in-law to translate it.

Despite the Third Republic's recent misfortunes in Egypt, the French consul retained his status as one of the most recognized men in the province. European consuls in the Ottoman Empire were no mere diplomats. Thanks to an old imperial convention known as the capitulations, the Ottomans, who still nominally controlled territories that today compose significant parts of the Near East (Syria, Lebanon, Iraq, and Kuwait), granted extraterritoriality rights, including protection from the Ottoman justice system and taxes, to settlers who could demonstrate their connections to one of the European powers there. As a result, these officials operated much like chief executives of their respective national settler communities, among whom they enjoyed prestige and plenipotentiary powers.

Paris bestowed upon Kleczkowski, a lifelong diplomat, the vital task of determining Pranzini's whereabouts and criminal antecedents going back to 1879 at least. In Paris, Guillot needed to know whether Pranzini *could* have committed the murders of which he was suspected. The suspect claimed to have arrived in France the previous summer, but this needed to be verified. If Pranzini had traveled to France anytime in the past couple of years, he could have had a hand in the deaths of the demimondaines Lucie Alhiaume and Marie Aguétant. The latter victim had been found dead just a few months before Pranzini said he arrived. If it turned out that he was lying and had come earlier, then the Parisian cases that had gone cold would need to be reopened.

The consul, a bald man with a thick neck, was nothing if not thorough. He promptly assembled trans-Mediterranean ship passenger lists and examined Pranzini's school records, military documents, and job history. He mobilized business and diplomatic contacts and obtained records from Egyptian, Italian, and British administrators. He received and took statements from Enrico Pranzini's childhood friends and their parents. He combed through testimony from co-workers, French doctors, Ottoman state employees, and high-ranking officials in the British occupation army in Egypt. He indulged tipsters and sifted through letters denouncing Pranzini. He set up a mail interception at the Egyptian Post, and he queried banks.

Mrs. Pranzini appeared before Kleczkowski as requested, at 10 a.m. on April 17, 1887, precisely one month after the murders in the rue Montaigne.

"How long have you been in Egypt?" Kleczkowski began, through a dragoman, or interpreter, an employee of the consulate.

In the course of the interview that followed, Mrs. Pranzini was forced to reckon with her family's failures, which in some ways caricatured those of the Italian colony in Alexandria. She revisited her arrival in Egypt three decades earlier with her husband, Gandolfo. She discussed his death and, more obliquely, the shame of her poverty as a widow whose only material possessions were apparently limited to the old furniture that she took with her whenever she changed addresses, which she had done rather often in recent years.

She handed over a pair of her son's recent letters, sent from Paris. "I wonder what you're living on," he asked her in one of them, referring to her financial hardship. Pressed, Mrs. Pranzini elaborated on her son's travels during the preceding decade, information that the investigative magistrate was trying to extract from the suspect at that moment thousands of miles away. She provided the basic elements of a timeline. Some of the information was quite specific. It gradually became clear that Pranzini had not been in Paris during the time of some, if not all, of the demimondaine murders.

"My son, who was in Italy during the events of June 1882, came back to Egypt to get me," she said, indicating her son's moral character. He brought her with him to Bologna, where he held a job. They found an apartment and lived there together for about 15 months, until September 1883.

And between September 1883 and the summer of 1886? The consul bore down. "You never lost track of him during that time?"

"No, except for the one month he spent in Florence shortly before our return to Egypt."

"Personally, you never had reason to object to anything he did?"

"No, never. He was always a good son, very affectionate, and I can't see how he could have committed the murders he's being accused of."

"You're sure that your son never went to France before his voyage there in 1886?"[2]

For the French consular staff the Pranzini investigation presented the chance to salvage something uplifting—a contribution of some sort to the metropole—in a decade defined by humbling setbacks and other bad news: The French, having enjoyed significant, informal imperial influence in Egypt since Bonaparte's invasion in 1798, were struggling to maintain a toehold in the 1880s. Kleczkowski witnessed the sudden degradation of the Third Republic's political position in 1882. He was at his post during the uprising of indigenous Egyptians against Franco-British colonial rule that summer and stood by helplessly as London made a drastic counterinsurgency move. The British lobbed shells into Alexandria, let the city go up in smoke, and then seized the port—and the rest of Egypt along with it soon after. Paris sat back too long and was presented with a fait accompli. Ended was the so-called Condominium of the mid-1870s, which had established Franco-British control of Egypt's finances and promised spots for French and British nationals in the Egyptian cabinet.

In 1882 the British thus became the de facto rulers of Egypt, which they named a "veiled protectorate" of Queen Victoria's empire.[3] It was a bitter pill to swallow for Frenchmen reared on tales of Bonaparte's victory at the Battle of the Pyramids. It was also a contributing factor to the hostile treatment accorded to Pranzini in Paris. The French response to the Egyptian question illustrates the strained logic of the new imperialism of the 1880s, whereby humiliating colonial failure begat *more* colonial adventurism. Rather than slowing the republican imperialists in Paris, the loss of face in Egypt galvanized the movement by allowing them to play on anxieties about French inferiority on the world stage. Jules Ferry, the most powerful among the republican imperialists, said, "Everywhere, and in every manner in which our interests and our honor are engaged, we want—we must—maintain France at the rank that is hers."[4] In the same vein, Gambetta, a convert to the colonialist cause, spoke on February 23, 1883, of an obligation to blot out "our horrible political failure in Egypt."[5] Heeding their injunctions, the Republic turned its sullen gaze toward lower-hanging fruit in Asia and Africa.

More immediately, Kleczkowski's investigation armed Parisian prosecutors with evidence that undermined Pranzini's credibility. The consul's impressive research testified to the efficient circulation of information through diplomatic channels and entrepreneurial networks and across continents connected by imperial sinews—notwithstanding the common image of the colonial world as a free-for-all peopled by crooks and get-rich-quick scams. In a stroke the consul mobilized sources allowing him to retrace Pranzini's steps over three decades. There were, in fact, mechanisms for holding individuals to account, and a bad reputation could follow a man no matter how far he ran.

Looked at from yet another angle, the consul's dossier contained the elements of one family's biography, the story of the hard times suffered by people who had left Europe to avoid the same. In a letter Pranzini sent to his mother from Paris, dated February 15, 1887, the son makes vague promises of financial support. Although he first left home as a young man, his relationship with his mother remained the most important of his adult life. At a continent's distance, he could only assure her of his concerns about her failing health.

He also had good news to share: He had taken a lover who was French and generous.

> But I don't like to go so long without giving you news from my end, which are, happily, quite satisfactory, thanks to my girlfriend [*petite amie*]. She is

making sacrifices in order to help me break into high society [*le monde de Paris*], which demands quite a lot of image making if one wants to get anywhere. The process is long for sure, but it will bear fruit. . . .

Not a day goes by without my thinking of you, my dear mother, and as long as good fortune eludes me, I channel my pain in the hope of the future that I want to make—through honorable means—for your happiness. I am not promising anything, but one of these days my girlfriend, by making a sacrifice for me, will be able to lend me 100 francs, which I will send to you.

Congratulations to Giulia—I hope that she and her infant are in good health.

A thousand kisses from your loving son.

Enrico

P.S. I have never in my life suffered such a rigorous chill as that which we have had in Paris this year—it is still happening now. Oh! If you only knew how unbearable it was! Brrrr!

The Pranzinis were commoners whose experience was highly representative. Like tens of thousands of other settlers from southern Europe, they were treated by colonial elites as socially and racially dubious; as Levantines, they were often viewed as the undesirable by-product of conquest and expansion. Perhaps it goes without saying, then, that theirs was not the sort of biography commonly featured in Parisian newspapers alongside the pro-colonial coverage of military men battling in the scramble for Africa. Nor did the Pranzinis, petit bourgeois strivers, lead an existence that even remotely resembled those of ordinary European migrants who headed to the western frontier in the United States.

For centuries the Levant, a term evoking the rising sun (in French the verb *lever* means "to rise"), referred to what is today commonly called the Near East. As an adjective, *Levantine* modified the rich trading in the region; it also denoted the pockets of European Christians who settled there, often as merchants. Because of the capitulations, these people had an incentive to safeguard "European" traditions, even as they assumed the practices (food, dress) of the dominant Islamic culture. Cultural hybridity was less a choice than a matter of course.[6]

But with the rise of the modern nation-state during the nineteenth century, the demand for national purity and allegiance became more stringent, and the term *Levantine* became increasingly pejorative, connoting the "semi-Orientalized" European. Despite a European lineage, then, the Levantine became a major figure of Otherness in the Mediterranean world, as the historian Claude Liauzu has remarked.[7] The spread of the colonial cliché of "Alexandrian cosmopolitanism" coincided with and reinforced cultural connotations of Levantines.[8] Partly as a result, researchers interested in these colonial settlers contend with the fact that the label was mostly exogenous, meaning it was applied by outsiders to people who themselves had little use for it. Pranzini, whom Parisians would rate among the most notorious Levantines in the city's history, did not use this identifier in reference to himself.

Lower-class and southern European settlers confronted a cultural paradox of empires shaped by modern nationalism: French and English were the languages of colonial power in Egypt, but gaining fluency in them inevitably called attention to one's own hybridity. But fluency was hardly a requirement to become the object of class- or ethnicity-based scorn. In the view of some metropolitan purists, the mere act of permanently displacing oneself from European soil was cause for concern about the loss of national identity. In a widely read account of a voyage to Egypt in the 1860s, the French feminist Olympe Audouard asserted that it was rare to find a Western European in Egypt who was from a good family. The French settlers were all "adventurers, failures, poor devils of bad extraction who came to get rich"; worse, the Greek and Italian settlers were "plagues on Egypt," for they were gamblers and nightclubbers and "crooks and murderers by profession."[9] In a typification of the cosmopolitanism she encountered, Audouard wrote that "Mr. Zizinia, of Greek origin, is a French protégé and a Roman count, [and] the Consul of Belgium, and simultaneously an impresario at the Italian theater to which he gave his name: the Zizinia Theatre."[10]

Travel guides popularized views of Levantines as venal, fond of cheap novels, dubious in business relations, and maddeningly difficult to identify racially.[11] This was enough to inspire in racial purists a sharp eye for the biological risks of the imperial project, because in the terms of their own choosing, the French burdened themselves with measuring the suitability of "other" races to *civilisation*.[12] The diplomat Arthur de Gobineau, in his influential 1855 treatise *The Inequality of Human Races*, sketched the "tertiary" peoples (the products of racial mixing) in a manner that would be used to describe Levantines and countless other colonial hybrids. Gobineau saw tertiary types as harbingers of the "racial anarchy" found in the colonies and in port cities and capitals: "One man will have the Negro's hair, another the eyes of a Teuton, a third will have a large Mongolian face, a fourth a Semitic figure; and yet all these will be kin!"[13]

Lord Cromer, consul-general of Egypt during the Pranzini investigation and one of Britain's towering imperial figures, ruminated more precisely on the "danger" of what he called "levantinization," conceived as a degeneracy that diluted national-racial purity. Some people in Egypt were more prone to it than others; Europe's "southern races" were most vulnerable to the malady, whereas the robust nature of British racial stock provided a greater level of immunity against slippage into what Lord Cromer also referred to as "Egyptianization."[14] Predictably, the Pranzini investigation revealed that some in Paris did not share Lord Cromer's confidence in the English race. For them, Pranzini embodied a levantinized Englishness every bit as much as he presented with hybridized Frenchness. Pranzini, noted one critic, had "an English air and the soft gracefulness of an Oriental."[15] Leaving aside the intrinsic absurdity of these conjectures, what discussions about Pranzini drove home most poignantly was the flaw in the basic premise of "national" empires, in which the subject-object relationship between colonizer and colonized was believed to hold a stable meaning (thus making it possible to "civilize" or to "liberate" a people).

Pranzini, as the consul's investigation would make plain, was *simultaneously* the product of the Ottoman, British, and French empires, as well as, of course, of the Italian colonial settler community in which his parents were well-known. What elites and metropolitan settlers pathologized about his biography was the intractable social essence of empire itself.

NINETEENTH-CENTURY Alexandria was a colonial boomtown in the way that Paris and London were imperial capitals, New York City a hub of imperial aspirations, and Salzburg a relic.

At first, European newcomers fancied themselves the bearers of industry and progress to a port that had been, in the time of Cleopatra, a center of learnedness and beauty. In the view of Napoleon Bonaparte, France was uniquely suited to revive ancient splendor and decay and to reconcile republicanism and Islam (to which he converted, in an oft-told episode of political calculation). The city's demographic shifts trace the arc of unfettered colonial settlement after the general's ignoble departure: When Bonaparte sailed into the port in 1798, he found only 8,000 people living there; 70 years later, by 1868, the population had inflated to 200,000. In 1887, more than a fifth of the city's inhabitants had come from abroad, including 10,000 Italians.[16]

When Antonietta and Gandolfo Pranzini disembarked in 1857, their move from Tuscany to the Nile River was typical of the demographics of trans-Mediterranean migration. Gandolfo's hometown of Livorno, where he worked as a coal merchant, was a vital link for the steamship traffic between Europe and Egypt that proliferated during the Industrial Revolution (in earlier times, Livorno had been a prosperous importer of spices from the Levant).[17] The Arno River served as an inland waterway connecting Livorno to Florence, bringing British coal inland to the new factories of industrializing Italy and giving young men access to a new order of shipping.[18]

But the Revolution of 1848 and its aftermath disrupted the Duchy of Tuscany, which was riven by a costly foreign occupation that decimated the city's commerce. The movement to unify the Italian peninsula soon spurred thousands of middle-class Tuscans to emigrate, among them political exiles, engineers, and military men.[19] At the time, Egypt still exercised a stronger pull than North America. When European men dreamt of glory and wealth abroad, it was not onto the Great Plains but into the Orient that they projected themselves. The far shorter journey to Egypt offered an insurance policy if things did not work out, and there were religious considerations as well. For Tuscans like the Pranzinis, the ingrained American hostility toward Catholic immigrants, explicit in most of the colonial charters and still generations from extinction, made the United States less welcoming than the Islamic Ottoman Empire, where tolerance was the norm. The Pranzinis would have spotted evidence of Alexandria's plurality from the sea; mosques, Anglican and Catholic churches, and Jewish synagogues together stamped the skyline in a manner yet unthinkable in the West. Indeed, European consuls had historically felt compelled to discourage European settlers from converting to Islam, which they did of their own volition, sometimes for cynical gain; some of the most prominent army leaders of the Napoleonic invasion converted (thus did General Jacques-François de Menouchange his name to General Abdallah de Menou).[20]

Egypt held numerous other advantages for upstart businessmen: a strategic location for trade, fertile soil, cheap land, exploitable indigenous labor, pliable administrators, and slack defenses against rapacious financial practices.[21] Industrialization and staggering growth in the 1830s and 1840s made Egypt a welcome home for a coal merchant; despite a lag in the local economy, the

British completed the Alexandria–Cairo railway in the 1850s, and the French engineer Ferdinand de Lesseps lobbied for a new canal in Suez.

It was said that Lesseps's success was a result of ingratiating himself with Said Pasha when the latter was still a child. Said was an overweight boy; seeing that his father, Muhammad Ali, imposed a strict diet on him, Lesseps secretly passed the lad plates of spaghetti. The Suez Canal, a huge source of Gallic pride, is arguably the most important nineteenth-century imperial construction, renowned for trimming more than 4,000 miles off the journey from Europe to India. (One hundred thousand Egyptian laborers perished digging the canal in the desert sand with their bare hands—they were not provided with tools.) By the time Enrico Pranzini was an adolescent, Alexandria was one of the Mediterranean's premier ports—the U.S. Civil War in the 1860s created a dearth in world cotton markets from which Egypt benefited—but strains on the environment became apparent in land and water shortages in the Nile Valley.[22]

THE ITALIAN CONSULATE furnished Kleczkowski with Pranzini's Tuscan army conscription number. He never served Italy and referred to the new Italian state, tellingly, as "my parents' homeland," that is, not his own. Unfortunately, that is the extent of Pranzini's recorded reflections on his own colonial identity. Given the dynamic historical context, we can surmise that his sense of belonging in the Ottoman Empire was informed by the empire's steady recession from Egypt, in addition to the matrices of class and ethnicity. To borrow Benedict Anderson's famous formulation, the question of identity was on the minds of all "imagined communities" in Ottoman Egypt. Greeks, for instance, argued among themselves over what it meant to call oneself Greek in the Orient. In general, European settlers differentiated themselves from Syrians and indigenous Egyptians, to whom they referred indiscriminately as "Turks." Equally indiscriminately, Ottoman subjects lumped the Europeans, whom they viewed as foreigners, together under the rubric "Franks." All the while, Alexandria's Arabic-language press vented a collective frustration over the Europeanization of the port.[23]

Socially, Europeans in Alexandria were preoccupied, if not inordinately, with social class mobility; culturally, they remained very much under the spell of France.[24] Cafés displayed images of Bonaparte. The French language was seen as a ticket to social advancement. Italian immigrants easily outnumbered their French counterparts in the latter half of the nineteenth century, but Italian *usage* actually declined relative to French.[25] Italian and Greek settlers communicated with their own national consulates in *French*.[26] This practice reflected the de facto hierarchy that existed among the different national settler groups. Roughly, the Italian community, which was particularly stratified, straddled the ground between the Greeks (the most populous and poorest of the settlement groups) and other groups who were "protected" by the British and French consuls.[27]

France's imperial strength was in culture, which had a hand in Enrico Pranzini's upbringing. French Catholic missionaries did much of the legwork of the "civilizing mission" during this period, diligently transmitting French culture, technology, and political ideas to the territories of the Ottoman Empire and beyond.[28] In Alexandria these well-funded missionaries founded international schools rooted in French curricula. As a boy, Pranzini boarded with the Christian Brothers School (L'École des frères chrétiens), which had been established in 1847.[29] The consul's dossier hints that Pranzini's experience at the French school was not altogether happy or profitable. But his spoken accent in French was honed finely enough that the Parisian ear, readily identifying it as non-Parisian, could not rule it out as nonnative.

At age 15, Pranzini transferred to a British school. It is unclear why he did so. The decision may have been a pragmatic calculation, in sync with the increasing sway of the British over Egyptian affairs in the 1870s. The curriculum of Pranzini's new school included a two-year language program and an apprenticeship as a clerk in a British bank. Pranzini's ties to the British, which only strengthened thereafter, would not go unremarked in Paris. Did Pranzini have stronger proclivities toward one or the other of the two imperial powers? Hard to say. On the one hand, he wound up in Paris, not London. Yet he Anglicized his given name when signing sworn statements following his interrogations: Henry. At any rate, his schooling seems to have finished without major incident, and his parents were perhaps pleased with his chances for social advancement.

As the owner of a small business, Gandolfo Pranzini was vulnerable to the downturns of the streaky Egyptian economy. When the great cotton boom ended, his coal concern folded and he turned to the Italian community for work. One mark of excellence and prestige for Italo-Egyptians was the creation, management, and staffing of the Egyptian Post. A group of Italian entrepreneurs ably elevated a private courier firm, the European

Post, into a reputable national service by the 1860s. The elder Pranzini took a job as head of the Egyptian Post's record-keeping department, where he was a respected employee. With his father's aid, Enrico obtained a low-level position at the Egyptian Post in 1874.

According to a contemporary manual, Egypt's linguistic diversity placed polyglots in high demand at the Egyptian Post: Employees "must receive and deliver mail matter addressed in all the languages, Asiatic and European, spoken by larger or smaller groups of the population—Arabic, Turkish, Armenian, Hindustani, Greek, Italian, French, English, Maltese—and must be able to respond to enquiries in more than one of these tongues."[30] Enrico performed well enough to earn a promotion in 1875.

Gandolfo died sometime in the latter half of the 1870s, leaving his son a permanent financial burden. A restless soul of 20, Enrico Pranzini was beckoned by tradition to support his widowed mother with his meager clerk's salary. At this point, he began working on the Egyptian Post's Alexandria–Constantinople delivery line. For the first time, he visited the seat of the Ottoman Empire. More travel followed. His file notes certain changes in his comportment. Colleagues and acquaintances remarked on his fine clothing. He was reputed to be chronically short of money. A ship's doctor who befriended Pranzini on the Alexandria–Constantinople line told Kleczkowski that the young man took to prostituting himself to "many Muslim men."[31]

Pranzini's tasks included the handling of sensitive packages, some containing valuables. He began to steal from the packages. "It was then," Pranzini admitted to Guillot in Paris, that "I made a mistake." In 1877 he was arrested for the first time. According to the Italian consul's records, he admitted to filching 950 pounds from packages in transit. He was fired on New Year's Eve 1877, convicted of theft, and sent away to prison for nine months. "Despite this sentence, and thanks to my father's good name, I was freed after three months of detention," Pranzini later recalled.[32]

Having squandered the career set before him, Pranzini left Egypt to embark on what he called his "adventures," which spanned imperial war and commerce, tourism, and government bureaucracy. He seems never to have had trouble finding either a job or an investor willing to cut him into a deal. He traveled eastward and then back, working in trading concerns of all sorts. In Alexandria he partnered with Egisto Sibaldi and Cesare Frangini, and the three planned a business venture in South Asia. They pulled together 3,000 francs—Pranzini had no money to contribute—and took off for Bombay in

May 1879. The journey took 4 months, which was sufficient for Pranzini to pick up some Hindi. "Once in Bombay we got into contact with the princes in the Raj, thanks to our knowledge of the Indian language and for 7 or 8 months we sold them products of all sorts," Pranzini recalled, including hectographs, a gelatin-based system for copying documents that was developed in Russia in the 1860s. These dealings turned a nice profit. In Paris, though, Pranzini told Guillot that he separated from Sibaldi and Frangini because they turned out to be "petty crooks."

Because of the geographic expansion of press coverage during the late nineteenth century, news of the rue Montaigne murders made it all the way to South Asia, which is how the other side of the story echoed back to Kleczkowski. Sibaldi had settled in Calcutta in the interim. While reading one of the colonial newspapers there, he first learned of Pranzini's troubles in Paris. He followed the story and grew incensed—and not a little worried—when he read that Pranzini had besmirched his honor in his statements to the Parisian investigative magistrate. To repair his reputation, Sibaldi asked for an audience with the French consul in Calcutta. Flanking himself with a professor from a Calcutta art school to vouch for his character, Sibaldi signed the following statement: "Pranzini was luckier than us. He found a job as soon as we arrived at a hotel in Bombay. I noticed that he gambled a lot and was losing significant sums playing billiards, and I thought it was imprudent to keep him as an associate. We ceased our relations, little by little. Learning today of the despicable lies Pranzini has told, I have come to ask you to save my honor and my reputation with respect to the French justice system." In the document later forwarded to Alexandria from Calcutta, Sibaldi added that he was prepared to make the weeks-long trip across the Indian Ocean, through the Suez Canal, to continental Europe to back up his version of events, if need be.[33]

Pranzini's next move was to partner with an American named Archer. The two organized a caravan heading east from India. They brought domestic servants, horses, elephants, and camels, all carrying merchandise to sell in Afghanistan, Baluchistan (today a Pakistani province), and Persia. The trip was profitable, but Pranzini had to cut it short. "After one year I fell gravely ill, and I returned to Bombay having earned a certain sum of money; I met a German called Stein who must still be abroad today. We became associates and set out for Singapore. After visiting almost all of India, we came back through Suez and I left my friend to return to Alexandria."[34]

THE ALLEGED TRAITS that made Levantines seem shifty to elites were often precisely what made them vital middlemen in the maintenance and banal operations of empire.[35] The reasons for this are self-evident. For empires to carry on constant dialogue with local farmers and laborers, business owners, and Ottoman administrators, they needed go-betweens with more than a passing knowledge of the cultural codes and languages of the terrain. These middlemen served as a buffer between elites and the indigenous people. As a result, elites commonly associated European middlemen with the empire's dirty work; they liked to blame Levantines especially for the underhandedness and abuses that were the hallmarks of imperial exploitation. Here is Lord Cromer: "The upper-class Levantine naturally considered the upper-class Egyptian as his prey. The lower-class Levantine tricked the fellaheen."[36] Beneath armed force and civilization-bearing colonial administrations lay the colonial netherworld of levantinism.

Of all the working people tossed into this netherworld, interpreters and translators were among the most visible to tourists, businessmen, and military officers alike (employment in the consular networks was generally viewed as more respectable, but not by much). The children of Alexandria learned languages as a matter of everyday life, and their skills were much in demand. Between flashes of business prosperity, Pranzini used this avenue to earn a living, most often as a hotel or military interpreter, a job typically providing room, board, a modest salary, and daily exposure to Europeans of a certain social standing.

According to his mother, Pranzini returned to Constantinople after a brief stint in the administration of the Ottoman *wali*, or governor, of Syria. In the Ottoman capital he found an arrangement as an interpreter at the Hôtel d'Angleterre. He made the acquaintance of some Russian army officers, and they offered him more work as an army interpreter. In 1877–1878 the Russian and Ottoman Empires were locked in another of their territorial disputes, and Pranzini accompanied the officers, arriving in time for the Treaty of San Stefano, which ended the conflict. He then continued to Odessa and, according to records obtained by the French consul from the British occupation army in Egypt, he served the British army during the Second Afghan War.

The colonial phobia of cultural and racial hybridizations, which fed the stereotype of the duplicitous interpreter in the East,[37] foreshadowed and probably aggravated the chronic shortage of native British officers willing

Figure 8. In a studio photograph taken in Cairo (note the Great Pyramids in the background), Pranzini wears an interpreter's uniform. Archives de la Préfecture de Police de Paris.

to live among indigenous peoples for the time required to become bilingual. Did true bilingualism not require, in effect, living as a cultural go-between quite in the manner of the "vile race of interpreters we are now forced to employ," as one British naval official described the non-British middlemen whose "evil practices" made them less than ideal employees?[38] The British Archives contain numerous letters from military leaders during the latter half of the nineteenth century decrying the shortage of interpreters and, following the advent of new officer programs and incentives, lamenting the failure of these. "Considering our present complications in the Persian Gulf," wrote one military officer in 1866, "one is reminded that, we see no signs of our scheme for encouraging qualifying for Interpreters."[39] Nearly two decades later, in 1883, Lord Cromer—a few months before quitting his post in India to oversee the expanding British position in Egypt—co-authored another such letter requesting even greater incentives to attract British officers.[40] The interpreter problem persisted, and before long Pranzini was working under Lord Cromer's supervision.

Lord Cromer met with the British general Charles "Chinese" Gordon in Cairo in 1884 to discuss the deteriorating situation of the British garrison in Sudan, where an anticolonial uprising led by Mahdist rebels was gathering steam. A colonial "hero" of the first order, Gordon insisted on heading up the Nile to oversee the evacuation of the British unit; military positions along the river were being abandoned in a coordinated retreat. But the enigmatic Gordon abruptly changed his mind and decided to shore up the British hold on Khartoum. His hubris quickly got him surrounded by the rebels. A long siege commenced, killing thousands. Only under pressure did London come to the aid of Gordon. Lord Cromer helped organize the Nile Expedition late in the summer of 1884.

Pranzini, living with his mother in a small Cairo apartment at the time, was working odd jobs when he heard that the British were desperate for interpreters. Interpreter Second Class Pranzini was immediately dispatched and, according to the records of the British general Stephenson, he made it past the Second Cataract to the British camp at Wadi Halfa, the base of the expeditionary force. He then headed south to the village of Saras (more than halfway to Khartoum, in northern Sudan), where he spent the whole of December 1884 and January 1885 at the service of high-ranking British officers.

By the time the expedition arrived in Khartoum, Gordon's beheaded body had been cut to pieces and Sudan lost. The cleanup would require

months of work, and Pranzini and other Egyptian contractors found themselves in limbo in the desert. Some of them, recalling the sand, wind, in-
sects, and intense heat of the previous September, began leaving their posts
in anticipation of the hot season. Pranzini had heat stroke, he later told
Guillot, and suffered some memory loss. He wrote a handful of letters to
his superiors, begging for release or a promotion to Interpreter First Class
(which paid better). He mentioned his needy mother and a job she had
found for him in Italy.

"We cannot go without interpreters," replied a colonel in an internal
memo from Wadi Halfa. Pranzini's requests were twice denied, but he
persisted.

"I offered my services to the British government at a time when interpreters were in great demand," he replied.

Finally, after seven hellish months, he was issued his release documents
on April 11, 1885, along with a glowing testimonial letter containing an administrative summary of his skills—he "speaks French, Italian, Greek, Turkish, Arabic, Russian and Hindu, and he writes English, Italian, French and
Greek,"—and the observation that he was "kind-natured, obliging, and energetic" and came "recommended by Captain King."[41] Pranzini returned to
Lower Egypt, working for a time as a casino dealer. His money was soon gone.

In the spring of 1886, Pranzini chanced on the rising Orientalist painter
Rudolf Swoboda the Younger of Austria, who had made six different trips
to Egypt since 1879 and was at the time shuttling between Britain and India
through the Suez Canal. The painter was making his way back to the court
of Queen Victoria, who had recently gushed over his work—in her journal
she had written, "He is only twenty-six, of the name of Swoboda, and is
full of talent"—and had commissioned much of it.[42] Pranzini and Swoboda
were roughly the same age and struck up an easy friendship, with Pranzini
serving as Swoboda's interpreter and helping him organize an exhibition to
sell his work in Cairo. Swoboda planned to make a stop in Paris en route to
London, and he offered to pay Pranzini's fare. Pranzini had a cousin, Enzo,
who worked as an interpreter at the Hôtel du Louvre. He agreed to accom-
pany Swoboda. According to Kleczkowski's final report, the duo left the port
of Alexandria on June 15, 1886, on a ship bound for Marseille. The diligent
consul could thus declare with some certainty that Pranzini had not been in
Paris between 1879 and 1886. The prime suspect in the case of the murders in
the rue Montaigne was not a serial killer.

CHAPTER SIX

Criminal Detection as Colonial War by Other Means

Investigative Claims on the Latin American Rastaquouère

> *Rastaquouérism* is the order of the day.
>
> —*L'Illustration*, July 16, 1887

> It was in this embryonic city, in the middle of savages, that I learned about the defense of society and the hunt for robbers.
>
> —Deputy Chief François Goron, on how life on the colonial frontier in South America prepared him for a career as a Paris police detective[1]

> A French detective has been here for some days back searching for the man Geissler, suspected of complicity with Pranzini in the late triple murder in the Rue Montaigne at Paris, but hitherto without success.
>
> —Berlin correspondent, London *Times*, April 21, 1887

"We at Security were irked that the man had been caught in Marseille," confessed Deputy Chief Goron.[2] Instead of redounding to the benefit of the maligned inspectors under their command, Pranzini's arrest unleashed more adverse publicity on the chief and deputy chief of Security. The Marseille police were hailed as superior for having nabbed the suspect, and within weeks rumors of Chief Taylor's imminent firing trickled into major Parisian newspapers such as *Le Temps* and *La Croix*. "If Mr. Taylor were to leave his post," cracked one journalist, the "decision would be taken only after the investigation of the crime in the rue Montaigne." Then the punch line: "If we wait for the end," the chief will keep his job "for eternity."[3] Taylor, perhaps not wishing to dignify the press with a response, stood by as justice ran its course, doing the minor research tasks and fact checking that the magistrate Guillot demanded of him.

Goron was neither so readily consigned to menial work nor disadvantaged out of a chance to shine in the public eye. He had journeyed to Marseille along with Inspector Fortuné Jaume to retrieve the suspect and had been the first Parisian investigator to rifle through Pranzini's meager belongings. Among these were handkerchiefs bearing the initials A.S., for Antoinette Sabatier, Pranzini explained, a Parisian lover with whom he happened to share an apartment. Goron also obtained the report of a Marseille prison doctor who, having observed that the liner of Pranzini's overcoat was ripped out during his first night behind bars, wondered whether the suspect had attempted suicide. Questioned about this, Pranzini explained that he had suffered a headache in the middle of the night. He called out for help but received no attention from prison guards; so to relieve the pain, he tied the liner around his forehead.[4]

On the overnight train ride back to Paris, Goron attempted an impromptu interrogation of the suspect that yielded nothing of substance. The following morning, Taylor ordered the diversion of Pranzini's arrival from the Gare de Lyon to the Charenton station to avoid the newspaper reporters (a few still found their way to the platform). And, almost from the moment he disembarked with Pranzini in tow, Goron saw himself marginalized: The arrest of a colonial migrant caused the investigation to balloon, with experts from a variety of fields discerning a rare opportunity. At the top of the pecking order stood Guillot, a saber-toothed questioner of suspects who, despite decades of experience, encountered snags in his approach to Pranzini. Then came the "scientific" police, the doctors, criminal theorists, and, of course, the newspaper reporters.

As though to compensate for this marginalization, Goron hatched a plan that would highlight his cosmopolitan knowledge, which carried with it the whiff of imperial military glory that he and many of his subalterns believed to be central to their work. The idea, a transnational quest for the rue Montaigne suspect known as Gaston Geissler, had the benefit of whisking Goron himself to the foreground. If the novelty of Goron's search for Geissler was clear only in hindsight, it was because of the embarrassment it caused in the short term. Yet as the deputy chief came out from Taylor's shadow, he positioned Security as an agency fit to combat the cosmopolitan criminality and sexual danger purportedly presented by the figure of the rastaquouère. By dramatically expanding Security's geographic reach—and the public exposure to it—Goron set an important precedent for future transnational criminal investigations.[5]

FRANÇOIS GORON grew up in the western city of Rennes. The milieu was conservative. His mother saw a future for him in the priesthood. He read crime fiction and also Hugo and Sue. His uncle had been a surgeon in the army of Napoleon I, and he was bathed in imperial nostalgia at an impressionable age. "My mind was occupied by the glorious memories of the First Empire; I dreamt of becoming the aide-de-camp of a new Murat, galloping and superb in the glory and smoke." Although he wished to attend the prestigious military school at Saint-Cyr, his performance in school was mediocre and he had no clue how to operate a gun. Under these circumstances his parents pushed him into a career as a pharmacist. His first job was in that field, although he soon grew restless and left town.

News of Napoleon III's invasion of Mexico revived Goron's fantasies. He wanted to make his name as a warrior in French Latin America: "I already imagined myself on the route to Puebla, gun in hand, hunting guerillas." He quit his job and enlisted. As a soldier, he never amounted to much. By his own account, he ran afoul of his superiors, who in turn prevented him from departing for Mexico. Goron responded by joining the navy and requesting to be sent to war in Asia, but again he was kept away from the field of battle and was instead dispatched, in 1867, to Martinique, "the most tranquil of the colonies," where he was kept for two years. When the French looked to expand their sphere of influence in West Africa, it looked as though Goron might be sent to Dakar. This time his mother intervened to keep him out of danger. Fearing for her son's life, she prevailed upon him to reject the mission (which in those days entailed buying a replacement) and return to Rennes.

Although Goron would later emerge as the predominant advocate of veterans at Security, his own military career ended in a clutter of snubs and chagrin. Almost as soon as he had returned to Rennes, the Prussians invaded France, and he excitedly donned the uniform again. At a street parade organized to send the local sons off to war, Goron was in a familiar place

M. GORON

SOUS-CHEF DE LA SURETÉ

Figure 9. François Goron, Deputy Chief of Security, 1887. *La Revue Illustrée*, 10 April 1887.

at the trough, slaking his thirst for attention. "It was a superb demonstration and I was very proud because I got to carry the flag. All along the path women clapped and threw flowers on us. I shouted 'To Berlin!' with all my might." But a group of workers standing along the parade route chafed at the sight of a young bourgeois monopolizing the *tricolore*, and they jumped Goron, beat him bloody, and then snatched the flag and left him in a heap, humiliated.[6] Not until the Geissler investigation nearly two decades later did Goron make it to Berlin. In 1870 the army deployed him not to the eastern border but instead to Algeria, where he was forced to train Arab recruits for the war against Prussia. Longing for the war front, he protested. But by the time he and a small corps of African soldiers made it back to Paris, the French had lost the decisive Battle of Sedan (and Napoleon III was captured).

His army career over, Goron made the acquaintance of John Lelong, a former Argentinean consul in Paris and a high-profile figure in the Latin American community there reputed for his efforts to induce French emigration to Argentina. French imperialism in Argentina was informal, but as in Egypt during the latter part of the nineteenth century, Argentinean elites, an increasingly cosmopolitan population, held French culture in the highest esteem. As in Egypt, the French language was the pinnacle of cultural knowing. The French colony in Buenos Aires viewed their influence in Argentina as a version of the official colonial mission of civilization. Migration helped sustain a durable, if mostly one-sided, cultural exchange between the two nations; the French constituted the third largest immigrant group in Argentina, with 230,000 Gallic settlers, a figure unmatched by any formal French colony in the world except Algeria.[7]

No French invasion of Argentina was in the offing, yet the South American nation lay squarely within the French colonial imagination. Lelong "painted such a warm painting of the future of the country, and the chances of success for the audacious ones who went to colonize it, that I decided to liquidate my belongings and leave with my wife and two children." The Gorons, accompanied by their domestic servant, joined the boatloads of ambitious Europeans on the weeks-long journey to northern Argentinean territory on the Paraguay River, about 750 miles from Buenos Aires. There, they contributed to the development of a new colony called Formosa, in which Italian immigrants formed the largest European contingent. "A city! We designed it, and we built some houses, or rather some *ranchos* with palm trees and mud."[8] Goron sought fortune as a cattle rancher, a vocation that Parisians associated with the new-moneyed and flamboyant rastaquouère social type. (Goron seems to have remained innocent of the irony.)

In the beginning Goron found frontier life invigorating. He saw himself enacting the stories of Gustave Aimard, the author and noted French adventurer in Latin America. But harsh realities soon set in. Formosa lived under the constant threat of attack from indigenous tribes. There were gun battles. "Over there in the desert, I made my debut" in police work, Goron would later recall, a wildly Panglossian assessment even by Goron's standards. In fact, the colony confronted disasters of biblical proportion. Goron's livestock was wiped out by an epidemic and his crops were decimated by a flood. The Tobas tribe overran the land that the Europeans had claimed. The national government in Buenos Aires was unable to act because of political chaos, which sealed Goron's fate and "completed my ruin."[9] His servant fell ill; then his 7-year-old son was infected, caught fever, and breathed his last in Goron's arms. The family returned to France on a German ocean liner and, for many years, Goron was unable to speak about the child he had buried overseas.[10]

BEGINNING in the 1870s, the Paris Police Prefecture was drawn into society intrigues involving Latin Americans (some of them war veterans) who had returned from the rubble of European outposts in Latin America.[11] Like the cases involving Pranzini and the other so-called "lords of crime"— though on a much smaller scale—these investigations depended on colonial knowledge. Still, Goron understood that it would take a fierce advocate to demonstrate that the colonial war veterans at Security could make a valuable contribution to public safety.

The challenge was complicated, given the Third Republic's tendency to distance itself from earlier regimes' dependence on a militarized police force and its echoes of authoritarianism. Like their counterparts across Europe, civilian police forces in nineteenth-century France were heavily stocked with what leading policing historian Clive Emsley has called "military elements." In Paris, police and military personnel effectively shared duties; the gendarmerie (a hybrid of military and civilian police created by Napoleon I) and the army were routinely called on to bolster the uniformed beat cops (*gardiens de la paix*) in ways both visible and quotidian—to stand guard at a theater, say, or at a prison or prefecture.[12] But this sharing of duties, together with the Paris police's gratuitously violent antirevolutionary crackdowns, risked perpetuating the common (and justified) view of the Paris police as an oppressive force staffed by brutish army retreads, rough-cut men of little promise.[13] In its first fifteen years the Third Republic slashed Parisian gendarmerie posts by more than half, from a height of 6,100 in 1871 to 3,000 in 1887. At the same time, the number of beat cops increased to 8,000 by 1887, and training programs were conceived for these latter.[14]

Despite these shifts, in the 1870s and 1880s the Third Republic got swept up in a massive wave of militarization, a development whose implications for the Paris Police Prefecture have not been fully measured. What is clear is that soldiering remained the formative training for Paris policemen.[15] What sorts of military experience did military veterans bring to their police work? The Republic launched its military buildup assuming that another war with the Germans was forthcoming. Events did not go according to plan, however, and French forces wound up vectored in just about every direction but Germany's during the four decades before World War I. In other words, the wars fought by veterans-turned-cops were *colonial* wars, yet historians are only beginning to inquire into the relation between colonial expansionism and the professionalization of metropolitan policing.[16]

In principle, "l'empire" remained a dirty word among republicans, tarnished by the antidemocratic regimes of Napoleon III and his uncle. But from the point of view of Goron and other colonial war veterans at Security, the distinction between France's glorious (i.e., Bonapartist) imperial traditions and the Third Republic's colonial project was a question of semantics, much like the distinction between soldiering and policing. It followed that criminal detection in the metropole was colonial war by other means. Goron's understanding of police work as an extension of the duties of colonialism was rooted in firsthand experience. After all, French colonial soldiers typically doubled as the local police force in their stations at least until a civil administration could be established.[17] It also carried a far-reaching implication: The practitioners of state-sanctioned colonial violence—soldiers—were embedding themselves deep in the Third Republic's criminal repression apparatus.

Unflinchingly self-promotional, police memoirs and pro-Security publicity were integral to the advancement of the police agenda and the improvement of the agency's image. They valorized overseas experience and transmitted it to a mass public—memoirs were published serially in newspapers before their release under respected Parisian imprints.[18] These works carried on a kind of public conversation and, at their most ambitious, constructed police culture and consciousness while offering alternative perspectives to those found in the official histories commissioned by the Police Prefecture.

A lingering glance at these publications indicates that colonial war service was a shared reference point in Security, and colonial violence reverberated back to metropolitan France. Colonial war veterans held many of the agency's most prominent posts during the first two decades of the Third Republic. Some inspectors had been practically raised in the military; among the most recognized members of Security, *les enfants de troupe* (the offspring of low-ranking soldiers) were not uncommon. Some spent much of their careers shuttling between armed conflicts in the metropole and in the colonies. There was Inspector Bazard, for instance, who began as a soldier in the African campaigns from 1864 to 1869 and then returned to fight the Prussians in 1870, for which he won an award for bravery.[19]

Inspector Rossignol, a stellar detective and a friend of Goron's, traced a comparable trajectory. At age 20 he joined the Zouave battalions in French North Africa. In 1870 he returned to the metropole with his battalion and was subsequently taken prisoner by the Prussians. Then, in 1871, he returned to North Africa, this time to take part in the bloody campaign to put down the anticolonial insurgency in Kabylie, Algeria. Afterward he tried to join the Senegalese Tirailleurs in West Africa, but when that didn't work out, he caught on as a military musician for a time before his hiring at Security in 1875 for the modest annual salary of 1,200 francs.[20] Rossignol's initial move to Security came on the heels of an undesirable career event. It was not, to put it mildly, a sought-after job. "I started with the police force by chance," said Goron; it is likely that many others could have said the same.[21]

In a thick, fawning profile of Security published in the late 1880s, Horace Valbel held up the inspectors' combat experience as a prelude to, and sometimes an explanatory accounting of, their outstanding investigative work in Paris. In some instances, tracing the inspectors' career paths meant revisiting the Commune. In a departure from official police histories, Valbel's profiles did not paper over the divisive legacy of that civil conflict. Antoine Claude, who was chief in 1871, worked on behalf of the Versailles government and was arrested by the Communards, whom he viewed as criminals.[22] In memoirs published under Claude's name but not in fact written by him, we find a startling equivalence that the former chief would have undoubtedly endorsed, namely, between "the final hour of the Commune" and "the final hour of the empire of Mexico," each of which unloosed a "cosmopolitan brigandage" on Paris.[23]

Hostility toward the Commune was not limited to Claude. Inspector Archimbaud also served Versailles and was likewise imprisoned.[24] Among the notable colonial war veterans who took up arms against the Commune stood future Inspector Gaillarde, who had served in China during the Second Opium War, where he was recognized for bravery.[25] Gaillarde rose to become part of Security's elite *brigade spéciale*, and he was regularly mentioned in the press during the 1880s for his participation in transnational investigations.

Yet the conversion of war veterans into criminal detectives had its drawbacks. Security leaders such as Gustave Macé (1879–1884) complained that many of the men had never called Paris home and were unable to find their way around the city; others drank absinthe or lived in flophouses under assumed names.[26] To corral them, Macé resorted to military idiom. He called them his sacred battalion and spoke, in his first address to them, in almost farcically Napoleonic language that would not have been out of place in a general's speech to a division that was about to invade and occupy a foreign capital. "From this day forward, you are my general staff. France has her eye on us," said Macé, before imploring the men "to work for my glory, [and] it will reflect back on you like rays of sun on the universe."[27]

Goron liked to draw parallels between the flair demanded by criminal detection and the heroic masculine ethos of the colonial frontier. His subalterns followed suit, clinging to military culture and idiom, particularly the self-assigned superlatives of investigative zeal and sacrifice that were meant to resonate with the hardships and drama of the colonial frontier.[28] When searching for a suspect, inspectors at Security said they were on a "manhunt" or a "homeric race" or simply a "campaign." When successful, they received awards that approximated military commendations, and their captures were tabulated as a matter of public policy.[29] Like soldiers, they counted their injuries, and these tallies were publicized too.[30] Like bounty hunters, they were rewarded financially for catching dangerous suspects.[31]

When Louis-Alois Kuehn stepped in as Macé's successor (in 1884–1885), he became the first colonial war veteran to head Security, having joined the agency after a tour in the Crimean War, where he had been wounded five times (at the Battle of Sebastopol, he lost his left arm and was fitted with a prosthetic limb). Just 19 months into his tenure, Kuehn died suddenly in his office on the Quai de l'Horloge; Ernest Taylor tried to fill his shoes.

Goron's memoirs leave little doubt about Taylor's uneasy fit in the colonial subculture at Security. Goron's frigid appreciation of his boss's professional conduct essentially questioned Taylor's fitness as a leader. Taylor was a republican bureaucrat, stiff and cerebral, like a "professor" whose rationalism and timidity curtailed his abilities; he was "too rigorous, too puritan" and preferred to batten down the hatches when a situation called for risk taking. At his most explicit, Goron suggested that Taylor "perhaps wasn't the ideal Chief of Security; he would surely have made a better investigative magistrate, because he lacked the physical prowess vital to the hunt for bad guys, as well as a taste for the picturesque—the artistic instinct, if you will—that keeps a policeman entirely dedicated to the solution of a problem until he has succeeded."[32] Physically, Goron went on to clarify, a chief should be brawny like a "general" but at the same time possess "premonition, instinct."[33] In contrast to Taylor, Goron possessed these Romantic qualities in spades, by his own estimation. The "luck and the intuition that is indispensable to policemen served me more than the savant's deductions."[34]

"WITHIN FIVE MINUTES of laying eyes on him, I had no doubt about the man's guilt," wrote Goron of Pranzini, who, he added, was "made for crime." Applying his colonial knowledge, the deputy chief considered himself an able decipherer of Pranzini's "craftiness" and of his manifest indications of "imbecility" and "savage cold blood." Pranzini, he concluded, belonged to a "special category of criminals: the rastaquouère, murderer of loose women."[35]

Goron was a reader of colonial physiognomies and an adherent of the commonly accepted view of criminality as innate to certain men and legible to the expert eye. But what was the rastaquouère?

Because of its murky etymology—the term *rastaquouère* was often shortened to *rasta*—the type has resisted historical analysis; the last serious attempt to map its early usage was published more than a half-century ago.[36] *Rastaquouère* was at first the argot of the elite Parisian *boulevardier* and was probably familiar to few beyond the quarters of central Paris before the 1880s. In practice, the term delineated racial difference at a time when the

Atlantic Ocean was becoming a migratory conveyor belt, thanks to cheaper and faster maritime transport coupled with New World fortune seeking that attracted Europeans and enabled those who succeeded in the Americas to return to Europe and live comfortably. Specifically, rastaquouère was a racial slur when aimed at Latin American men in Paris; yet it was, like all enduring stereotypes, essentially untethered from complex social realities and hence malleable. It hardly mattered that Pranzini, who became the most famous embodiment of the rastaquouère, never set foot in the Americas; he was of "Latin" ancestry, in the same sense that the French and the people of Central and South America were. As a social type, the racialized category of the rastaquouère evolved in correlation with ideas about colonial ambition and migration but also gender and forms of criminal and sexual danger.

In 1886 Baron René-Jean Toussaint confabulated the rastaquouère out of the colonial upheavals happening in the Western hemisphere. Toussaint, who wrote under the pen name René Maizeroy, was a military man and was said to have inspired Maupassant's antihero Georges Duroy. On the eve of the Pranzini affair, he defined the rastaquouère as "a modern leper, a contagion dating from the Empire [of Napoleon III]." Toussaint was patently referring to citizens and representatives of Latin American nations freshly liberated from European rule, migrants who settled in the French capital "as though for a victorious conquest . . . establishing a loud colony in the newly opened neighborhoods" that Haussmann created.[37]

Anecdotal evidence corroborates Toussaint's dating of the rastaquouère type and exposes the racism that Latin American immigrants encountered when reverse migration brought them back to the metropole. In 1863 the acclaimed actor Jules Brasseur, playing the role of the title character in a comic piece called *Le brésilien*, took the stage in blackface. Then he launched into a grunting flourish that brought down the house. An account of Brasseur's performance and its fallout is worth quoting at length.

> To begin with, he looked pretty much like a Negro [*à peu près nègre*], with an outfit of all the colors of the rainbow spread over an incredible vest, plus earrings. He opened his mouth and then resounded the most horrifying syllables—like a hailstorm on windows: *Astaquer bonastaquer*, and then finally *rastaquouère*, which wasn't in the text. This cascade made the chandelier tremble, and it got the crowd laughing. At the exits, and later in restaurants and cafes, the spectators imitated and popularized the loud terminology.

And consequently, several members of the distinguished Brazilian colony [*la colonie brésilienne*] in Paris were so disturbed by it that that they went to the Palais Royal two days later to boo Brasseur. Their legation paid a visit to the Quai d'Orsay [the French Ministry of Foreign Affairs]. The state censor intervened, and the management at the Palais Royal pushed Brasseur to make an act of contrition. But by then it was too late. The term *rastaquouère* had already entered our slang. So then the [other] young people of Latin American origin complained, not without reason, that this sobriquet lumped them together with the Brazilians. Brasseur had to assure all of Central and South America that he meant no harm by it.[38]

The remarkable reaction of the Latin American community to racial stereotyping is an early example of the challenges of postcolonial identity in metropolitan France. The story also serves as a point of departure in a rapid transition from early stereotypes of the rastaquouère as a figure of evident racial Otherness to what it represented two decades later when it entered print, namely, a more numerous, less innocent brand of criminal.

The journalist Aurélien Scholl estimated that 40,000 rastaquouères were prowling the city in 1887. (For Scholl and other writers who studied Pranzini, Levantines were a subcategory of *rastaquouèrisme*.) Far from the babbler portrayed by Brasseur, these men were "masters of the art of pulling the wool over one's eyes." At their lowest, Scholl added, they were "gatherers of cigar butts" who subsisted on coffee and whatever else they could cadge. The rastaquouère owned only a few shirts, but these were flashy. He dawdled on café terraces, people watching and scanning the crowds for jewelry and wallets to pick. Crucially, he could converse with almost any Parisian or visitor: "The man of prey speaks three or four languages."[39]

The nomadic interpreter was the most likely sort of rastaquouère; hotels were full of "all order" of Pranzinis, wrote Scholl.[40] The journalist Hugues Le Roux confirmed that Pranzini "was very well known" at the Hôtel Continental. Le Roux, in his exploration of the international "brotherhood" of linguistic interpreters, expressed relief that the Pranzini case had helped call attention to a "category of people passably suspect and generally unknown to Parisians." The rastaquouère-interpreter roamed in train stations, lay in wait in ports for the arrival of ocean liners bearing tourists, and loitered around the gates of the national museums; he could be spotted beneath the arcades lining the rue de Rivoli, where he proposed guided visits to theaters, monuments, streets, and palaces.[41]

Alongside these "rastaquouères by vocation" were "rastaquouères by blood," according to the columnist Bachaumont, adding that the rastaquouère could operate from an upper-class station. Eighty percent of all Latin Americans were rastaquouères—European emigrants typically fell into the category, no matter their nationality—but that left a substantial proportion of them who could operate as a kind of corrupting force operating from within—not foreigners but home-grown rastas. As a point of clarification, Bachaumont listed some well-known examples. His inclusion of the half-Jewish star Sarah Bernhardt suggests an amalgamation with anti-Semitism. Bachaumont was writing in the early 1880s, when the word *anti-sémitisme* began to circulate in the press and in Catholic publications.[42] A few years later, Edouard Drumont would begin to use the term *rastaquouère* almost interchangeably with "the foreigners and the Jews" who got involved sexually with French women of the *bonne société*.[43]

As with stereotypes about Levantines in Alexandria, rastaquouères were viewed as shallow imitators of Parisian style; as colonial settlers, they remained attached to Europe for the sake of prestige. And, just as anti-Semites conjured Jews with exaggerated racial traits as well as Jews who could pass in stealth, so could the rastaquouère stereotype simultaneously accommodate Brasseur's performance on the one hand and, on the other, Pranzini, who embodied the "veritable proteus" of feral allure, dubious financial means, and nouveau-riche fashions. Two more self-styled experts, Paul Belon and Georges Price, elaborated on this point.

> On the boulevard—between the rue Drouot and the Madeleine—people mean by *rastaquouère* any individual of foreign origin whose means of subsistence are problematic and who, in reality, lives by his wits amid tainted luxury. The rastaquouère can be English, German, Belgian, Russian, Balkan, or Levantine; but he may also be Neapolitan, Spanish, Portuguese, and most often South American. In that case he has a copper complexion, black hair, fiery eyes, and a feline look: he exaggerates stylishness in the tailoring of his clothes, and he wears charms and diamonds on all of his fingers. He's a classic type who can vary infinitely and one has trouble keeping up with all of his diverse transformations.[44]

The first sightings of Pranzini in Paris sparked more fanciful conceptions of this protean rastaquouère, with newspaper descriptions of his anatomy and physiognomy resting on a paradox: If the rastaquouère's essential formlessness made him socially dangerous, then investigators needed urgently to fix the physical traits that would indicate his presence. "Pranzini added a new type to the history of crime," a journalist wrote, because his was the "face on which *internationalism* meets itself."[45]

Giving themselves a wide berth, reporters combined colonial stereotypes with the lexicon of biological determinism from criminologists and other social theorists. *La Petite République* claimed that it spotted the demeanor of a merchant in Pranzini's gait. Other papers projected the *métissage* of East and West onto his countenance and, in turn, sussed glints of danger back out of it. *Le Figaro* saw steely blue eyes beneath Pranzini's "Chinese eyelids."[46] Others saw eyes of black, brown, or green—it depended on the news outlet.[47] "Yes, the eye is terrible," concurred another journalist. "It is light, piercing, menacing, derisive. . . . You only catch a glimpse of it, sometimes, beneath the undergrowth, or roll of flesh, that is produced by the folds of the forehead. But it is there, always worried, always anxious, always aroused, always illuminated and brilliant like a whitish flame."[48]

In a quasi-Lamarckian twist, then, the cacophony of the *fait-divers* lent credibility to the idea that Pranzini's physiognomy could rapidly evolve to the point that it remained indecipherable, neither colonial nor European and yet both at once. Goron's notes are a case in point. Goron studied Pranzini from close range and observed in him the "Oriental languor that the Levantines have in their eyes." As deputy chief, he had easy access to accurate data and years to get his facts straight. And yet, within a handful of pages, he followed the conflicted path of the reporters, first recording Pranzini's eyes as dark blue and then as black.[49]

Anatomy and "origins" were inextricably tied in these investigative fictions, as both derived from Pranzini's rangy biography, a subject that pulled the *fait-divers* onto new terrain. Known conventionally as the quintessentially *local* news genre, the *fait-divers* seldom carried news from abroad. The Pranzini case, however, forced reporters to broaden their geographic horizons.[50] Newspaper readers, agog to retrace Pranzini's routes, consumed a story in nonsequential bits as these streamed into France.

The jigsaw format of the *fait-divers* gave the ominous impression of a pleating of colonial space into Parisian space. On any given day one might absorb stories of the suspect's gambling losses in Cairo casinos and of his first months in Paris, when he kicked around in flophouses near the Champs-Elysées and canvassed the small Egyptian expatriate community in search of a job.[51] The papers recounted Pranzini's clubbing in Montmartre and his attempts to seduce women as he loitered in luxury hotel lobbies; still others reported his work as a tour guide and as a colonial importer-exporter as far away as Jakarta.[52]

Bolstered by these reports was the *fait-divers* crime reporter's claim to a prominent role in the tracking—and by extension, the criminalization—of colonial migrants and other alleged infiltrators who, as it was suspected of the rastaquouère, may have been involved in the international sex trafficking of French women and girls: *la traite des blanches*, or "white slavery."[53] "If there is one subject in which it is difficult to disentangle myth from reality," writes the great French historian Alain Corbin in his classic history of prostitution in France, "it is certainly the white slave trade. Indeed, this is a theme made more significant by the fear-ridden literature that conveyed it than by the reality that it concealed. It was the crossroads of all the obsessions of the period, a subject on which the most balanced minds of the era lost their bearings."[54]

The sexual treachery of the rastaquouère type counted among these obsessions in the 1880s and 1890s. As Corbin shows, the myths and realities of global sex trafficking stemmed from the skewed demographics of colonial mobility—the "vast movement of emigration that took millions of Europeans to every other part of the globe" during the period—and particularly the waves of southern Mediterranean migrants, mostly male, who settled in such places as Latin America and Australia. These men demanded European prostitutes, a "fairly large number" of whom were shipped (sometimes having been duped beforehand about the nature of the voyage) to such trafficking hubs as Buenos Aires and Alexandria.[55]

Debates about how to handle the problem occupied newspaper columnists and lawyers alike. Predictably enough, the Parisian mass press fixed the blame for sex trafficking on a few groups of outsiders: South Americans, Levantines, and Jews. What were their sources? Corbin notes that the antitrafficking movement's leaders at the time were chiefly "aristocrats and members of the upper bourgeoisie."[56] That these Parisian elites may have profited from or otherwise promoted xenophobic or anti-Semitic sentiments may have reflected the changing dynamics of the elite sex trade in Paris from the 1860s onward, when a noted influx of prosperous foreigners acquainted themselves with the stars of the demimonde.

Even if never explicitly acknowledged, a consequence of the increasingly cosmopolitan sex trade on the Grands Boulevards was the intensified competition for sought-after courtesans. Anxieties about the rastaquouère and the Levantine were fed by, and reflected, the realities of the market for sex, so it is logical that both types lurked in chapbooks such as *The Pretty Women of Paris*. The text drips with disdain for the Egyptian bankers, wealthy Levantines, Turks, and Latin Americans who frequented such high-class Parisian whores as Berthe Béranger. Readers were warned that Béranger was "well-known among the Peruvians, Chileans, and Bolivians who swarm in Paris," having given birth to the child of one of these "lusty, dark-visaged cavaliers," the "descendants of Montezuma."[57]

There was more than a tinge of resentment in the lament that Europeans might not measure up financially to flashy immigrants, such as Khalil Bey, from colonial lands—men who, in tapping their considerable resources, upped the ante beyond the reach of some men. The courtesan Cora Pearl, a neighbor of Marie Regnault's in the 8th arrondissement, reserved for Bey, a "Parisianised Oriental," an ecstatic passage in her memoirs. At Bey's splendid mansion, "I bathed in pink marble basins, I slept long hours on sofas with the smell of rare flowers, which conjured up dreams of enchanted palaces, and when I awoke, the reality was still finer than my dreams!"[58]

AS THE FACE of the rastaquouère in Paris, Enrico Pranzini presented scientific researchers with an important specimen amid ferocious debates about the social and biological origins of criminality. Rather than fading into obscurity, ancient practices involving physiognomies and examining skulls to determine criminal markers were rejuvenated in the 1870s. The era's most influential theorist was the Italian criminal anthropologist Cesare Lombroso, who devised highly influential, biologically driven explanations for criminal recidivism and devised research to discover the "born criminal."[59] But by the mid-1880s the French scientific community was breaking away from Lombrosian biological determinism and replacing it with research into the social conditions that begat criminality. Had Pranzini arrived a decade earlier, cutting-edge criminal theorists in Paris might have noted—which is to say, invented—physical abnormalities on Pranzini indicating that he was "made for crime," to use Goron's shopworn phrase. This did not occur.

Keeping pace with scholarly fashion—and dismissing the off-the-cuff physiognomic readings of their journalistic lessers—leading French theorists such as Henri Joly and Gabriel Tarde underscored instead the *normality*

of Pranzini's body. They pointed to the absence of irregularities and defor-
mations commonly believed to be intrinsic to the criminal body. By no
means did these thinkers seek to challenge the assumption of Pranzini's
guilt—quite the opposite. Pranzini, wrote Tarde, was one of the "true and
perfect criminals" who were as "minimally degenerate as possible" and, in
some cases, as beautiful as "studio models." To comprehend Pranzini, the
scientist must scrutinize not his physique but the "social conditions, the nation, and the historical time" that had made him.[60] Pranzini's physiognomy
was pleasing, agreed Joly, but it was only relevant insomuch as it opened the
doors of demimondaines.[61]

Pranzini's identification as a migrant, a colonial, and an alleged recidivist
criminal generated great interest among the scientific policing bureau in the
Paris Police Prefecture, where Alphonse Bertillon, the father of the mugshot,
was on the rise. Bertillon personally photographed and measured Pranzini,
taking advantage of the occasion to showcase his spacious new "sanctuary
of criminal anthropometry."[62] During the 1880s, Bertillon emerged as the
standard-bearer of *bertillonage*, the onerous system of recording the body
measurements of criminal suspects, generating a massive database, and pre-
venting recidivism.

Bertillonage should be understood within the context of a series of
bureaucratic shifts during the 1880s that saw more forms of registration,
police controls, and identity documentation. Bertillon's system had been
used to track migrants before its application to criminals, a fact that speaks
to the easy amalgamation of mobility and criminality, which was in itself
nothing new. Still, as the means of collecting information about people
changed, so did the agenda of the classifiers. National borders were hard-
ening, and regional boundaries were beginning to fade. Concomitantly,
the old suspicions of "interior" migration (mobility within France mainly
because of urbanization) were displaced by preoccupations with "international" migration and how to police it: Unified France would be a nation
of immigrants.[63] *Bertillonage* was indebted to the colonial imagination too.
Like the fingerprinting system devised contemporaneously in Britain, the
techniques used in *bertillonage* had origins on the colonial frontier; Bertillon, an amateur ethnographer, had published work on the anthropometry
of the "savage races."[64] Thus Pranzini's criminal record and use of aliases
appeared to be precisely the phenomena that *bertillonage* was designed to
snuff out.

The relative scarcity of colonial migration toward the metropole may partly explain Bertillon's deference to the social theorists with regard to Pranzini, whose anatomical ordinariness he affirmed. Pranzini's thumbs were normal, that is, smaller than those of "machine workers" like the murderer Troppmann, Bertillon observed.[65] Two decades later, Bertillon returned to the Pranzini file one last time, characterizing him as a chameleonic rastaquouère. By then, the racial epithet was almost entirely void of anthropometric significance. The finding that Pranzini's body was normal, even attractive, had added another alarming layer to the colonial antihero. The inference was that an ambitious male migrant could very well pass as a respectable and desirable gentleman.

Consequently, anatomists like Dr. Brouardel were left with the final word. Brouardel, who likewise examined Pranzini soon after his arrival from Marseille, made a number of determinations. To the certain frustration of prosecutors, he held that the cuts found on the suspect's fingers did not prove that he had wielded the murder weapon. Nevertheless, to the excitement of the press, Brouardel located a single physiological trait that marked Pranzini as a threateningly exotic Other, if not a criminal. The genitals, wrote the doctor, "are very voluminous. The penis is long and thick. It is more than four centimeters in diameter at the base; the scrotum hangs rather low."[66] In the coming months, rumors relating the size of Pranzini's genitalia contributed to the making of a criminal archetype and became a permanent part of his legend. Perhaps unwittingly, Brouardel had construed an Otherness that lay beyond the view of all investigators—Bertillon did not use phallic metrics—thereby privileging his profession.

PRANZINI got his introduction to French criminal procedure the day he was escorted into Adolphe Guillot's chambers in the Palais de Justice on the Île de la Cité.

Guillot could not have divined the challenge awaiting him. Pranzini bewildered and frustrated the magistrate. The interrogation transcripts seem to obscure him at least as much as they reveal him or his motives, as though Guillot was viewing the suspect through a large scrim. The two men spent countless hours jousting in a space decorated with little more than books, their grinding stalemates recorded by a clerk, signed by both men, and relayed in increments to the public.

They had stacks of evidence to get through.[67] In addition to the consular files from India and Egypt, Guillot had information from French diplomatic channels in Italy, where newspapers carried coverage of the rue Montaigne case and local police launched investigations on behalf of Paris. The interrogation transcripts bear the markings of Guillot's red highlighter on a witness statement from Bologna, where Pranzini had worked for several months as a conductor for the Pullman Company on the new Bologna–Brindisi railway that spanned the Italian peninsula. A bartender recalled the suspect as an occasional client of his: "On a personal level I can't say anything about Pranzini, who, despite earning 150 francs per month seemed to lead the life of a 'Monsieur' and to be working for the Pullman Company on a whim more than out of necessity. He dressed with elegance and showed his diamond rings, one of which was worth 600 or 700 francs."[68]

Early on, the magistrate tested the waters by revisiting some of the suspect's more recent misbehavior. The interrogation sessions typically began with Guillot proceeding in neat syllogisms, cornering Pranzini and then needling him for a confession; the sheer repetition of this pattern can make for tedious reading. Guillot was aware that Pranzini suffered the tremendous financial burden placed on him by his mother and that he had moved to Italy at her request to make money to send back to Egypt. He spent some months in Naples near the end of 1881, working as an interpreter and clerk at the Hotel Caprani. After several months there, he fell out with the owner, Mr. Caprani, who discovered that 1,200 francs had gone missing from an envelope safeguarded by the hotel. The bank notes had been replaced by pages from a foreign-language book.

Guillot said, "Confronted with such a theft, as Mr. Caprani puts it, one experienced the same shock as that one sometimes experiences when viewing a magician's sleight of hand."

"I simply told Mr. Caprani, 'If you think I did it, then I'll reimburse you'; but I never said, 'I did it,' since I was innocent of this theft and I simply wanted to avoid trouble because Mr. Caprani knew of my sentence in Alexandria." Caprani threatened to damage Pranzini's reputation locally, and Pranzini grew frightened. That was when he left Naples for Bologna.[69]

Guillot's head resembled a chunk of carved alabaster ringed with a narrow strip of curly locks. He had heavy jowls, thick bags beneath his eyes, and a pronounced chin; his manner was acerbic and irritable. He had

UN INTERROGATOIRE DE PRANZINI DANS LE CABINET DU JUGE D'INSTRUCTION

Dessin d'après nature par Henri Meyer. — Gravure de Tilly. — Voir l'article, page 122.

Figure 10. Pranzini answering questions in the magistrate Adolphe Guillot's office at the Palais de Justice. *La Revue Illustrée*, 10 April 1887.

been trained in investigative procedures that still reeked of the Inquisition's methods; suspects in 1880s France did not have the right to have an attorney present during questioning, nor were they granted full access to the evidence against them before the criminal trial. Journalists who observed Guillot as he questioned suspects summed up his technique: Guillot analyzed the suspect first and then the crime, the better to "pull the truth from the heart."[70] As Guillot himself phrased it in a legal treatise, the tears of an interrogated suspect are "more useful to justice than the most tightly assembled arguments."[71] A suspect's female mistress was the most effective conduit to his emotions and should be leveraged against him, he added: Pranzini's lover, Antoinette Sabatier, was in the magistrate's sights posthaste.

French procedure depended on, and aimed foremost at, the extraction of a suspect's guilty confession—the "queen of evidence," as it was known. Investigations did not operate on the granular level of crime scene clues, forensics, and argumentation, all of which carried much less evidentiary weight. Indeed, the criminal investigation, in the modern sense, remained marginal to magistrates and police, who were largely left to their own devices when it came to the gathering of evidence and the treatment of suspects.[72] The record of Guillot's questioning of Pranzini is consistent with a conception of material evidence as more of a means than an end tool for breaking down the suspect's will until a confession was signed.

Guillot told Pranzini that the coachman who helped lead police to him in the opera house later made a damning statement. According to the coachman's story, Pranzini spent an inordinate amount of time in a public restroom during one of the stops on his brief tour of the city that day. Moreover, having entered the facility with a package in his hands, Pranzini returned to the taxi empty-handed. Later, reporters and police combed the sewage and found a package with some jewelry inside. Pranzini was unfazed. The story left open the question of why he would go to the trouble of dumping booty when he was hundreds of miles away from the crime scene and not, as yet, a suspect?

Was Pranzini aware that it was commonplace for the police to offer rewards for helpful statements and evidence, a practice that could produce a glut of "witnesses" in cases like this one? Pranzini dug in his heels, denied the coachman's account, and kept a mental record of the "false witnesses" that he would later accuse Chief Taylor of delivering to Guillot.[73]

Other vestiges of the Inquisition served as levers of power in the hands of the investigating magistrate, who in nineteenth-century France could use a variety of means to "cook" a suspect, as it was said, including physical force. Or, while awaiting trial, a suspect might be cut off from other prisoners and the outside world. Prison guards could place him in isolation in a dark corner of the prison if he refused to give way under questioning. False confessions were not unheard of.[74] Did any of these things happen to Pranzini? It is impossible to say. That no evidence of such treatment has survived in this case is not terribly surprising, and it means little.

Guillot's feints led Pranzini into needless self-contradictions, stonewalling, and backtracking. Without notifying Pranzini that investigators had found his calling card at the crime scene, for instance, Guillot asked him if he had ever met the victim. (The card, a simple impression bearing the Boulevard Malesherbes address of an art gallery where Pranzini had worked as an interpreter, was one of many that Regnault kept in a box in her boudoir.) Perhaps calculating that a reply in the affirmative would condemn him, Pranzini answered that he had never met her. On cue, Guillot brought in the calling card, and, within seconds, Pranzini admitted that he had met the victim through an intermediary, a certain Monsieur Alfred. He told of meeting Alfred, a high-society gentleman who mentioned an art exhibit happening at the Mirlitons, the ultra-exclusive gentlemen's club. Pranzini managed to find his way into the exhibit, and it was there that he first met Regnault. More than once in the weeks that followed, he called on her in the rue Montaigne, but platonically, he said.

Then Guillot laid a trap by probing into the nature of these visits to the rue Montaigne. He angled toward the Gaston letter found in the boudoir. Chemical tests done at Dr. Brouardel's lab found microscopic traces of blood on the back of the envelope, meaning that the killer had probably planted it as a decoy. When shown the letter, people in Regnault's inner circle could confirm that it demonstrated a shallow knowledge of Regnault's life.

"When I went to her apartment building, I asked the concierge for 'Mme Montille,'" said Pranzini, "and when I spoke with her I called her 'Mme Montille'—I wasn't sure about the spelling of her name."

Guillot pounced. "You've just pronounced the *nom de galanterie* of this woman, and like several times already, I have noticed that when you speak of her, you say 'Mme Montille.' . . . Everyone who knew her called her '*de* Montille,' yet you say just 'Montille,' exactly as it is written on the envelope?"[75] Guillot added that he suspected that the murderer had placed the letter in plain sight in order to send investigators in pursuit of "Gaston Geissler."

"Whether someone put it there on purpose is not my business because I've got nothing to do with it," said Pranzini.

"Everyone in Regnault's intimate circle is convinced that the letter was fabricated," continued Guillot, perhaps stretching the truth a bit, "if for no other reason than the fact that it does not mesh with her life, save for her relations with Mr. Paul Lemoine, which was of public notoriety and which you could easily have known about."

"She never said anything particular [about it] to me. But she did tell me she was divorced from her husband, a noble who was to arrive in Paris any day, which surprised me, since Monsieur Alfred had told me that she was an independent woman."

"In the letter there was mention of a trip to Nancy, . . . of a portrait and some tailoring done on a dress; of a loan of 500 francs; of a man called Gustave; of a Marie who was in her last days; and finally of several details which, if true, would have been known to the intimates of the house" but were not. "If this letter was not a substitute for a real one and Marie Regnault read it before her death, she wouldn't have understood anything at all—so would she keep it in order to decode the enigma?"

"What should I know about this? I couldn't possibly know anything," said Pranzini. And like that, Guillot, pressing hard and seemingly on the brink, watched his carefully constructed path to a confession vanish before his eyes. Unable to pull back, he kept on a few seconds too long on the specifics of the letter, and Pranzini landed a counterpunch.

"The letter is signed 'Gaston' and it mentions a Gustave," said Guillot. "You have said that a certain Gaston Combemorel put you in contact with a certain Gustave who was never found."

"You're confusing things," retorted Pranzini, now turning the tables. "During the voyage [from Marseille to Paris], Monsieur Goron told me that a letter signed 'Gustave' had been found in the boulevard Malesherbes." Here was an illustration of Pranzini's most potent defense tactic, neutralizing the aged magistrate with an air of impatience verging on righteous indignation. This counterattack was used again in his reply to accusations that he had stolen some money from a traveler on the Bologna–Brindisi train line.

Guillot charged, "One day, a traveler caught you in the act of filching his wallet—you had in your hand the 24 pounds you'd just taken out of it."

"I'll leave it to you to consider how absurd that is," came the reply, and the topic was dropped.[76]

Having no evidence linking Pranzini to the earlier prostitute murders or any news on the Geissler lead, Guillot would have to settle for just one indictment for triple homicide, he focused all his energy on it. He brought in dozens of witnesses, including the conflicting statements of two coachmen who claimed to know something about the killings. His file contains testimony from a lemonade-stand operator, a hair stylist, and a knife salesman. He also staged "confrontations" between Pranzini and a host of people, including, most movingly, Sabatier. After several weeks he concluded his investigation; he came away with no confession.

SOMETIME in mid-April 1887 Taylor and Goron returned to the Gaston Geissler lead. Goron remembered it this way: "We were very curious to see if Geissler wasn't just a myth. That guy, at least, we would have liked to arrest ourselves."[77] Taylor allowed himself to be convinced that a transnational investigation could break open the case. There was good reason to keep the Geissler lead open. The description of him provided by the employees at the Hôtel Cailleux matched the one provided by Marie Regnault's staff. Pranzini looked nothing of the kind.

But there was also a rationale for forgetting about Geissler. Revisiting the Geissler situation courted risks at this point in the investigation: Pranzini was under lock and key, so prosecutors could pretend that he was the sole culprit and then stitch together enough circumstantial evidence to get a good shot at a conviction. The press, obsessed with Pranzini, no longer mentioned Geissler much, making it more likely that the public would raise questions about the lead. Goron, on his return from Marseille, had told Taylor, "Geissler doesn't exist." One imagines that this was accompanied with a wink. What he meant was that it would be wise to forget Geissler's name: If investigators were settling on the theory that Pranzini had acted alone, Geissler *had better not* exist.

Taylor at first signaled his intention to play it by the book, replying, "All the same, we must find Geissler."[78]

Not a month later, Goron changed his mind and, setting aside his certainty of Pranzini's guilt, concocted a flamboyant plan to stalk Gaston

Geissler through Belgium and Germany, all the way to what are today parts of Poland. A "manhunt," he called it. True to form, Taylor dismissed as "crazy" the idea of locating Geissler with only the bespoke shirts and small photograph found at the Hôtel Cailleux. That is when the duo struck their compromise: Goron could launch his border-crossing investigation, provided that he kept it discreet. His goal would be to prevent Geissler's strange disappearance from becoming a "dangerous arm in the hands of Pranzini's defense."[79] If word got out that Security was still actively pursuing Geissler, it could have been seen as a tacit admission of doubt that Pranzini was the sole killer, if he was involved at all.

Goron unburdened himself of that tactical restraint and transformed his trip into a public relations event; the farther he got from Paris, the less direct control Taylor exercised over him. Goron wrote vividly of his "fantastic adventure." As he crossed the border into Germany carrying photographs of the three mutilated corpses—his "passport"—he thought back to the war of 1870. The veteran in him was "living a dream."[80]

A crack group of Parisian crime reporters were again tailing Goron, which guaranteed that the trip would bring him the publicity he had promised to avoid. Soon, the international press was covering his eastward movement. The stops along the way—cities such as Brussels, Cologne, and Berlin— lacked the exotic ring of Egypt or Argentina. But this would not keep him from trumpeting the voyage across Germany—amid an escalating espionage crisis with Chancellor Bismarck—as a "difficult and almost impossible mission." This was not pure exaggeration. Goron encountered stories of unruly Geisslers in almost every German city he visited: The surname, he learned, was "as common in Germany as Dubois or Durand in France." By coincidence, these Geisslers bore a penchant for skipping out without paying their hotel bills. The quantity of dead-ends was impressive. Basking in the exposure, the deputy chief could even appreciate this "burlesque side" of the path leading to Geissler. "I recall an article" that had "me chasing Geissler in [the eastern Russian peninsula of] Kamchatka."[81]

For their part, Parisian crime reporters keenly seized the opportunities presented by the transnational hunt, and in doing so, they helped lay the groundwork for a budding generation of traveling newsmen, called *grands reporters*, who become a vital, and far more prestigious, part of Parisian newspapers in the 1890s.[82] Among the *petits reporters* who shadowed Goron "on tiptoes" was Félix Dubois of *Le Soleil*, who later launched a successful career as a *grand reporter* and "celebrated explorer" in colonial Africa.[83] It was Dubois who ultimately broke the news of Goron's astonishing discovery in the city of Breslau.

The announcement that the mysterious Geissler had been found soon made all the Parisian newspapers. It proved a slight embarrassment to Taylor, whose superiors, learning of the breakthrough at the newspaper kiosk, were upset that he had not kept them abreast of Goron's progress. (Goron did not admit to having been the source for Dubois's story, which he likely was.)[84]

Dogged sleuthing brought Goron to the tailor who recognized his handi-work in the "G.G." shirts. He had made the shirts for the Guttentag family, he said. Goron consulted a Breslau address book and knocked on the door of an Issac Guttentag. A servant opened. "I admit that my heart was beat-ing hard, and I felt an infinite satisfaction when the servant recognized the shirts, the handkerchiefs, the socks, and the collars, which she herself had washed several times."[85] He showed her the picture of the woman in the locket: Mrs. Isaac Guttentag, the mistress of the house; the soiled laundry belonged to her son, George—George Guttentag.

Isaac Guttentag, the aged patriarch, returned to his home later and de-clared with certainty that the handwriting etched onto the cufflinks in the rue Montaigne, "Gaston Geissler," was that of his son, who had, he de-duced, taken an alias. "Curse my son," said Guttentag. "He is dead to me." Goron stood listening to the father, who continued, "He left here at the beginning of March without saying goodbye to me. I didn't give him any money so I don't know how he got to Paris."[86]

Goron found out that George Guttentag had contacted a cousin, who also lived in Breslau, to ask for money and aid. He told the cousin that he had been arrested and remained captive because he was unable to buy his freedom. Without alerting Isaac Guttentag, the cousin sent 250 francs to Paris, part of which was to be used for a one-way ticket to America.

So Guttentag was in prison. *In Paris.*

Guttentag's cousin, whose name was also George, handed Goron a piece of paper recounting the events with partial accuracy. On the night of March 16–17, George Guttentag, age 32, was arrested by the Municipal Police of Paris. After leaving the Hôtel Cailleux, he had gone out drinking. Later that night he attempted suicide by leaping into the icy River Seine from the Pont d'Iéna. But he "did not succeed in dying," to quote the report filed by the policemen who fished him out and promptly jailed him for vagabond-age.[87] He languished for weeks in the panopticon Mazas Prison near the Gare de Lyon, an inferno according to its humanitarian critics.[88]

Goron rushed to telegraph Paris. Guillot and Taylor then hustled to Mazas Prison, cell 85, where Guttentag still stewed.

As the deputy chief made his way back to France, the Parisian press began to herald the arrest of the true rue Montaigne murderer. Based on the physical descriptions, they began to posit that Pranzini had been Gut-tentag's "accomplice."[89]

But that hypothesis was short-lived. By the time Goron arrived at Mazas Prison, Guttentag had explained what had happened. He had been calling himself Henri Geissler, not Gaston. He had no jewelry, and no knowledge of the rue Montaigne. Police were able to verify his whereabouts on the night of the murders. It was a staggering setback.

Complicating matters, yet another Geissler, Arthur Geissler, "spontane-ously introduced himself in Guillot's office" within a few days of the dis-covery. Arthur Geissler was a former colleague of Pranzini's from his days in Naples, and he wished to attest to Pranzini's underhandedness. There were now two Geissler narratives, and something needed to be done about it. The realization that Guttentag had been in custody throughout Goron's manhunt suddenly made Security's bid for investigative greatness look ri-diculous. To forestall other inconvenient disclosures, the police made the decision to rid themselves of Guttentag.

Three steps were taken to deflect attention from the Geissler lead. First, the police tinkered with Guttentag's arrest date, which was backdated to the night of the rue Montaigne murders (as in Goron's memoirs). An un-published investigation and archived police reports reveal that Guttentag was, in fact, arrested on March 22, several days after he had abandoned the Hôtel Cailleux. (According to these same reports, police verified that he had slept in "several flophouses" before the night of his arrest.) Having endowed him with an alibi, the police then generated a report ruling out Guttentag's involvement in the murders based on his alleged mental feeble-ness. According to the report, Guttentag was "timid, of weak mind, and sad nature—incapable of conceiving and executing the sort of infamy we're dealing with."[90] On May 4, the police escorted Guttentag directly to the German consul for immediate repatriation. That way, his release attracted little attention from the reporters, who, having never been granted access to the "faux Geissler," merely relayed what the police told them: Guttentag's mental faculties, reported *Le Matin*, "were not well balanced and he never understood the accusations" against him.[91]

Having cleaned up, not to say covered up, the Guttentag situation, investigators soon ran aground with Arthur Geissler. He did not recognize the infamous cufflinks or the belt that Pranzini was thought to have stolen from him—or the other Geissler—and placed in plain sight near Regnault's body. Little of his conversation with Guillot was recorded, and during the summer trial his testimony was brief and hardly a factor.

CHAPTER SEVEN

The Trial of a Gigolo

Intimacy, Foreignness, and the Boulangist Crisis

> Gigolo, Gigolette,
> Little god of lovers,
> Come to see me every day.
>
> —Popular song, 1861[1]

At 12:05 p.m. on July 9, 1887, Judge Georges Onfroy de Bréville began the much anticipated examination of Enrico Pranzini, the sole defendant charged in the rue Montaigne murders. Pranzini had just celebrated his thirty-first birthday in cell 1 of the Conciergerie, a medieval structure that provided easy access to the courtrooms of the Palais de Justice. The Conciergerie was haunted by the ghosts of Parisian history. Dethroned Queen Marie-Antoinette was held captive there before being led away to the guillotine in 1793, soon to be followed by her nemesis, Maximilien Robespierre, whose beheading took place mere hours after his arrival in the dungeon.[2] Pranzini seemed likely to share their fate.

Georges Grison arrived at the gates early that morning. In his trial notes he tells of the picturesque scrum that ensued when hopeful spectators, some having arrived hours in advance with tickets in hand, realized that they would not *all* be admitted into the courtroom. In those days the opportunity to lay eyes on a defendant as unsettling as Pranzini was rare indeed; murder trials typically finished in only two or three days, and the newspapers did not yet print photographs. Scores of descriptions and sketches had appeared in the press, but they agreed on just a single point: Pranzini was the handsomest defendant in living memory.

The throng grew ornery. Men in top hats surged forward, caroming against the makeshift barricades. Palace guards lost control, and a stampede spilled down onto the place Dauphine, where several women, trapped and crushed, were crying out and, in a few cases, losing consciousness. When the space was pacified and cleared, Grison took inventory of the dross they had left behind: jackets, scraps of food, umbrellas, camp stools, and a solitary shoe.[3] To those who made it inside, the stifling heat of the July courtroom seemed a stiff price of entry; it felt "Senegalese" in there, wrote a journalist, reaching for an apt colonial allusion.[4]

Grison's notes, published on the heels of his volume on the rue Montaigne investigation, stand as the most complete record of the four eventful afternoons of the Pranzini trial. Historians may be grateful for the many notations he included, especially his registration of the courtroom audience's audible reactions. This sonic record reads like a puzzling sidebar. Technically not of a piece with evidence and testimony, public outbursts of emotion in the courtroom lie in tension with these; indeed, they form an undeniably potent element of any trial, which is why presiding judges everywhere strive to control them. In the Pranzini case, Grison's notations convey the tonally erratic quality of the proceedings. Curiously, the record is pocked with instances of collective laughter, nearly thirty outbreaks. On occasion, Grison thought that the standard insertion of the italicized word "laughter," common also in parliamentary records, did not adequately capture the guffaws, so he substituted "general hilarity" (*hilarité générale*).

Did the fierce Judge Bréville preside over the most uproariously funny murder trial in modern French history? The audience was there to watch a death penalty case, one that would determine responsibility for the slayings of two women and a young girl, which raises the basic question: What was so comical?

The function of this laughter begins to emerge when we consider the Pranzini trial through the lens of politics. The first half of 1887 heralded a period of tectonic shifts in Paris. The nationalist New Right, destined to affect European history in profound ways, coalesced to confront a plethora of modern bugbears, cosmopolitanism foremost among them.[5] The centennial of the French Revolution of 1789 was approaching, though its legacy was as contentious as ever. Ideological clashes took to the air, throwing literal shadows on the urban landscape. On the Right Bank, workers had just finished laying the foundation of Eiffel's scandalous tower project; as the Pranzini trial commenced, they were building upward. French liberals hoped to showcase the trial at the World's Fair of 1889, a monument to rationalism, modernity, and—dwarfing, as it did, the exhibits of colonial peoples—the renascent republican empire.

But from the start Eiffel's design inspired an acute loathing among the conservative and Catholic currents of the New Right; critics dismissed the Eiffel Tower as an iron "suppository."[6] Meanwhile on the other side of the River Seine, atop the working-class and bohemian stronghold of Montmartre, the forces of reaction were busy erecting a massive structure of their own: the Sacré-Coeur basilica, which neighborhood residents interpreted, justifiably, as a gleaming expletive directed at the left-wing rabble-rousers in their midst.

Into this simmering conflict entered the truly puzzling phenomenon known as Boulangism, a word coined in 1887 and parsed since. In the months leading up to the Pranzini trial, a political movement coalesced around General Georges Boulanger, who, after service in Asia and North Africa, had remade himself into France's most vocally anti-German revanchist (so-called because he sought to regain the lost eastern provinces of Alsace and Lorraine and avenge the defeat of 1870). General Boulanger was a strikingly attractive man who rode a gorgeous horse; beyond this there was little to recommend him to politics, except, of course, the clot of adorers who materialized, seemingly ex nihilo, whenever he appeared in public. Whether by design or dumb luck—historians have never agreed—the general managed in a span of months to seduce factions of the extreme left (Jacobins and anarchists) and the New Right (old royalists, militarist nationalists, and Catholics).[7] His eponymous movement was a cocktail of paranoia and rage appealing to people who fretted about the erosion of national borders and the intrusion of the outside world. Personally, General Boulanger was obsessed with foreign infiltration, especially spies, and as war minister he set out to create a "territorial secret police"; ultimately, secret internment camps were envisioned for the imprisonment of foreigners deemed suspicious.[8] In the spring of 1887, it was Boulanger's saber rattling that inflated a minor espionage dispute on the German border into a diplomatic crisis known as the Schnaebelé affair.

Historians have never mentioned Pranzini in connection with Boulangism; granted, the pairing of the populist general with an accused murderer is odd on its face. But the Pranzini trial, which became a platform for the public ridicule of deviant sexual and ethnic identities, may have helped galvanize the disparate forces of the New Right. Consider Édouard Drumont, whose ferociously anti-Semitic tracts historians consider as essential to the New Right as Boulanger himself. In fact, Boulanger began his popular ascent in 1886 just as *La France juive* transformed its author, an enterprising journalist, into a publishing dynamo. Yet Drumont, throughout that year and the next, saw in Boulanger a potential rival, particularly after the Schnaebelé affair drew attention toward the general and away from the attention-hungry Drumont and his minions. Their differences were important. Boulanger was neither openly anti-Semitic nor Catholic, major distinctions for Drumont, who had little interest in provoking Germany as the Boulangists were wont to do. Drumont's response, for months on end, was to ignore Boulanger.[9]

A subtle shift was evident in Drumont's next book, *La fin d'un monde*, which was published in 1889. By then, Drumont had become an ardent Boulangist, having come to view the general as a useful reinforcement of his own appeal to the petit bourgeois; both men whipped up fears of a common enemy: the cosmopolitan infiltrator. Pranzini was not Jewish, but his purported Levantinism accorded well enough with Drumont's anti-Semitic obsession. The exclusionary jibes aimed at Pranzini during the trial functioned as the basis of an entente: Laughter fused voices and forged consensus across ideological divides; the anecdotes of a gigolo's sexual transgressions could also function as a cautionary tale about the trespassing of national and class boundaries. The presiding judge's performance came under sustained fire from critics; in *La fin d'un monde* Drumont stepped up to defend the "playful examination" of Pranzini and to applaud, among other things, Bréville's humorous, ironic use of "mon gentilhomme," a stodgy honorific, when addressing the defendant.[10]

Boulanger and Pranzini shared newspaper column space for months, with the investigation of the murders in the rue Montaigne often serving as a subtext to the general's grab for power. A succession of parliamentary crises ensued; in late May a backroom coup ran Boulanger out of his cabinet position. The Boulangists fumed. Their ire intensified when the government announced that it was reassigning Boulanger to Clermont-Ferrand, a provincial backwater where, it was hoped, his political aspirations would die on the vine. To Boulangists, this "deportation" was a transparent attempt to get rid of a political nemesis—doubly irritating because the general learned of it through the press.[11] The Boulangists called for a protest against the government on July 14, the national day of celebration.[12] In a tit for tat, the government told General Boulanger to be on a train out of Paris on July 8.

Boulanger's departure, a tale often recounted by historians, was a singular event in Parisian history; it shook the city into an awareness of Boulanger's popular clout and seemed to foretell yet another strongman's coup d'état.[13] When Boulanger arrived at the Gare de Lyon on the morning of July 8, he was swamped by tens of thousands of supporters—one estimate had them at 100,000—who, upon spotting the general, took the station by storm, blowing past a meager police contingent of 25 men. They disconnected the train car in which the general had a seat reserved, lay across the train tracks, and demanded an end to President Jules Grévy's tenure.[14] Authorities concluded that there was no breaking through. They offered to whisk the general out in a secret convoy and send him from the Charenton train station instead. This was the simplest way out, and Boulanger was not resisting a departure in principle. But he did not like this plan, he explained, because Pranzini had made *his* arrival in Paris by way of the Charenton station.[15] The general's rumination is astonishing and perhaps stands as the strongest evidence of his own thin skin. He was, after all, vulnerable to the charge of being an ambitious usurper, an unprincipled political seducer, and a meritless climber—that is what Jules Ferry meant when he quotably disparaged the general as a flashy two-bit conspirator (he called Boulanger "Saint Arnaud de café-concert," by which he meant a lesser version of General Saint Arnaud, the famous colonial adventurer who served Napoleon III).

In view of the nation's taste for authoritarian regimes, commentators speculated on Boulanger's intentions. Were the days of the Third Republic—just 16 years old and already France's longest experiment with democracy—coming to an end? The extraordinary attention devoted to the Pranzini case led some to wonder whether it might be a political omen. "The July Monarchy, on the eve of its fall, had the Praslin affair; the Second Empire, just before folding, had the Troppmann affair. Is the Pranzini affair likewise destined to become a historical date, as well as a great criminal trial?" asked the critic Edmond Biré. "The historian who one day writes about the men and events of the Third Republic will perhaps have to confront the murders in the rue Montaigne."[16]

Judge Bréville seemed to sense that the Pranzini trial might be used as a rallying point for Boulangists, not least because the defendant symbolized much of what the movement hated about the Republic, foremost the internationalism wrought by imperialism. Bréville's silver hair and patrician-like mien lent a thin veneer of due process, but the opening remarks he prepared surely delighted the Boulangist spirits present, among them the future prime minister Georges Clémenceau and the acerbic newspaperman Henri Rochefort, who sat cheek to jowl with "loudly dressed" demimondaines.[17] For example, by insisting, despite a lack of evidence, that Pranzini knew the German language, Bréville brought sexual fears of the "Oriental Don Juan" in line with the right-wing suspicion of border-crossing spies and infiltrating Jews.

If Bréville was on board with the Boulangists, then his pretrial preparations betrayed his cunning instincts. When officials at the Palais de Justice scheduled the trial's opening for Monday, July 11, Bréville petitioned successfully to have the date changed to July 9, the morning after Boulanger's departure—and a Saturday. It was a shift "nearly without precedent in criminal procedure," according to a court observer.[18] The upshot was that Parisians could experience Boulanger's infamous departure and the opening of the Pranzini trial nearly as a single event, with crowds draining from the hours-long ruckus at the Gare de Lyon to the Palais de Justice.[19] Parisians and foreign observers alike estimated that the Pranzini trial "caused Parisians to forget the 'idol of Clermont'" rather than the reverse.[20]

Fate handed Bréville an irresistible opportunity for self-aggrandizement, a chance to go out with a bang on an international stage (foreign journalists were trumpeting Pranzini as one of the "the most remarkable criminals that even Paris has ever produced").[21] The judge (in French, *le président*) was a descendant of the *petite noblesse*, an ancient family that lost everything in 1789 but managed to rise to public prominence in subsequent generations. Bréville's long, undistinguished career was first overshadowed by that of his famous father and later by that of his own son.[22] Yet he was skilled in public relations and knew how to manipulate the press. His background as a prosecutor began under the Second Empire (1851–1870), and he played a minor role in the 1869 Troppmann murder investigation, where he received a lesson in the power of the newspaper crime columns to elevate a murder case into a cause-célèbre.[23] Bréville amused journalists with his penchant for mock solemn admonishments, which he planted in the newspapers in the days before the trial. Playfully, he announced that he would not allow lorgnettes in the courtroom, and he warned that only women in "decent" clothing would be admitted, references to the flashy, fleshy world of the theater, a clichéd metaphor for the courtroom.[24]

In this and other ways Bréville telegraphed his decision to orient the trial around the theme of sexual intimacy. He leaked parts of the love letters that had been found in Pranzini's belongings and from which he intended to read during the trial.[25] Behind the scenes Bréville threw himself headlong into the investigation of Pranzini's intimate encounters in Paris. In the archives there is a confidential letter that Bréville addressed to Ernest Taylor, chief of Security, on June 21, 1887. In it the judge alerts Taylor, "Word has come to me, in a roundabout way," that a woman who "knew a lot of things" about Pranzini was living on the southern end of Paris. Bréville provides her address and recommends that the police proceed with caution: "It would be good to look into this *unofficially* and with great prudence; and only to act *officially* if the initial investigation produces a serious lead."[26]

In another unusual move that was sure to chafe some observers, Bréville stipulated that he alone would be signing and issuing tickets to the trial, personal passes that the press dubbed "invitation cards."[27] This required that Bréville procure spare public omnibus tickets from a nearby office and have them numbered to designate seating assignments. Like a savvy showman, he then issued a number of tickets roughly equal to three times the courtroom's capacity—hence the agitated crowds outside the Palais de Justice and the air of exclusivity inside the courtroom.[28] Nary a worker could be seen on the trial's first day; celebrities and powerful politicians were shown to their seats, along with artists, actresses, and men of letters.[29] The trial preparations were a smash. "The Théâtre-Français could not have drawn so many Parisians in midsummer," remarked the *New York Times*; no murder trial there in the last half-century had generated this level of interest.[30]

AS BRÉVILLE began his examination of Pranzini, the judge struck the keynote of the trial: "We are going to study your past. It will be long but indispensable. The jurors must know your entire life; they will see that you were always a crafty liar who loved to gamble and who, most of all, loved women. . . . You were always this way—resorting to the saddest means to get by, and that was the genesis of the crime."[31] Bréville, in the role of social anatomist, was signaling to the defendant that his sworn statements concerning the night of the murders would no longer stand after an analysis of his character. Pranzini claimed to have spent the night of March 16–17 with a respectable society woman whose name he could not, as a matter of chivalry, divulge. It was a bold gambit. Pranzini's chivalrous posturing flew in the face of received ideas, foremost that chivalry remained a source of *French* male honor and identity, one laden with class privilege.[32] From Bréville's perspective, Pranzini's status as a lowbrow cosmopolitan strictly precluded any such knowledge or status. From the defense's point of view, Pranzini's sworn statements, even if true, risked rubbing jury members the wrong way, given that they were uniformly products of the anxious and unstable lower bourgeoisie—artisans and small business owners who might aspire to the old masculine codes in a democratic society but who at the same time felt social pressure from below.[33]

Wisely, Bréville set out to undermine Pranzini's plea with an argument based on gender and class privilege and blended with national exclusion. The strategy was to focus on Pranzini's intimate past to expose him as a faux-gentleman and sexual deviant, thereby forestalling the chivalry defense. Within the trial's first few hours, it became clear that Bréville's strategy meant painting Pranzini simultaneously as dangerous and ridiculous, as a social and criminal threat and a laughably effeminate gigolo.

Jokes and taunts that emasculated Pranzini arose from the allegation that, rather than supporting himself financially, he had used his sex appeal to live off the women he encountered during his travels, the "saddest means to get by." And there was a good deal of evidence to support the notion that Pranzini fit this definition of the gigolo. Bréville cited a letter from a witness who had known the defendant in Egypt, a French doctor. The doctor told investigators there that Pranzini was always an "overdressed hunk" who "fussed over rich women."[34]

More recently, according to prosecutors, Pranzini applied himself rigorously to the pursuit of social status and money through women. This brought him into contact with his victim, Marie Regnault. Investigators contended that early in 1887 Pranzini became Regnault's *amant de coeur*, the term for a courtesan's nonpaying client who stands to gain materially from her prodigious wealth and who could, in turn, be kept by her.[35] All the while Pranzini lived with his devoted girlfriend, Antoinette Sabatier, in her Montmartre apartment. According to the prosecution, Sabatier unwittingly served as a stepping-stone in Pranzini's quest. Sabatier's testimony, scheduled for the trial's third day, would be vital to the prosecution if Bréville was unable to extract a confession from Pranzini during the first two sessions. Bréville made it known that this was the point of the event, even if that meant he would have to ask for it explicitly at key junctures in the trial and thus come across as desperate or outdueled.

Realistically, Pranzini had faced the duress of long interrogations on dozens of occasions; the chances that he would cough up a confession at the trial were remote at the outset. At the least, Bréville may have hoped that the airing of Pranzini's love letters, followed by sustained question-ing, would neutralize Pranzini's attorney, Edgar Demange, the era's great wizard of courtroom rhetoric. As defense counsel, Demange had earned an international reputation for daringly selecting long-shot cases—and for winning them. Square-jawed and bearish, Demange wore thick sideburns that drooped all the way down over his collar; his eyelids opened to slightly different apertures, giving his face an emotive, asymmetric shape. But by far his most remarked-on gift was his voice, a booming bass that melted juries and mystified foreign observers, on whom his persuasive powers were often lost in translation.[36]

Demange remains something of a mystery to historians. Little has been written about his career, except his epic defense of Alfred Dreyfus, which began seven years after the Pranzini trial.[37] Like his American contempo-rary Clarence Darrow, Demange believed fervently in the constitutional rights of the defendant, an article of faith instilled in him by the legend-ary Parisian attorney Charles Lachaud; Demange was the most dazzling of Lachaud's disciples.[38] As a young attorney, Demange roared onto the scene with a defense of Prince Pierre Napoleon in 1870, a ne'er-do-well cousin of Emperor Napoleon III who admitted to gunning down the republican journalist Victor Noir. In a brilliant sleight of hand, Demange won acquit-tal by reinterpreting evidence at the scene of the crime to demonstrate that the prince had acted in self-defense.

It was the lot of the public defender to draw accusations of moral rela-tivism, and Demange, who sought high-profile cases, sparked controversy wherever he traveled. To his detractors he was always "the eleventh-hour accomplice." But *this* professional choice—the defense of a man vilified, tried, and convicted in the press—led some of his admirers to suspect that Demange was motivated by baser instincts, such as the thirst for celebrity. "The defender of a man like Pranzini has abandoned any pretension to the benefit of the doubt," complained one of the disappointed. "He is, for France and Europe, the great, the illustrious, *l'éminent*. The cartoonists draw him in every illustrated magazine. The photographers hang his image along the boulevards."[39] Demange was also an ardent Catholic—a pure social product of the Second Empire—but he won over the republicans for his devotion to the "cult of liberty and justice."[40] To conservatives who felt a sting of betrayal in Demange's choices, the most that could be said for him was that he was the son of a French soldier.[41]

The Pranzini trial held special challenges for Demange, who did what he could to interject skepticism about the evidence during the first two days, usually to be shut out by Bréville. The circumstantial evidence that investigators had compiled was significant: Pranzini left Paris within two days of the murders; investigators found his calling card in Regnault's apartment; once arrested, he gave conflicting accounts of his actions.[42] And then there was the jewelry. How could Pranzini have come by it so quickly unless he had killed Regnault?

Yet the case against Pranzini was not airtight, and Demange's adversary, Georges Reynaud, had little experience in the media-saturated courtrooms of the Palais de Justice. Reynaud had recently arrived from the provinces, where he had worked ably for two decades. Observers were quick to point out that he lacked Demange's oversized presence and thundering voice, the "one natural gift" believed to be essential to great oration.[43] Would the buttoned-up prosecutor, who possessed a "tact that protects against excesses," wilt in the atmosphere of an epoch-making trial?[44] Reynaud's greatest hurdle was to demonstrate that Pranzini, a linguistic interpreter with no history of violence, had taken a midlife leap into premeditated murder.

Pranzini admitted that he occasionally received money or gifts from women—Antoinette Sabatier put a piece of her own jewelry in hock to help him pay for a one-way train ticket out of Paris—but, as Demange objected, womanizing and petty theft were a distant cry from murder. And Pranzini's calling card, found at the scene of the crime? It was tucked into a stack of other gentleman callers' cards, which only proved what everyone already knew: Regnault was a courtesan in demand. Pranzini called on her a few times, but he had not known her carnally: "My visits were brief and punctilious," he said. "I barely had the time to talk with Madame Montille [*sic*], since she was in such a hurry on the first visits; and it was only during the last visit that we spoke about things—banalities. I played the piano on her request; she asked me what I thought of the great book she'd just got, *La dame aux camélias*."[45]

The prosecution had other vulnerabilities. The bladed murder weapon was never found. The testimony of a cab driver from Marseille, while initially promising, did not add up: Pranzini, the hypothesis went, would have taken Regnault's jewelry with him to Marseille after the murders and, having no reason to believe that he was a suspect in the case—which, in fact, he was not—would then have suddenly decided to dump his hard-earned loot in a public toilet before heading off to the local opera to take in a show. Furthermore, no witness could place Pranzini in the rue Montaigne on the night of the crime. On the contrary, the physical description taken from the concierge and his wife the following morning did not match Pranzini's. They described an "homme brun"—a mysterious, dark-haired fellow—who had frequented Regnault in the weeks leading up to the murders and who was for a time believed to be a man called Gaston Geissler. Some believed that the whole thing was a case of mistaken identity. And yet, why would Pranzini have left Paris so abruptly in the first place?

From the bench Bréville gave early signs that he would not take a chance on either disputable crime scene clues or a prosecutor who was an unknown quantity. Bréville kept his focus on the trove of intimate correspondence that investigators had found in Pranzini's belongings when they arrested him in Marseille. The love letters were the first pieces of evidence that Bréville admitted, and he milked them for every bit of humiliation they could bear. In the nineteenth century a true gentleman knew to burn the letters of a woman when their story reached an end; Pranzini, by hoarding them, appeared caddish. Bréville read the letters at length, the audience swooned, and for many years Parisian journalists quoted them like a shared book of jokes that never stopped being funny.[46] The most widely cited phrases in the correspondence were those written by a young woman, Edith Drake, who lived on East 78th Street in Manhattan. In one of her letters she mentions that Pranzini took her virginity during her tour of Paris in the summer of 1886. "God! When I think of how I gave myself to you immediately! My fatal destiny! You, who never wanted to believe that it was the first time of my life! . . . I would have done better to wait for you to promise marriage, and then to keep my body from you until that blessed moment."[47] In other quotable passages the New Yorker praises Pranzini's "iron muscles" and alluring "foreign aspect" while trying to convince him of the superiority of New York City over Paris.[48] There were pages upon pages more. At one point, Pranzini lobbed a complaint about the duration of his examination. The judge conceded the point—and carried on as though no objection had been raised.

Through the trial's first two sessions, the defendant was unruffled. During witness testimonies he sat still and expressionless. He arrived in the courtroom impeccably dressed, each day in the same white piqué vest beneath a fashionable jacket. Although he had spent three months in custody, he did not look at all the part of a prisoner facing a possible death sentence; with his easy presence and his evening wear, he more resembled a fellow who had inadvertently wandered into the proceedings in search of a waiter to refill his champagne flute. "He's patently a handsome fellow," thought Grison, "well-proportioned" and tasteful, reminiscent of a "boulevardier in love with elegance."[49] A journalist from Le Gaulois scribbled that Pranzini's unflappability was actually a mark of "arrogant bravado."[50]

Pranzini wore his hair freshly cut and parted down the middle "à la Capoul." The style was named after the great French tenor Victor Capoul, who popularized it in the 1880s, and it helped conceal his receding hairline. Pranzini sported a thin, tightly upturned moustache and groomed the curls of his beard, which clung to his pronounced cheekbones.[51] The press, as they had throughout the spring of 1887, continued to scrutinize Pranzini's appearance for clues. A great deal was said about his facial hair, in which the average Parisian man invested time and resources—mutton chops and goatees made a statement in a world saturated with drab colors, and facial hair was associated with virility.[52] General Boulanger's amber-hued beard inspired song lyrics, and his decision to lift the army's ban on beards was widely viewed as a political calculation.

Pranzini's presentation was a potential problem for the prosecution: If the jury found his cleanliness and demeanor gentlemanly, it hypothetically strengthened the defense's position. Sensing the danger, Bréville stepped up the insults. "Beautiful on the exterior, but nothing underneath," he scowled, "You didn't even own six handkerchiefs."[53] The judge harped on Pranzini's sartorial choices and played up any piece of evidence that might hint at shiftiness or artifice, even the defendant's handwriting. All the drapery of social aspiration could be ripped away, the judge believed, and the lower-class colonial migrant laid bare. In a way, the energy that Bréville devoted to this project paid a compliment to Pranzini, because it indirectly acknowledged the deftness with which the defendant had mastered the codes and manners that the judge was trying breathlessly to police. Lest the jury reach an undesirable conclusion, Bréville called witnesses who could demonstrate Pranzini's fraudulence in clinical terms. Foremost among these was the graphologist Alphonse Gobert, of the Banque de France. Gobert took the witness stand midway through the second afternoon to discuss the affectionate letter found on a bedside table in Regnault's boudoir. Of all the letters brought as evidence, this one, signed "Gaston," was the most consequential, because it proposed a meeting with Regnault on the day of the murders.

Was the writing in the now infamous Gaston letter in Enrico Pranzini's hand? Gobert reiterated what he had told investigators: This was not Pranzini's native handwriting, but that did not rule out Pranzini's authoring it. According to Gobert, Pranzini possessed not one style of handwriting but instead multiple, "quite variegated handwritings." In a perfect reflection of the cosmopolitan shape-shifter, Pranzini's handwriting had unstable identities too. He was, according to Gobert, an "extraordinary calligrapher of prodigious skill." Pranzini could have purposefully concealed his own style: The Gaston letter was written in "very studied characters revealing a clear intention to modify the ordinary handwriting" of the author.

"In sum, whoever its author, this is a letter written by someone who disguised his handwriting," said the judge.

"Precisely," Gobert replied.[54]

OF "ALL THE GIGOLOS WHO PLEASED" Antoinette Sabatier, Pranzini was the most memorable, said a journalist.[55] Scholars have found gigolo-like males in a variety of historical eras. Gigolos are understood in a general sense as womanizing bachelors, or more pointedly as men who provide sexual services or companionship in exchange for remuneration. But the term's coining and usage in Paris during the latter half of the nineteenth century remains unexplored.[56] This is strange, given the controversy that tainted bachelorhood in the late nineteenth century. The predominant gender norms of the Third Republic discredited and denied the bachelor's masculinity. Sexual promiscuity made him more problematic, because it was believed that all men required the socialization of marriage in order to pretend to virile strength and personal investment in social order and indeed in French civilization itself.[57]

Spatially, the term *gigolo* evoked the freewheeling erotic underground of Montmartre, where Sabatier and Pranzini regularly went out in the evening. The bourgeois chronicler of the Parisian night, Alfred Delvau, posited the gigolo as a "completely modern type," a product of the dance clubs up on the butte.[58] The gigolo and his female partner, the gigolette, or dancing girl, personified the city's permissive "new morals." Young and beautiful and recently arrived from the provinces, they spruced up the doldrums of their new lives in the urban working class by creating a hedonistic culture. Delvau dismissed them—they are "ignorant as a carp," he wrote—but his prose suggests that he found them more engrossing than that.[59] Their codes were unusual and effortless; they did not comport themselves like hardened professionals of the sex industry but instead took the work that came to them.

Of the dance clubs in the area, the most welcoming to the gigolo was the Folies-Robert, a bohemian outfit located on the boulevard Rochechouart and named for its owner, a cross-dressing impresario named Gilles Robert, who had earned the capital required to launch the place by selling himself to men.[60] Gigolos at Robert's dance club were easy to spot, as Delvau notes: They dressed better than the other male patrons; for a night out, the gigolo put himself together well enough to lightly conceal his working-class identity and please the gigolette, who sold herself to male patrons. The two types were partners in gabble and in commitment-free sex. The gigolo could also be useful; as an "inconsequential lover," he might be called on, in a pinch, to act as a go-between between the gigolette and one of her paying clients. The gigolo would take no offense in this role, which other men would have found degrading or emasculating.[61] The gigolo might even make himself sexually available to the gigolette's male customers, should they wish it.[62] In this instance the category of the gigolo blurred into that of male homosexual prostitution, an unspeakable commerce in the nineteenth century.[63]

By coincidence, on the second day of the Pranzini trial, the press carried reports of the arrest of a "pretty gentleman" in northeastern Paris whose biography was said to contain "marked points of resemblance" to that of Pranzini: "Well-dressed, he has seen all the great cities: Venice, Nice, Lyon, Algiers, Bordeaux; he admits that since leaving school—since the age of 16—he has lived off the generosity of women, or worse, through unspeakable relations. Last year he lived in the Latin Quarter, where, he says, a well-known physician, whose name he would only give as 'Camille,' paid him 200 francs per week."[64]

Although homosexuality remained a crime and although prostitution was merely tolerated in Paris, the gigolo's licentiousness and abject sexuality were leavened by his risibility. He was, in Delvau's rendering, a trifling "little" man who "occupies the middle ground between the cherub and the Don Juan—half nitwit and half lover [*greluchon*]."[65]

The gigolo became a social threat when he wandered out of the enclosed sites of illicit sex and took to the boulevards, where he might try to transform his nighttime activities into something like a lifestyle. Leaving the working-class dancing girls behind in Montmartre, he became sinister, predatory, and more difficult to identify—at least to the uninitiated. This is what Bréville was driving at when, near the end of his examination of Pranzini, he asked why the defendant had emblazoned his calling card with the address of a part-time employer for whom he had done translation work, an art dealer in the boulevard Malesherbes, when in fact he was residing with Sabatier in the rue des Martyrs.[66] Pranzini replied that he had done this as a matter of convenience.

Interrupted Bréville, "You had another reason. The boulevard Malesherbes is an elegant address. Number 11 is a beautiful building. You are completely superficial, and this was yet another of your contrivances. This was the little game that you frequently employed. When you met a woman who seemed rich and able to satisfy your tastes—with her largesse—you slipped her your calling card and asked for a meeting. But you left instructions in the boulevard Malesherbes to say that you had gone out whenever someone came looking for you."[67]

Here again, prosecutorial strategy merged with politics. Bréville was using Pranzini to articulate the sentiment that the elite culture of the boulevard was being vulgarized by lower-class phonies, a major preoccupation of the "politics of resentment." If the Eiffel Tower symbolized "vulgar cosmopolitanism" in the sky, men like Pranzini personified it in the game of seduction.[68] Furthermore, the Pranzini case transformed the gigolo as a social type, namely by globalizing it. Because the term *gigolo* was imported into English and other European languages, it was exported to the colonial world and later the developing worlds, where it designated the young men who provided sexual services and companionship to Western tourists.[69] A fictional prototype of this postcolonial gigolo, likely based on Pranzini himself, appeared in a turn-of-the-century novella in which a male character is described as an "exotic gigolo born on the banks of the Nile."[70]

How, precisely, was the gigolo understood to coarsen the stylish Grands Boulevards? Once more, Pranzini's intimate correspondence provided the court with culpatory evidence. It turned out that Pranzini had met his lovers in a most unorthodox manner. His techniques of seduction, befitting the new morals decried by Delvau, were breathtakingly modern—and, by extension, effeminate. Pranzini typically began by approaching a woman in the street. Then he spoke to her. In broad daylight and unaided by either drink or the requisite social introduction. The French verb for this is *draguer*, or "to chat up," and as it pertains to the random heterosexual social encounter, it is a modern urban phenomenon, a symptom of a fluid social world in which the stiff banter of the provinces would no longer do to seduce.[71] Observers speculated that Pranzini had won over Antoinette Sabatier with the "charm and diversity" of his conversation. He knew how to tell a good story, it was supposed, and he had a "pile" of them at his disposal.[72]

For trial spectators the airing of Pranzini's correspondence provided as candidly vivid a depiction of modern seduction as could be found anywhere. "Monsieur," huffs one letter, "I find it surprising that you could be unaware that a society lady [*femme du monde*], whatever her nationality, does not easily submit to a discussion with a stranger in the arcades."[73] In what follows in the letter, observers could easily infer that Pranzini had approached this woman, whispered something into her ear, and handed her his card. To maintain good form, she feigned shock at this. As she continued, however, tradition accommodated modernity: "Yet I want to forget about this improper beginning. Your chance to beg my pardon will be at the Cercle, place Vendome. Come—I'll be in the *salon de conversation*. Approach me there and I will greet you as though you were an old friend."[74]

Obviously seduction was not new, but the brazenly public character that it took on in these years provoked dismay. The "flirt" was a term imported from English, where conservative French moralists would have preferred it to remain. In the 1880s flirting became part of random heterosexual encounters, and Parisians grew obsessed with it. Perhaps most troubling of all, flirting radically disrupted social boundaries, making it more possible for young upstarts like Pranzini to prowl and pounce. The flirt also acknowledged female desire in a way that struck conservatives as a "perversion," in that it involved not only spoken interactions but also subtle smiles, light caresses, and playful regards.[75] Readers of a Parisian journalist who decried Pranzini's Manhattanite lover as a "young emancipated woman" understood that he was flagging the American as the type to partake in flirtation.[76]

It became imperative to understand how Pranzini managed it. Outside the courtroom, commentators examined his love letters under the guise of detached social research. "We are led to ask how this shabby adventurer managed to catch the feminine gaze," wrote one journalist. What were the secrets of the "ladies' man" (*homme à femmes*)? Some held that Pranzini's success was due to the mimicry of masculine codes: Pranzini compensated for his innate lack of French spirituality and Parisian *gaieté* with clothing— gentleman drag—and "constant study." Others instead contrasted Pranzini's methods of seduction with the honorable norms of the day. Pranzini, they implied, had none of the pride that honor bestows because he could not take no for an answer. If he spotted a woman in the street, he immediately showered her with "assiduous attentions"; if she slammed the door in his face, he found her again "via the window." Shameless and without dignity, he persisted "with the patience of a Mohican."[77]

Figure 11. An advertisement for a forthcoming work of fiction, *The Memoirs of Pranzini.* The author credited is a "femme du monde"—a society woman. gallica.bnf.fr/ark:/12148/ btv1b9012679n (Bibliothèque Nationale de France).

Pranzini's conduct with women was nearly always glossed as effete cunning and in every way contra to the prevailing belief that boys should show a hard outer shell from a young age.[78] It was reckoned that Pranzini's approach to women was, on the contrary, "full of tenderness and skill."[79] Then he probed for vulnerability.

Pages from Marie Regnault's diary indicate that the difficult period she was going through at the time of her death had been intense—"I, who cried only at the death of my mother, of my sister, and three times out of anger; I cry everyday now"—and had involved a secret sexual abandon that was meant, as she put it, "to avenge myself."[80] It was just the sort of melancholic "psychological moment" that Pranzini was alleged to leverage, particularly when it pertained to older women, the best targets because they wished to "re-create lost illusions."[81] Strategy and circumstance conspired to bring the courtesan and the gigolo into congress; for Pranzini, the leap from the boulevard to the boudoir was really but a short step.

If prosecutors were right, Pranzini grasped that he could become Regnault's *amant de coeur*. This would have made the courtesan, in turn, a redistributor of wealth and, eventually perhaps, status. Delvau, ventriloquizing the salty patois of the Montmartre night, gave this definition of the *amant de coeur*: He is like a "servant, to say it another way, who mounts the horse of his master. The distinction between the simple *amant* and the *amant de coeur* is that the while the former is a lover who goes broke for his mistress, the latter is a lover for whom the mistress sometimes goes broke—if he fucks her well."[82]

Dr. Brouardel, whose testimony was also heard on the trial's second day, used more or less the same reasoning as Delvau, but in clinical terms. In Brouardel's view, Parisian society blurred Pranzini's upwardly mobile seduction into criminality. Following the suspect's arrest, Brouardel recalled, the "excited imagination was eager to charge him with all similar unsolved crimes in Paris in recent years. Soon we learned that Pranzini had had relations that his social station should have precluded—with young women and ladies—and a real legend grew up around him."[83] For the most part, investigators never located these women, whom the press derided as "les pranzineuses."[84] A few were deposed or gave witness testimony and quickly returned to anonymity after fulfilling their obligations. But for one woman, Antoinette Sabatier, the Pranzini affair was a cruel, unstinting drama.

THE COURTROOM AUDIENCE was abuzz at the promise of Antoinette Sabatier's first public testimony, slated for the trial's penultimate day. Apart from a brief pretrial witness registration, she had not been to the Palais de Justice to watch Pranzini's examination. Her absence, remarked in passing, had not quite registered with anyone as strange.

"Let's have no unwholesome indiscretions," declared Bréville in half-jest. "Bailiff, bring in Miss Antoinette Sabatier!"

The bailiff stepped out, and alone he returned.

"She has not come, Your Honor." Stirrings in the audience grew into shrieks of disappointment. Had Sabatier absconded?

"Go to her place and fetch her!" yelled the judge.[85]

Sabatier's ordeal had commenced on a quiet evening the week after the murders were discovered, when the Paris police came knocking on her apartment door. A tall and elegant brunette, Sabatier gave conflicting answers about what had happened on the night of March 16–17. Initially she told the police that she and Pranzini had slept in her apartment. Investigators did not believe her, and they intimated that she could also be considered a suspect in the case if she did not cooperate. Then they told her that they would be taking a look around her apartment; she fainted. A thorough search of the place, including the building's old-fashioned septic system, turned up nothing.[86]

Nonetheless, Sabatier was taken down to the Police Prefecture for more questioning. She talked about her first encounter with Pranzini, in the summer of 1886. She said that he accosted her one afternoon outside her workplace in the rue de la Paix. Before long, he installed himself in her rue des Martyrs apartment, carrying only a small valise and a briefcase. According to Sabatier, the couple spent nearly every night together in the following six months.[87] Investigators tried to wear down her resistance by showing her the admiring letters that Anglophone tourists had sent to Pranzini. Sabatier rebuffed them, stating that she had known about the correspondence and anyway she could not have read it because she did not know any English. Again, they threatened to charge her as an accomplice.[88]

Finally, after two days in custody, Sabatier agreed to sign a sworn statement that squarely contradicted her prior version of events. She now recognized that Pranzini had not spent the night of the murders in her apartment; she said that she did not see him after dinner that evening and that he did not return until the following day.[89]

Sabatier became the "object of a unique sort of curiosity," remarked a writer for Le Journal des Débats in characteristic understatement.[90] She was a well-spoken woman of arresting appearance, sophisticated and demure and not so easily read. Guesses at her age ranged from 40 to 51 and were usually accompanied with a qualification: She looks younger than her age.[91] Her sense of style was informed by a long career in the employ of Mélanie Percheron, a prestigious hat designer. In the 1880s hats were essential to men's and women's fashion; Percheron's designs garnered citations in the press. Perhaps it was the day-to-day dealings with the society ladies who patronized Percheron's boutique that sandpapered Sabatier's accent down to a point that it no longer marked her as working class.[92]

When the gist of her deposition became public information, Sabatier could not deflect attention. She was a controversial figure in her own right from that point on, although not for the reasons one might have supposed. Paul Bourget, a Boulangist writer and purported expert of female psychology, devised a poll for Le Figaro. Titled "The Sabatier Question," the poll asked Parisian women to imagine that they had been Pranzini's lover and then to reply by mail to the question of "whether Antoinette was right to give up her Levantine." Bourget named fellow author Alexandre Dumas fils to tabulate the results.[93] Also writing in Le Figaro, an organ otherwise emphatic in its law-and-order politics, Albert Bataille answered the question unequivocally: Sabatier, he wrote, was guilty of "betrayal."[94]

A few voices rose to denounce the besmirching of Sabatier, but their efforts may only have worsened matters for her. A writer for La Lanterne opined that Sabatier was the victim of overzealous investigators trying to salvage their own battered reputation; they "brutally jumped this poor woman, who was only guilty of yielding to a seductive man."[95] Her jailing without cause brought to mind the vice squad's abuse of common prostitutes, enough so that a journalist at La Justice found it necessary to assure readers that she held regular employment. She was a trusted employee of sixteen years for Madame Percheron, who also came forward to vouch for Sabatier's character. Sabatier had begun as a manual laborer, making hats, and then proved herself worthy of greater responsibility and eventually was put in charge of the sales register. She "easily covered her expenses," in short, and her arrest was "far from justified."[96]

The futility of these arguments was confirmed by reports that Madame Percheron had decided to relieve Sabatier of her duties, the better to maintain the boutique's pristine reputation.[97] The unavoidable paradox was this: Clearing Sabatier's name meant calling attention to her material independence, which is precisely what had angered conservatives in the first place. Sabatier was an autonomous, professionally successful, unmarried woman who had found sexual fulfillment outside marriage—and she made no apologies for it. The chance to make an example of her—to shame her—remained, never mind that authorities had concluded that she had no involvement in the Rue Montaigne tragedy.

Historians have long contended that the past's constructions of gender should be studied as a relational process, one in which "women and men were defined in terms of one another."[98] Upon closer examination, the "Sabatier Question" was really more of a web of contentious questions that arose when traditional norms of gender and sexuality began to erode in late-nineteenth-century Paris, a fundamental shift that is credited to the advent of the modern New Woman.[99] The emasculation of Pranzini was complemented by a stripping of Sabatier's claims to femininity. As a woman on the verge of spinsterhood, she became a symbol of female loneliness and vulnerability of the sort that Pranzini was supposed to expertly exploit. Caricatured in the press for years to come, she would be recalled as the "ageless mummy."[100]

In this way the couple became enmeshed in anxieties about the loss of control over female sexuality and a correlated endangerment of traditional masculinity.[101] If Pranzini's trove of love letters proved anything to traditionalists, it was that Parisian women were themselves eager to pursue secret sexual pleasures. What could be done about it? As the Pranzini investigation unfolded, a conference of French attorneys convened to debate one facet of the question: Does a husband have the right to open the letters addressed to his wife? The journalist Aurélien Scholl, a specialist of the rastaquouère phenomenon, contended that a husband who relinquished the "right to surveillance" essentially lifted the lid on his wife's sexual desire. Scholl, another Boulangist who published extensively on the Pranzini case, warned men not to "let mysteries circulate beneath the flap of an envelope." He counseled husbands to slice through the wax seal of envelopes addressed to their wives with a switchblade, read the contents, and reseal in secret. "Madame is none the wiser."[102]

The problem of adultery seemed mundane compared with that of declining birth rates. That Pranzini's sexual conquests had sapped the nation's sexual economy was beyond doubt; Sabatier, by partnering with Pranzini, had selfishly shirked her procreative duties. With the intellectual support of scientists and sexologists, the Third Republic was then embracing a vigorous pro-natalist agenda, based on the theory that the French could avoid decline only by channeling reproduction through marriage and that other kinds of sexual intimacy would leave France trailing its European rivals.[103] Hence one journalist's Darwinian reply to the "Sabatier Question" suggested that Sabatier was less than an authentic French lover, less of a woman, for having "so poorly gambled with the last favors" she had to offer a potential mate; her decision to turn against Pranzini was but another selfish act, a means to "pull herself out of the competition."[104] It was as though Sabatier's femininity was fading in the moment. It did not take long for bizarre whispers to make it into print: Pranzini's girlfriend enjoyed wearing fake beards in her spare time.[105]

Investigators believed that Sabatier would be the most reliable means of obtaining a dramatic courtroom confession from the defendant, but the pivotal courtroom encounter between Sabatier and Pranzini did not come with any guarantees. To the contrary, investigators had to wonder what Sabatier might say on the witness stand, considering her belief that Pranzini did not commit the murders. In her view, Pranzini was constitutionally incapable of violence, let alone the gruesome acts of which he stood accused. She had stated this and would continue to repeat it in the weeks ahead to reporters, friends, the police—to President Jules Grévy himself. Bearing this in mind, Bréville tried to keep Sabatier from mentioning her general views of the case in front of the jury and at the same time encouraged her to coax more forthright answers from Pranzini.

At long last, the bailiff escorted Sabatier into the courtroom. Where had she been when her name was called earlier in the day? No one present ever bothered to learn the excuse for her tardiness, if she offered one. She wore a modish hat, of course, and a black dress with a streamlined *cul de Paris*, flared sleeves and garniture that ran the length of the front seam, which opened as it met the floor. Around her neck was an oversized ribbon, hanging studiously to the left, with strings that dangled over that side of her chest. She placed her fine hands onto the stand and moved them when replying to Bréville's questions about her relationship with Pranzini.[106] Her answers were direct and articulate. "I found, in him, an intelligent, loveable, graceful boy."[107] She was not brooking any insinuation that their love story had been somehow abnormal, still less that she had been the naïve victim of exploitation or ruse.

But Bréville kept guiding her back in this direction. In one long exchange he pursued the matter of Pranzini's income and expenses, which was key to the establishment of motive. Sabatier explained that Pranzini had tried hard to find work. His friends had also helped him look for a job.[108] In fact, an economic crisis lingered and employment was scarce.

"What were his pecuniary resources?" Bréville insisted.

"I didn't ask him, not at first."

"Of course—you needed to get close before . . . "

"Later, he asked me for help," Sabatier allowed. "I granted him this."[109]

Bréville pressed on with his narrative. "By the month of March, his situation had become even more awkward. You, mademoiselle, had to co-sign for a rental suit, and when you went with him to the tailor's shop, you were yourself, it would seem, a bit ashamed."

"I'm the one who told him that he had to have a nice outfit in order to look for a job," replied Sabatier, contradicting the judge. "I did not co-sign on the payment of the items because they were never delivered."[110]

Bréville shifted focus to Sabatier's earlier statements to investigators, reminding her of her admission that Pranzini had not come home the night of the crime.

"You were not worried that night?"

"I slept rather deeply. It was only in the morning that I began to feel something. But I did not suspect infidelity." To which Bréville mentioned the love letters. "There was nothing in there to excite my jealousy," she demurred.

"True—they were written in English." (*Laughter*)

"He also showed me the letters of a French woman, but they were not signed," Sabatier added. "I forgave all of that: He was young."

In her responses Sabatier came across as dignified and firm. But in this exchange she had opened a door for Bréville and he pounced. He liked to taunt her by repeatedly employing the honorific "mademoiselle." His usage was technically correct; but when men used the word in such a stilted way, it called attention to a woman's unmarried status, even more so when her family name was omitted.

"And that is why, mademoiselle, I permit myself to observe, a propos of your love, that it doubled as a maternal love. When the two of you were together alone, how did he explain his absence [that night] to you?"[111]

Looking on from the press row, *Le Figaro*'s Bataille took note of a metamorphosis, as though Sabatier, a comely woman, was turning into an old maid for all to see. In the following day's edition he said that Sabatier had looked jaundiced, that she had "no shape here or there," and that her narrow lips were "topped with that unwanted fuzz that lends a masculine air—that which, on women, announces the late season."[112]

Then Bréville asked for Sabatier's recollections of the day after the murders. She told the court how Pranzini had suddenly broken down and cried that evening, March 17, after the pair returned from a show at the Cirque Fernando. In her account Pranzini said, "I saw blood last night," and then he confessed to having been in Marie Regnault's boudoir the previous evening when another of the courtesan's lovers arrived, unannounced, at the front door. Regnault shouted, "He's jealous—hide!" Pranzini told Sabatier that Regnault then led him to a large armoire in the corridor outside her boudoir and instructed him to climb inside and wait. He did this. When he emerged from the armoire, Regnault, Gremeret, and little Marie Gremeret all lay in pools of blood.[113]

That, Sabatier told the court, is what Pranzini had said.

Needless to say, this was highly damaging testimony for the defense. Bréville turned to Pranzini, who flatly denied every word of it. Grison had noticed that during Sabatier's testimony, Pranzini's eyes were blinking nervously; his lower teeth kept reflexively biting his moustache.[114] Seizing a propitious moment to corner the defendant, Bréville reached for the recording of the Pranzini-Sabatier confrontation. He began to read it aloud. In the selected passage Sabatier pleads with Pranzini to be forthcoming about where he had spent the night of the murders. "I don't want to believe that you are guilty," she says. "You were good, you were gentle. You would not have hurt a fly, you loved holding children and yet you would have killed that little girl?—No, of course it's untrue. But you must speak. You have to say where you were that night. I beg you, please."[115]

Bréville looked up to cajole Sabatier, "Come on, mademoiselle, look at him if you can, talk to him if you still have the strength, tell him to confess." The audience shuffled as Sabatier leaned against the bar, turning her head slowly toward Pranzini, who looked up to meet her eyes.[116]

"Don't try to mesmerize her, Pranzini," said Bréville.

"I'm only looking at her. Shall I lower my eyes?" Pranzini said, to the audience's murmurs. The courtroom grew agitated as the two paused in the presence of each other, Sabatier saying nothing, Pranzini keeping silent. Bréville had enough of it and ordered Sabatier out.[117]

AN ADMIRER once asked Edgar Demange why he did not publish more. The great barrister's reply, "I don't know how to write," was taken as modesty, yet a cursory look at his file at the Archives Nationales would seem to confirm that in addition to publishing nothing, Demange saved little in the way of notes or correspondence.[118]

Another admirer, wishing to discover Demange's secrets as a successful trial lawyer, went to observe him closely at work; he left the courtroom dumbfounded. Demange, the most formidable public defender of his era, did not prepare his courtroom remarks or statements in advance of trial. When it came time for the all-important closing argument, he arrived with a student notebook and a goose-feather plume. Only moments before taking the floor, he would scratch out some ideas: "Hieroglyphs pile up as his pen creaks and runs across the page; he writes in every direction, then crosses it out, underlines it, writes over it, and it's a marvel to think that this graphic confusion will, in just a moment, give birth to a discourse of dazzling order."[119]

As he listened to the prosecutor's closing argument on the final day of the Pranzini trial, Demange had difficult decisions to make. Sabatier's steady testimony was credible. It may have let Bréville down, but it tightened the screws on the defendant and diminished his counsel's range for a reply. The rhetoric of a defense attorney like Demange is a calculus of intuition. Did Pranzini's claim to have no knowledge of the murders in the rue Montaigne remain plausible to the jury?

Reynaud delivered the long, even-keeled argument that was to be expected. At one point he gestured to Demange and, in a backhanded compliment, warned the jury to beware of his adversary's "artifices of language." When he finished, Demange rose and began to refute the prosecutor point by point, pausing to recall for the jury that the police had erroneously suspected Pranzini of murdering other high-class prostitutes, mentioning by name Marie Aguétant in Paris and Marie Rigottier of Lyon. In one of those cases a witness had gone so far as to formally identify Pranzini as the killer, yet Pranzini had been at war in Sudan at the time.[120]

On the topic of Sudan and the "scramble for Africa," Demange moved against undue national prejudice. Pranzini was not an enemy of the French empire in Africa, said Demange. Admittedly he had worked for the British army, but this was not evidence of allegiance. Pranzini "provided services to all Europeans" in Africa. In an allusion to contemporary newspaper headlines, Demange assured the jurors that the tragic death in Sudan of the beloved French journalist Olivier Pain had not been Pranzini's doing (in a heavy-handed show of solidarity, Pranzini began to cry when Demange mentioned Pain).[121]

Next, Demange upended evidence advanced by the prosecution, beginning with the legend of the Oriental Don Juan. Pranzini had established himself in Paris, in a comfortable life with Sabatier; he wanted for nothing. Sabatier's love for him was not maternal, as Bréville suggested, but based on a bona fide desire. The couple's relationship was neither commercial nor irregular: Sabatier, "like the young American, loved muscles."[122] No, Pranzini was a harmless, carefree adventurer with no designs on Parisian high society. Didn't the prosecution's depiction of him as a lowlife beneath a polished carapace effectively say the same thing? If Pranzini was as ragged as Bréville claimed, then wasn't it far-fetched to suppose that an exclusive courtesan like Regnault would have chosen *him* as her *amant de coeur*?[123]

Returning to the night of the crime, Demange tapped into the key sources of reasonable doubt: two mysterious figures discussed by investigators who, no matter the trial's outcome, would leave an enduring mark on the Parisian investigative imagination. First, there was the society woman whose name Pranzini refused to divulge.[124] Bréville said, "If he would sooner see his head lopped off than betray the name of this woman, who can possibly make a crime of it?"[125] The prosecution alleged that Pranzini was trying to seduce his way upward, and the defendant's intimate correspondence had been exhibited as proof. But if this was so, Demange asked, then why had it been so easy to dismiss as "improbable," even laughable, the notion that Pranzini had been with a society woman on the night of the murders? He was from Egypt, after all, "land of the *almées*!" shouted Demange, in reference to the harem dancers who enchanted European painters in the East.[126]

The second credibly exculpating counternarrative, that of the *gringalet*, had also been circulating in the newspapers for months. This was the diminutive, skinny fellow who had been seen with Regnault in the days and weeks before the murders and who, all agreed, could not have been Pranzini. Was this the *real* Gaston Geissler? Pranzini may not have been entirely innocent in this case, but neither was he the culprit. There was plenty of room for doubt. None less than the former chief of Security Gustave Macé had arrived at the same conclusion. "Pranzini is not the killer," Macé declared, "but he must have been the lookout man nearby where the crime was committed."[127]

As he neared the end of his argument, Demange grew more animated, his voice a chain of exclamations. "You will remain deaf to the anger of the crowd, and doing the work of justice, you will say, 'Let him live!'"[128] Was the anger of the crowd an allusion to the Boulangists who were out demonstrating in the streets or to those seated in the courtroom or possibly the bench? Demange may have been throwing a line to the jurors who recoiled from the trial's crass politicization or who simply believed that Pranzini's right to a fair trial had been undermined by Bréville's high jinks.

French law gave presiding judges a lot of latitude, called discretionary power, when it came to courtroom procedure. In principle, the presiding judge's responsibility was to guide the two sides toward an equitable exhibiting of the evidence. But the prerogative was his to participate in a criminal investigation and to choose pieces of evidence to read during the trial, powerful levers with which to squeeze a defendant.[129] At the time, many critics shared the view that Bréville had abandoned all pretenses of "impartiality." "It seems to me," wrote one, "that the presiding judge at the *assises* court has a higher calling than clever remarks."[130] The trial was a show, agreed Paul Mougeolle, consisting of "only actors and *impresarios*."[131]

A chorus of international onlookers expressed shock at Bréville's conduct. A British journalist wondered whether Bréville was trying to "engender public sympathy" for Pranzini, a "vulgar libertine."[132] Editors at the London *Standard* felt "half driven to side against" the prosecution in view of Pranzini's unjust treatment: "Whatever he did showed guilt. If he lowered his eyes it was shame, if he wept it was breaking down, if he was silent in the face of damaging evidence the Judge reminded him that he was not only pale, but absolutely green."[133] Mindful of the stormy political backdrop, an American correspondent grew concerned about what Bréville's performance might say about the embattled French Republic. "For a great nation, especially a nation in peril, it is a pity."[134]

Did some members of the jury share the sentiment that justice was indivisible from procedure? Demange reserved for the end a final maneuver that would have met them halfway. In what must have been an improvisation meant as a compromise, Demange swerved in a new direction and casually entered a new plea for his client, one that Pranzini had not made himself and that conspicuously contradicted the defendant's sworn testimony. Demange, in essence, confessed that the defendant had not been completely ignorant of the murders. Instead, Pranzini had been a marginal actor in them. He killed nobody, but he *did* act as a fence for the stolen jewelry, and that is why he left Paris so suddenly. Pranzini, Demange was saying in so many words, was a liar. But a murderer he was not. Few attorneys would have attempted it. Perhaps no one could have pulled it off as smoothly. If forewarned, Pranzini surely would not have endorsed his lawyer's sudden impulse. Had Demange divined something in the eyes of the jurors suggesting that in order to rescue Pranzini, he needed first to hang him? Had this been Demange's own assessment of the mystery all along?

Bréville could do nothing to forestall the inevitable. Demange completed his argument. The stunned courtroom audience erupted, their applause sweeping from the back of the courtroom clear to the front. "This speech, so troubling, so energetic and hot, has again *thrilled* the audience," noted Grison. Laboring to regain control, Bréville shouted down the onlookers: "Silence! I cannot tolerate this applause in a hall of justice!" Having lost his grip on a spectacle of his own creation, he turned to the defendant. "Pranzini, do you have something to add in your defense?"

Pranzini, evidently swept up in the excitement, stepped up to the balustrade that separated him from the judge and struck it with great force, hollering, "Death or Liberty!" Then he swung his right hand into the air and again raised his voice, "I am innocent!" The audience was dumbstruck.

Bréville promptly declared the trial finished. The jurors were led out to deliberate. When they did not return immediately with a verdict, the effect of Demange's argument was confirmed. The room got rambunctious. There was speculation that the jury was hesitant to send Pranzini to the guillotine after all they had seen. Two hours passed, a long wait by contemporary standards. Finally at 6:45 p.m. the jury returned. The foreman stepped up to read the decision. Guilty on two of the three counts of premeditated murder.

Reynaud asked for the death sentence.

Bréville turned to Pranzini: "What do you have to say?"

Pranzini: "I have nothing to say."

The court announced that Enrico Pranzini would receive the penalty of death. Pranzini joined his hands and looked toward the sky, as though to pray. Bréville informed him that he had three days to file an appeal. Again Pranzini declared his innocence. Guards came to escort him back downstairs to the Conciergerie, and the Pranzini affair came to the first of its endings.[135]

CHAPTER EIGHT

The Skin Affair

Punishment and the Colonial Body

> If you feel an attachment to your skeleton
> Don't do as Pranzini did.
> Die in your bed instead
> Of keeling over at the Roquette prison;
> Then carved up your body won't be
> For the men of Security
>
> —Satirical verse, 1887[1]

> Moreover the Pranzini affair is quite a specimen, as it were, of the most fantastic and fascinating kind of crime drama. One finds in it the horror of Edgar Allan Poe's stories, the cynical backdrop of a corrupt fin de siècle, and a display of all that the police is, and is not, capable; and finally, [there is] the triumph of luck, building up and then unknotting the intrigue, directing and explaining it like the choirs of ancient tragedy!
>
> —François Goron[2]

"I believe he's innocent," repeated Antoinette Sabatier throughout the summer of 1887.[3] The verdict had done nothing to shake her faith in Pranzini, an insistence that was shared by Edgar Demange, who prepared for several weeks of appeals and petitions to save his client from the guillotine. Pranzini was transferred to the Grande Roquette Prison in eastern Paris, designated for death row inmates and other dangerous criminals. He languished in a cell with a slatted door, a desk and chairs, a bed, a large rectangular window, and a pipe to smoke. Angered by Sabatier's testimony, he refused to speak to his lover. Nevertheless, she resolved to campaign for his pardon. Mélanie Percheron offered to introduce Sabatier to an acquaintance in the government who might be of aid, but, barring a successful appeal, Pranzini's only chance at survival was to convince President Jules Grévy to commute his sentence. Sabatier decided to petition Grévy personally. On an August morning a few weeks after the trial, she headed down to the Elysée Palace, the president's official residence. She had no appointment.

"On the way there, I had to think things through. Who would I ask to see? Who would I ask for help?" One name came to mind. "I thought of Madame Wilson, whose goodness I had heard much about. Also, a woman would be better able to understand the feelings that brought me there."[4]

Alice Wilson (née Grévy) was the president's daughter. Although married now for several years, she still lived with her family at the presidential palace. Her husband was Daniel Wilson, a newspaper mogul, government deputy, and incorrigible philanderer who had wed his way into the palace—he asked for Alice's hand when she was 32 years old—and who, according to rumors, had his own designs on the presidency. Dubbed "Mister Son-in-Law," Wilson was rakish and scandal-prone. He had been embarrassed when the vice squad found his name in the infamous black book of the Widow Rondy, the notorious Parisian madame who had once employed Marie Regnault—not that this discovery came as a surprise to the police; for many years they had kept tabs on the vast sums that Wilson doled out in exchange for the privilege of deflowering young women in the capital's brothels.[5]

Sabatier entered the Elysée Palace, made her requests, and was shown into the antechamber of Madame Wilson's apartment, where she composed a note asking Mrs. Wilson to arrange an audience between herself and the president. Doubtless she mentioned the Pranzini case in her note, for her wait was remarkably brief. An army general in charge of palace security emerged to greet her.

"There are many here today with letters requesting an audience," he said, "but you will be the first in—I promise." At noon, Sabatier found herself in a small, out-of-the-way office that the president usually used for napping and letter writing. Grévy strode into the room, motioned sympathetically to her, and she took her seat. The president's informal manner put her immediately at ease.[6]

In his eighth decade, President Grévy looked very much the part of the elderly gentleman. With his bushy white sideburns and provincial plainspokenness, he was the epitome of old-school bourgeois republicanism. His life had spanned three different kings, the two Bonapartist empires, an assortment of revolutionary uprisings, provisional governments, and, for that single incandescent spring, the Paris Commune. Through it all he demonstrated staying power with a milquetoast political persona that one journalist summed up in a few words: "simple, modest, and horrified by noise."[7] He breezed to reelection in 1885 and seemed destined to live out his days peacefully at the Elysée Palace, were it not for the political strife caused by General Boulanger. The dual tasks of muting the general's hot-blooded declarations in foreign policy and conspiring with other centrists to mitigate Boulangism's threat had begun to take a political toll: The Boulangists' chants at the Gare de Lyon had been for Grévy's removal from office.

Sabatier and Grévy spoke of the Pranzini verdict for a half-hour. Grévy required no debriefing. "I had to see you, madame," he replied when he sat down.

"I have come to ask you to pardon Pranzini, because—in the name of my conscience—I do not believe that he is guilty."

"Madame, I will do everything within my power, and I will examine the matter conscientiously, I promise you."[8] Sabatier left the palace filled with gratitude and hope.

"Do you believe it, sir?" she asked a reporter. "He agreed to meet with me even though I had no introduction letter—I, who had no title or standing to request a pardon for Pranzini?"[9] Questioned by yet another reporter, she said, "I don't know that I was eloquent, but I am sure I made a good impression."[10] News of the tête-à-tête made the front pages, but it also raised eyebrows because of Sabatier's unblessed relationship with the convict. Aghast, one newspaper falsely claimed that Sabatier had fallen pathetically to the president's feet, incapable of uttering a word except, "Pardon!"[11] "That old witch," seethed a *Gil Blas* columnist. She used "to bring home young men who are 25 years younger," and here she was trying to obtain the condemned man's body like Mathilde in Stendhal's *The Red and the Black*, who retrieves the guillotined head of Julien Sorel and fashions a shrine for it: "It inspires in me a mix of disgust and horror."[12]

This strange remark was unwittingly prescient. During the summer and fall of 1887, the battle over the symbolic control of the Pranzini investigation evolved into a struggle over the fate of the condemned man's body, coded at once as criminal and colonial. In this chapter I revisit that scandal-plagued season of Parisian history and show how the battles over the significance of Pranzini's body helped to precipitate the fall of Daniel Wilson and the collapse of Jules Grévy's presidency. My contention is that this unprecedented turn of events, a scandal known as the skin affair, was in certain respects a logical coda to the preceding months.

IN A CONSCIOUS REJECTION of concentrated executive power, the constitution of the Third Republic granted the president relatively little sway; Grévy had endeared himself to republicans by advocating for weaker presidential powers against his own self-interest. One presidential prerogative that he jealously guarded was the right to commute death sentences, which he occasionally—and controversially—exercised during a period when the debate over capital punishment attracted strong partisan voices on both sides. Victor Hugo, the patron saint of the Third Republic, agitated against it. One reason for Sabatier's optimism may have been that the president's misgivings about the procedures surrounding the death penalty were well-known. As Pranzini sat on death row, some wondered whether the "end of the guillotine" might be on the horizon, or whether perhaps a modernizing compromise might be reached with the newly patented electric chair, America's recent contribution to the global debate.[13]

Even though Grévy was by no means an outspoken "abolitionist," he typified the "age of sobriety" in capital punishment, a broad nineteenth-century move toward the modernization of the death penalty as represented by the curtailment of public torture and attempts to quash the carnivalesque atmosphere of public executions that had been the hallmark of the Old Regime.[14] One of Grévy's first legislative initiatives as president was a bill proposing to suppress the "scandalous spectacles" around the guillotine by holding them at dawn and by strictly limiting the number of journalists— "delegates" of the press—in attendance. He disagreed with the assertion that the public viewing of executions served as a deterrent to crime; it "instead awakens bloody instincts in the spirits of those in attendance," he told the Chamber of Deputies.[15]

As Pranzini's weeks on death row demonstrate, the endeavor to cloak the death penalty in this sort of high-minded rationalism was probably doomed from the start. No matter what Grévy did to discourage the throngs crying out for an execution, they materialized like weevils in rice every evening outside the place de la Roquette. The newspapers carried advertisements by companies such as Savon du Congo, a soap company claiming that Pranzini was requesting its product ("On my bloodied remains a Savon du Congo, to make sure that I smell good when I go!").[16] By August 24 a false rumor had made the rounds: Grévy had rejected Pranzini's plea for clemency; the execution was imminent. Within 48 hours, some 10,000 people clotted the streets around Roquette Prison, which was located on an inclined patch of Paris between the place de la Bastille and Père Lachaise Cemetery. Jean-Marie Caubet, head of the Municipal Police, had the unenviable task of maintaining order around the prison. According to Caubet, the execution crowd mainstays sprang up in greater numbers than usual: Street singers provoked pockets of applause; *camelots* sold moist, paper-wrapped croissants and cakes; and there were pimps, three-card monte dealers, pickpockets, fugitives, and drunkards as well as workers and bourgeois types who streamed in alongside taxis full of "rastaquouères of the Grands Boulevards."[17] A heavy police contingent surrounded the throngs and tried to disperse them. More than a hundred "leaders" were rounded up and jailed, but the festivities continued unabated.[18] Gallows chants droned through humid dusks.

It's his head, his head, his head;
It's his head that we want
Oh! Oh! Oh![19]

According to a foreign correspondent, conditions grew "intolerable" as the wait dragged on for days, with thousands of people refusing to go home.[20] Grévy's careful review of each death penalty case, kept secret from the public, had precisely the effect that the president wished to avoid. He left Paris for his annual summer retreat in the Jura mountains, where he had access to newspapers but refused to dignify rumors about his decision by refuting them.

So the place de la Roquette became fertile soil for bookmakers doing a brisk business, due to lingering doubts about the verdict, which many believed would figure into Grévy's decision on the Pranzini pardon.[21] The unnamed lady with whom Pranzini claimed to have spent the night of the murders, for instance, remained part of the public discussion, thanks in part to Georges Grison. The journalist provoked a related scandal a few weeks after the trial by proclaiming that he had a list of sixteen Parisian reporters who were blackmailing Parisian women; these reporters alleged that the women had known Pranzini and could have spent the night of the murders with him. The report triggered a witch hunt among the city's larger papers, a scandal known as "The 16 Affair."[22] Then in late August there were rumors that a mysterious woman from Versailles had rented an apartment with a view onto the place de la Roquette at the rate of 150 francs per day—was she the "unknown lady"?[23]

The other counternarratives that pointed to a mistaken verdict (the *homme brun* theory and the mysterious Geissler lead) also persisted and later appeared to find evidentiary support with the arrest of a suspect named Anatole Romanoff, a polyglot migrant presumed to be a Levantine. "Despite the assurances of the *parquet* [public prosecutor's office] and the police, many people continue to believe that the crime of the rue Montaigne was not the work of an isolated criminal, but instead a band of wrongdoers working together to exploit wealthy hookers. Information gathered on Romanoff following his October arrest seemed to confirm this hypothesis, since it established that he was at the very least Pranzini's accomplice—the famous dark-haired man whose existence was categorically affirmed by diverse witnesses and denied by the official investigation."[24] Romanoff, reportedly well spoken and with a face that was "most distinguished," told Goron that he knew something about Pranzini and the murders in the rue Montaigne, but then he refused to cooperate.[25] According to archived reports, Goron chased the Romanoff lead for several months.[26]

The unruly political climate, lack of public sympathy for Pranzini's defense, and long-standing grievances with Grévy's careful review of clemency pleas increased the pressure on the president to go forward with the execution. Grévy was sometimes called Papa Pardon[27] by those in the press who viewed his close scrutiny of death penalty cases as an "abuse" of power in that it positioned him as a supra-juror who did not show sufficient deference to the court's verdicts.[28] Reporters and police alike denounced Grévy's "capricious clemency."[29] The writer Victor Fournel speculated that "the Levantine's force of dissimulation" would permit him to "snatch a pardon from the weak" president.[30]

Pranzini's dossier did not reach Grévy's tiny village, Mont-sous-Vaudrey, until August 25. Demange, unaware that the president was in the Jura, had addressed his request for an audience to the Elysée Palace, whose staff replied with a boilerplate letter stating that the president was gone and unavailable. Demange, beside himself, went to the press, and Grévy, learning of the misunderstanding in the papers, telegraphed the attorney with an invitation to join him in the mountains. Demange took a train from Paris on the evening of August 27.[31] The next morning, the two men shared breakfast. By then Grévy had already given the dossier a close reading. To Demange it seemed that the president was giving Pranzini every consideration, but still he remained inscrutable.[32] Two days later, on August 30, Grévy wired a message asking Demange to return to Roquette Prison to plead with Pranzini for more information about the night of the murders. The president was throwing Pranzini a lifeline, but Pranzini would have to compromise—Did he serve as a fence? Was he a co-conspirator? Demange raced over to the prison.

From inside his cell Pranzini could hear the cantankerous sea of bloodlust beyond the prison walls. He received visits from the prison chaplain, Abbé Faure, who wrote of their intimate chats in a tell-all memoir about life on death row. "I considered this beautiful face, full of intelligence and distinction," recalled the chaplain, "and I found largely justified the flattering assessments" of the prisoner.[33] When he learned that Pranzini was a smoker, he began supplying him with tobacco. At least once the preacher tried to coax a confession out of Pranzini, who did not seem to take him too seriously, preferring instead to discuss liturgical music or the books of Alexandre Dumas, his favorite author.

Pranzini was no more forthcoming with Demange than he was with Faure. Demange would likely have advised his client that Grévy was leaving the door open a crack if Pranzini was willing to cooperate. But Pranzini's gamble had always been freedom or death, and he was not about to veer off course. At any rate, death, Pranzini mused aloud, was preferable to a penal colony overseas. Demange left their eleventh-hour consultation emptyhanded. Pranzini sat at his desk and penned a letter to Grévy requesting a grace period of 30 days so that his mother would have time to travel from Egypt to embrace him once more before he died. The missive arrived at the Elysée Palace and was forwarded to the Jura, but by the time it arrived, Pranzini was dead.[34]

At 6 p.m. on August 30, 1887, an officer from Security arrived at Madame Percheron's boutique with an official letter for Antoinette Sabatier. The letter announced that the execution of Pranzini would take place the following morning and invited her to attend. One can imagine that it was Grévy who extended her this courtesy, though there is no hard evidence of this. When she opened the letter, she cried out, "Oh! It's over!" Her co-workers ran to her. "They're going to kill him . . . Oh!—if only I'd known . . . he, so sweet . . ." They put her in a taxi to her sister's apartment in the rue Rochechouart.[35]

The execution's many spectators did not have the benefit of a public announcement that their long wait was over, only the rickety test drop of the blade before sunrise. A small group of executioner's aides had wheeled guillotine parts onto the place de la Roquette and erected the tall contraption atop five level slabs set into the pavement for this purpose. Mounted guards sealed off the place de la Roquette to prevent spectators from pushing too closely. A kite swirled in the gusting winds above the prison. The sky, clogged with dark clouds, began to clear its throat; a summer thunderstorm was setting upon the city.[36]

Inside the prison a group of eight men, including Abbé Faure, Chief Taylor, and Deputy Chief Goron, entered Pranzini's cell. Guards reported that Pranzini had read until around 10 p.m. but did not manage to fall asleep. They told Pranzini that his final appeal for clemency had been denied.

He said, "I'm innocent! It is you who are about to commit a crime!" Someone handed him a pair of shoes. He asked for cold water to wash his face and hands. While he was cleaning himself, Pranzini spotted Taylor standing discreetly in the half-light. "Well, there we are, Mr. Taylor, don't try to hide yourself. You planted false witness testimonies in my file. Curse you . . . you, you . . . "

"Pranzini, up!" interrupted the guards.

"Oh, relax!" he said, donning the blazer he had worn to trial. Next they led him into a separate room, a humid nook with bare stone walls, where the executioner, Louis Deibler, was waiting with his aides. The prison warden forced a sleeveless undershirt over Pranzini's head. An aide reached into his pocket for a cord to bind the legs. Deibler, a stout man who walked with a pronounced limp, reserved for himself the job of clipping the collar clean off Pranzini's shirt, opening ample space for the blade to engage the vertebrae; if a second drop was required to finish the job—and this was not unheard of—it spelled harsh criticism and even ridicule for the executioner.

His thick, pale neck exposed to the crowd, Pranzini ambled into the square. He could be heard grousing about the guards' overtight grip on his wrists. The chaplain offered him an embrace but was rebuffed. Pranzini asked for his crucifix instead and kissed it. Deibler, in a single brusque motion, hoisted

Pranzini onto the teeterboard and then lowered him parallel to the ground. An aide yanked Pranzini's hair downward to fit his neck in the copper-lined groove of the lunette. Pranzini lay face down, waiting for Deibler, whom Grison once described as agitated and nervous whenever the moment came for him to perform his duty.[37] Only several years later did Deibler's latent hematophobia—he suffered debilitating hallucinations of blood—finally bring his career to a close.[38] His laborious movement gave Pranzini a few moments to contemplate the basket placed inches below his face for the purpose of catching his severed head. Deibler groped his way along the slot, struggling to find the trigger mechanism that released the blade.[39]

When it was done, an aide took the head by the ear and tossed it into a rectangular box alongside the torso. The box was placed in a hearse, which was pulled by galloping horses to the Ivry Cemetery in southeastern Paris. With fat sponges, Deibler's men scrubbed the blood from the blade before it had a chance to dry. Deibler oversaw the guillotine's disassembly. Once that final step was complete, the police broke their cordon and onlookers flowed onto the reddened cobblestones.[40]

A FEW SUMMERS AGO, I had a much dreaded appointment in Paris's Jardin des Plantes. I needed to find out what had become of the corpse of Enrico Pranzini.

Typically, when an execution took place in nineteenth-century Paris, noisy anticipation gave way to silence as the media moved on to other topics. Even in a case as exceptional as Pranzini's, there would have been no reason to expect the execution to veer so wildly off course.

And for several days no one was aware that it had. According to accounts that appeared the following morning, things had gone according to protocol. After the beheading the usual mock burial was held at the cemetery on the outskirts of the city; this was a concession to religious tradition involving a priest, a doctor, and the chief and deputy chief of Security. Pranzini's body and severed head were then briskly returned to the faculty of the famed Medical School of Paris. Like the cadavers of many executed convicts of that era, Pranzini's body would be studied by doctors and their students (and a select group of journalists) before an autopsy was undertaken to determine whether his anatomy bore the markings of intrinsic criminality or race. After the autopsy his cadaver was dismembered so that parts of his anatomy could be preserved or molded by members of the Société d'anthropologie, a leading center for the study of human origins and "races" during the nineteenth century.[41] Pranzini was of particular interest to such anatomists as Dr. Brouardel.

But then awful rumors began to appear in the newspapers. There had been irregularities in the cadaver's handling, and parts of Pranzini's anatomy had gone missing—or worse.

The body was not snatched in its entirety, as a plethora of research publications attest. For a number of years scientists returned to the remains for study; they scrutinized his foot bones and scribbled observations about his pickled brain. Some parts, or casts thereof, became display objects for museum and exhibition crowds; a bust of Pranzini's skull was featured in an 1889 World's Fair exhibit. After 1929, though, scientific interest waned.

Although Pranzini's execution figures into official histories of crime and punishment in Paris, the crisis sparked by the desecration of his corpse figures nowhere in these. There is no mention of it, for instance, on the plaque that accompanies the last visible trace of the man in public Paris: a plaster cast of his head (one of the two made on the morning of the execution) on permanent display at the unfrequented Musée de la Préfecture de Police in the 5th arrondissement. The cast has been enhanced with a wig of thick, wavy hair, a moustache, and studiously inset whiskers. At the base of the neck, strokes of blood-red paint have been added for dramatic effect. Behind the glass is the likeness of a man in his prime, freshly struck by the guillotine's razor. A photograph of this cast was featured in an important 2010 exhibit, "Crime and Punishment," organized by Robert Badinter at the Musée d'Orsay, which assembled images and texts pertaining to capital punishment in France from the revolutionary era to 1981, the year Badinter, as minister of justice, successfully argued for its abolition.

The related questions of how the desecration of Pranzini's corpse took place, why it triggered a scandal, and how the entire episode slipped into the realm of forgotten anecdote lead us back to the nineteenth-century study of criminal and colonial anatomies. Physical anthropology and criminology, which mutually informed each other, always contained colonial racial and political dimensions in their public displays. Both were intrinsically bound up in questions of crime and punishment in the broadest sense of those terms. Indeed, as with many facets of European empires in the East, an important precedent for the intersection of the French colonial and criminal imaginaries can be found in Bonaparte's invasion and occupation of Egypt.

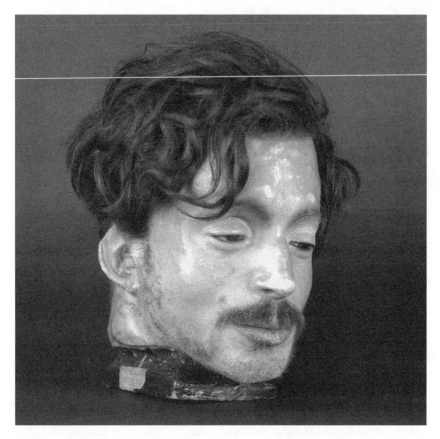

Figure 12. Cast of Enrico Pranzini's head. This cast is prominently displayed at the Musée de la Préfecture de Police de Paris. Archives de la Préfecture de Police de Paris.

In June 1800, after Bonaparte had absconded, the Muslim anticolonial activist Suleiman al-Halabi assassinated France's leader, General Kléber, in Cairo; following Halabi's execution, the French savants brought his remains with them back to Paris for display at the new National Museum of Natural History in the Jardin des Plantes. His anatomy instructed generations of Parisians and tourists in the ties between European colonial order, racialized anatomy, and punishment. His skeleton was situated alongside examples of European racial types for comparative anatomical purposes; in a single phrase, the placard fixed above his skull reinforced a conflation of colonial race, religion, and criminality: "Skeleton of Solyman, educated but very fanatic, Kléber's assassin."[42]

Since about 1900, multiple reorganizations and transfers of the physical anthropological collections of Paris, which contain tens of thousands of human and animal remains, have made it difficult to trace the movement of individual specimens such as Halabi's and Pranzini's. Inventories are spotty or nonexistent. In addition, reports that followed in the wake of the scandal indicated that certain parts of Pranzini's corpse were likely lost forever. His eyes, the subject of relentless fascination when he was alive, were the first coveted pieces to vanish in the hours after the execution, it was said. At least one ear was also likely purloined.

In itself, such mischief might have gone unnoticed beyond the walls of the medical school's amphitheater, where cadavers were routinely dissected. Rumors of students and doctors collecting discarded body parts as souvenirs were hardly the sort of thing to scandalize Parisian society. But the charged quality of Pranzini's remains set them apart from the curriculum. Also, the grotesqueries visited upon the cadaver occurred *outside* the medical school. Parisians were horrified when the news broke that parts of Pranzini's anatomy were circulating in the city like *articles de Paris*—fine artisanal goods.

I contacted Dr. Philippe Mennecier, who oversees the physical anthropology (*anthropologie biologique*) collections at the National Museum of Natural History. Mennecier confirmed that Pranzini's "post-cranial skeleton" had been absorbed into the museum's collection, though he could not say when or under what circumstances. Pranzini's bones are kept in a group with several other "suppliciés," he added, putting this term in scare quotes. Once the primary signifier of "executed criminal," the term *supplicié* is now archaic—France has abolished the death penalty—but it persists in old classification schemes. Pranzini's bones were available for consultation in the laboratory on-site, said Mennecier, but beyond that "I won't have much to tell you."

Mennecier gave me the address of a research facility, a cube-shaped building of modest size nestled alongside similar structures near the periphery of the Jardin des Plantes, a lavish greenery traced with immaculately straight pathways that has always functioned as a node of transnational France. The Jardin was founded by King Louis XIV, who used it as a medicinal herb garden. Since that period, the site has been home to leading researchers in the life sciences; it houses a menagerie and leisure spaces, which are all integrated into a massive botanical garden where tourists and Parisians stroll beneath tree varietals brought back by French explorers, merchants, and scientists. The Museum of Natural History was added during the French Revolution, and it quickly became an important center for the study of comparative human and animal anatomy, in which the display of the booty of imperial wars helped drum up public pride and support.[43]

I met Mennecier, an affable, tall and thin, middle-aged man, in the doorway of a second-floor office abutting a space that is akin to an ossuary. He told me that he had not heard of Pranzini before my inquiry. That morning a group of Russian scientists were scheduled to arrive at the lab, he said, so his time would be limited.

A veteran curator, Mennecier is not a scientist. He holds a PhD in linguistics and turns out to have a reputation among researchers from a wide variety of fields, who acknowledge his aid and hospitality in numerous publications. I assured him that my visit would require little time: Historians are not trained to *physically* behold the people they study, whose bodies, more often than not, have moldered away before we get around to them.[44] The purpose of my visit was not to observe the properties of Pranzini's remains—the laboratory was stocked with instruments of measurement—but more prosaically to account for them.

Recent years have seen mounting criticism of the possession and display of remains that were collected on the grounds of discredited racial theories and research agendas, whether in colonial or criminal anthropology or related fields of biological fields. Museum specialists are now raising ethical concerns about the circulation of the remains of executed convicts such as Pranzini.[45] These critics may find support in historical scholarship that undermines the scientific earnestness of those who amassed these collections in the first place; in practice, the line between anatomical research and trophyization in museums of criminal anthropology was flimsy from the beginning.[46] This insight has direct bearing on the political scandal that engulfed Paris in the autumn of 1887.

Going further back, legal disputes over individual cases or groups have resulted from campaigns to repatriate remains to a host of countries in Europe's former colonies.[47] Perhaps most famous among these was the case of Sarah Baartman, the "Hottentot Venus," a woman whose tragic plight in Europe has become synonymous with the inhumanity of colonial racism and its implications for the history of gender and sexuality. Baartman's "primitive" anatomy was examined at the Museum of Natural History and was displayed in pseudo-scientific representations as "unbridled" sexuality.[48]

Following her death, French scientists preserved her brain and sexual anatomy for a museum display that ran until the 1970s.[49]

I should clarify that the citation of individual examples of colonial and criminal specimens alongside each other is not done to equate their respective provenances and still less done to reiterate the confused biological constructions of them as sexually, racially, or criminally Other. A central aim of this book has been to elucidate these confusions, from which we are still trying to recover.

THE MORNING AFTER Pranzini's execution, the daily *La Justice* probably spoke for many Parisians when it expressed relief that the summer of Pranzini was over. "We are going to have to find another subject to read about and discuss. Anything."[50]

Instead, the Pranzini affair took flight once more on September 14, when Georges Grison published his scoop in *Le Figaro*: Top-ranking officials at Security, soon identified as Chief Taylor, Deputy Chief Goron, and Inspector Gustave Rossignol, were in possession of souvenirs that had been fashioned from Pranzini's corpse.

The initial reaction of Grison's rivals in the press was to doubt the story's veracity. Grison batted them away with gloats and sarcasm: "Not much you can do! One can't always be lucky enough to arrive first on the scene."[51] Within days it became clear that Grison had landed a major blow, and the skin affair was under way. The details of the story were quickly confirmed as Grison had reported them: A leatherworker in the rue de la Verrerie, whose initials he gave as M.D., received a peculiar visit from a customer with a "military look" just a few days after Pranzini's execution. The customer handed over a floe of treated flesh that was "very white and very supple" and requested that two card holders be made from it. M.D. asked about the skin's provenance. The skin was Pranzini's, said the client, smiling as he handed over his calling card: Gustave Rossignol. Five days later, Rossignol returned to recover the card holders. He paid 15 francs for the service—inexpensive, in Grison's opinion: "Certainly there are Americans who wouldn't mind adding two or three zeroes to that figure to buy a curio like this."[52]

Even those in the press who viewed the piece as sensationalist fluff conceded that the Parisian public opinion was "violently upset" by it. There were rumors that Pranzini's skull was being reused as a punch bowl.[53] "This is the first scandal of its kind—ever," observed *La Justice*, whose men were busy poring over law books to find an infraction corresponding to what the men at Security had done.[54] Graphic descriptions of the card holders appeared in the press, shaded with dark humor. *Le Gaulois* commented that the card holders resembled standard leatherwork—"same cracks, same *goose bumps*. They smell like musk and are lined with a prosaic, shop-soiled satin. The leather is mottled with stains like those seen on old ivory; it looks as though the skin was still too fresh to be tanned satisfactorily."[55]

Elsewhere in Europe, the corpse's skinning was interpreted as an alarming sign of civilization's decline. The Hungarian physician and critic Max Nordau, in his landmark diatribe *Degeneration* (1892), wrote that the policemen responsible for Pranzini's flaying stood as early exemplars of fin-de-siècle decadence. In literature it became a scene-setting device, a note of banalized horror enmeshed in everyday life. For example, the novelist Alphonse Daudet sketched a fictional interior located near the Medical School of Paris.

> The smoking-room at that time was a small apartment on the second floor of the building on Rue des Écoles, with hangings of écru linen with Turkey red border; on the walls were divers black-framed lithographs representing romantic subjects, presented by the directors of the Beaux-arts. Crippled, broken-seated chairs stood against the walls. On the mantel, a long-necked bottle of spirit of wine, in which swam a bit of Pranzini the Levantine's skin, served as a pendant to the bust of Chevreul, disfigured by the scratching of many matches on the nose of the first French student.[56]

The national government was caught completely off guard. Cabinet ministers, still away on summer holidays when the story broke, scrambled to take action. Eugène Spuller, minister of education, ordered that the card holders be turned over to the public prosecutor and that Taylor, Goron, and Rossignol be fired. The interior minister, Armand Fallières, informed the Council of Ministers that the Paris Police Prefecture would be investigating all three policemen on suspicion of "violation of a grave," a plainly ill-fitted charge, given that the corpse never saw the inside of a grave.[57]

The internal investigation opened by the Ministry of Justice was an unpalatable embarrassment for Security, and it was a sign that the Pranzini execution had raised uncomfortable questions about crime and punishment. The skinning, opined a journalist, brought to mind the old justice system, a punitive regime with no place in modern society, *except* in the case of a "scoundrel" like Pranzini.[58] Herein lay the tension between the legal status of the executed criminal body and the unstable meaning of *this* criminal body about which so much ink had been spilled.

The ensuing public debate was based on the shared assumption that the skinning was a form of postmortem punishment. The policemen's actions were an affront to those, like Grévy, who favored "sobriety" in capital punishment and who saw in the guillotine a means of eliminating all physical suffering and therefore of targeting not the criminal's body but his soul. To them, "humane" execution meant the painless mechanical extraction of life in an "instantaneous event," the guillotine's trigger mechanism signaling the elimination of "contact between the law, or those who carry it out," and the condemned man's body.[59]

But the skin affair illustrates how the principles of sobriety gave rise to an intractable conundrum, which the sociologist David Garland identified as the "problem of the body." In modern capital punishment, Garland writes, the physical body "is the unavoidable *object* of state punishment even when it is avowedly not punishment's *target*."[60] The traditions of public mutilation and torture may have declined during the nineteenth century, but contemporaries, who did not agree about what happened to the soul at the moment of death, continued to leave the deceased convict's body in the hands of an expanding cast of state actors: doctors and autopsists, policemen, anthropologists, medical students, and low-level medical school staff, to name a few. To assert that Pranzini was the sort of scoundrel who merited postmortem punishment was to acknowledge that the prerogative to punish was somehow bound up in the investigative practices of these actors, who ascribed meaning to criminal bodies in death. On August 31, 1887, their rivalries spilled into the afterlife.

Pranzini's corpse was still warm when it arrived at the Medical School of Paris at 6 a.m. Standing by were Drs. Brouardel, Variot, Launois, and Chatelier, the staff in charge of preparing the body for preservation and study, and a few journalists with good connections. When the corpse was set on a zinc examination table, Dr. Brouardel prepared to cut, exclaiming, "This was a beautiful male!"[61]

Working on a separate register, the anatomy lesson would provide gravitas to the colonial stereotypes applied to Pranzini's body by the press without fundamentally departing from them: As with the Levantine and rastaquouère stereotypes, there existed a body of received ideas readily imported from the colonial world to be borrowed by anatomists. Medical studies of "colonized bodies"—that is, bodies located in colonial settings—had traditionally held other races to be "symbolic inversions" of the European ideal.[62] Predictably, Pranzini's Levantine anatomy was a study in fusions; it was understood by the doctors as an erotic ideal, one whose perversions could be found in its Oriental traits. The men gathered around Pranzini's corpse found in it Western virility, Oriental femininity, and African features and genitalia. The hands and feet were of a "great fineness," observed one journalist, adding that he resembled a *mulâtre*, a term commonly used for colonial people of mixed European and African ancestry: a "square forehead, flat cheekbones, short nose with spaced nostrils, thick and sensual lips."[63] Lab aides began cutting. "One of his organs, so to speak, had become legendary," wrote a journalist present; doctors were prepared with a large container to preserve Pranzini's penis.[64] They took two fingers from the right hand, the index from the left hand, the nerves from the arms, the spleen, the belly button—all of these were dropped into labeled containers filled with alcohol, destined for display cases.[65]

The society journalist Hugues Le Roux stood in awe of the headless cadaver on the examination table before him.

> He is beautiful—a beauty of incomparable forms. We have never seen a model of this purity and plenitude of line. The chest bulges and has the width of an organ buffet, the arms and shoulders are those of a fighter. The hips are straight, the legs have the harmonious grace of Antinous. The hands hang from the end of the arms, almost femininely, with fingers turned inward, lightly pointing. . . . As my gaze fell upon this superb being that lay there, I thought of that troubling passage from Renan's *Marcus Aurelius* about "the beauty that was equal to virtue."[66]

Pranzini's erotically charged anatomy reflected classical beauty but with hints of femininity and temptation for women and men alike.

Dr. Variot made an earnest attempt to cool the obsession with Pranzini's genitalia. Yes, he conceded, Pranzini's penis was "above-average in size," but it was, in death at least, "far from the colossal dimensions" of which reporters, following Dr. Brouardel's lead, were apprising their readers.[67] While the doctors squabbled, the colonial antihero set itself deep in the French imagination, the myth of his hypersexuality spilling into the fiction of Zola and the avant-garde alike. Writing several years later about the protagonist of

Alfred Jarry's *Le surmâle* (The Supermale), a force of nature who is able to copulate dozens of times in succession, one literary critic reached for points of mythical comparison: Jarry's character was a "Pranzini gigantesque," a "modern Hercules."[68]

In a mirroring of the institutional competition that had defined the Pranzini investigation, scientific and belletristic accounts of Pranzini's anatomy originated among a handful of elites on the third floor of the Medical School of Paris. That was where the prized parts of the cadaver were removed for placement in the nation's collections. Anthropologists and medical researchers placed the highest value on skulls and skeletons, always making sure to claim these first.[69] On the lower rungs of the investigative apparatus, policemen and crime reporters were left to rummage through the cadaver scraps downstairs in the dissection amphitheater.

Rossignol went down to the amphitheater the day after the execution to look for a memento because Goron asked him to do so, but Rossignol took credit for the idea he hit upon once he arrived. With the help of a worker, he sliced flesh from Pranzini's torso, which had been discarded and was sitting on the floor.

Goron happily received the finished card holder. He also insisted that Rossignol give one to Chief Taylor, who by all accounts had no interest in it and only reluctantly accepted it. None of three men believed that they were getting away with something offensive, and all were shocked to find their police careers jeopardized after critics in the press likened their actions to the violence and trophy collection of the colonial frontier. "In any case, the dignity of Justice is not consonant with such an act of cannibalism, and it must not go unpunished," charged the conservative Catholic daily *La Croix*.[70] The editorialist Albert Wolff, who also covered the trial for *Le Figaro*, hoped that fellow Europeans would find the "burlesque side" of the card holder scandal—it is "infinitely better for us than to pass for the last of the savages who make trinkets out of the skin of executed men, like the Redskins who fashion belts from the hair of the *petits blancs* that they've scalped."[71] Wolff's readers surely caught the biting reversal in this play on words: Pranzini was a colonial *petit blanc*; the policemen, savages.

It became a motif: The civilized had been overcome by savagery, or rather, the veil of French *civilisation* had been lifted, exposing the Other beneath. "If Pranzini's body had needed to be reconstituted, there would have been trouble," Rossignol responded years later, still bitter. Goron and

Rossignol never forgot Grison's role in igniting the scandal, which to them was every bit as hypocritical as the condemnations of government ministers and highbrow *chroniquers*. "One journalist took an ear, another a finger, a third a lip—everyone took a little, with a preference for thigh skin," remembered Rossignol. Still, consciously or not, his objections to the government inquiry that made him a criminal suspect do reinforce the imagery of colonial violence for which he remained unapologetic and to which his own overseas soldiering might have inured him. When a police commissary came around to ask Rossignol about rumors that other scraps of Pranzini's skin were being treated at local tanneries, he went mum. "I made quite sure not to tell him anything, or else he would have also found the skin of the thighs of a Negro [*nègre*] that [an amphitheater aide] was tanning in order to make slippers!"[72]

The job of defending Security fell to Taylor and Goron, who were appalled by the feigned horror of their supposed moral superiors. Later, in a thinly veiled swipe at Dr. Brouardel, Goron ridiculed the "very distinguished savant" who performed tests on guillotined heads to determine how long they retained consciousness. It was self-evident, wrote Goron, that a man whose body is "violently separated" from his torso is "incapable of expressing his opinion on the events of the day!"[73] In the immediate term, however, the deputy chief waited in the wings and let Taylor do the talking. The chief lashed out at the press amid further speculation about his job security: "They want to demolish me, and they'll use any pretext to do it."[74]

Then something quite strange and entirely unpredictable occurred. Taylor and Goron found an ally in Georges Grison.

Having watched his great scoop gnaw at the public's conscience for nine days, Grison abruptly stepped away from it—not the facts of the story but his decision to report on them. On September 23 his column contained a shocking mea culpa, which read in part, "We recounted—and we now recognize that we were wrong to do so—that two card holders were confected." In what reads like a personal awakening to the power of his humble *fait-divers* column to shape history, Grison admitted that he never "expected this type of noise" to come from the skin story, let alone the damage it was doing to Security, an institution to which he, despite his own vitriol, remained fundamentally sympathetic.[75]

Why would Grison reverse course so abruptly? It seems likely that, as the story spun out of control and reached the Elysée Palace, Grison and his editors made some larger political calculations. The police were the public face of the Third Republic, which suddenly appeared weakened by the Boulangists. Grison's own *Le Figaro* was well aligned with Grévy's conservative republican centrism, and his superiors were probably dismayed to find that the skin affair made easy fodder for antirepublican and anti-Grévy outlets like *La Croix*, which undertook a brief but biting campaign against Goron as a direct result of Grison's scoop.[76]

It was Grison who tried gamely to put Pranzini's desecration into perspective by pointing to the ambiguity between accepted forms of anatomical research (scientific and medical) and the more informal ones to which the police had resorted—in short, between high and low collecting. "Many well-known people—government functionaries even—possess objects made from executed criminals," he offered, and "guillotined skulls have found their place in private collections" in the past.[77] And he had a point. For centuries the criminal body had been the object of investigations that sought to impose meanings on it by finding evidence in it, for example, of a criminal spirit or "nature" or of other abstractions such as "monstrosity."[78] Picking over the cadavers of executed criminals for mementos was a normalized, if hidden, practice, even an established tradition.[79] Troppmann's execution had been no different.[80] Put another way, it was not the desecration that was new but rather the *publicizing* of it, as the press reached another frontier in the investigative imagination. Surely some in the *Figaro* newsroom recalled the last time rumors spread after an execution. It was four years earlier, when *Le Figaro* reported that the skin of Campi, another of the shape-shifting "lords of crime," was said to have been used by someone at the Société d'anthropologie to bind a book.[81] Nevertheless, Grison's mea culpa appeared too late to have any effect.

Staring at the real possibility of termination—the end of the only career at which he had excelled—Goron took it upon himself to strike back at the government ministers and investigators who were bearing down on him. Unlike Taylor, he understood that the press offered the only way out, provided that it was mobilized wisely and subtly—that is, without engaging in an unwinnable public showdown with hostile reporters who controlled the terms of the discussion, as Taylor seemed resigned to do.

Goron worked behind the scenes. He had a childhood friend in the popular-science writer Émile Gautier, who happened to write a biweekly column for the daily *Le XIXᵉ Siècle*. With Gautier's help, Goron concocted an opinion piece defending the policemen involved in the scandal and urging that they not become Pranzini's posthumous "victims." The newspaper's political director, Édouard Portalis, agreed to run the piece unsigned, on September 23, under the title "The Skin of the Monster."[82] A few days later, Gautier came to Portalis with another column he had co-written with Goron. This one explicitly credited Goron for Pranzini's arrest and lauded the deputy chief's rapid climb through the ranks at Security. It mentioned Goron's feats in South America, in a region where, according to the article, he had participated in the first colonization by Europeans in history. The article called attention to the military service of both Goron and Rossignol and highlighted that Rossignol was the descendant of a military "dynasty" of several generations who, like all his colleagues at Security, were military veterans. Strikingly, the article made no attempt to defend Chief Taylor. To the contrary, its title, "Two Accused," completely omitted Taylor's name.[83] Goron seems to have seen a professional opportunity for himself, so long as he weathered the crisis.

In addition to these defensive maneuvers, Goron devised an aggressive strategy that the right-wing writer Maurice Barrès would later summarize in a semifictional recounting of Goron's chosen course: "It was necessary to stifle one scandal with another that was worse."[84] What occurred during the next four weeks is an oft-told tale of unintended consequences that brought down the government. But until now, historians have not shed light on the crucial link between the skin affair and the scandal that felled Daniel Wilson and President Jules Grévy by early December 1887.[85]

Near the end of September, an anonymous letter stating that a person who managed a prostitution ring near the Champs-Elysées, a certain Madame Limouzin, was involved with German officers and spies in France. This was the secret denunciation that would trigger a major uproar. Goron went to Madame Limouzin's place in the avenue de Wagram. He saw no evidence of espionage, but he *did* find the calling cards of several illustrious figures, including that of Daniel Wilson. He also hit upon evidence to suggest that Limouzin was serving as a conduit to corrupt government officials who were selling government awards, or *décorations*, for personal gain. Goron could use this to strike back at his superiors in the government. But launching an official investigation in this political climate would have taken the kind of time that he no longer had. So he conceived an undercover sting operation with plausible deniability: Although a variety of sources credit him with the scandalous investigation that followed, Goron writes preposterously that he was thrust into the role of henchman because Taylor was out ill on the day—September 29, 1887—that the denunciation letter alerted the police prefect to the corruption.[86]

Goron first sent an officer, who posed as a silk dealer from the provinces, to inquire with Limouzin about procuring government honors. Limouzin introduced the officer to General Caffarel, a high-ranking official at the Ministry of War and a former surrogate of General Boulanger. Goron appeared to have his man. He took his findings to the prefect of police, Taylor's boss; the prefect went to the very top of the government, Maurice Rouvier, head of the Council of Ministers. Rouvier received Goron's report with a cool warning to "proceed with the greatest discretion," because it was unclear what advantage the Boulangists might draw from the situation. The prefect agreed, and the war minister, General Ferron, promised an in-house disciplinary action against Caffarel. That way the matter would be kept from public view.[87]

The cover-up meant that Goron needed something far more disruptive. He returned to Gautier, and the two concocted an article that turned the political establishment on its head.[88] "Décorations Trafficking at the Ministry of War," shouted the front page of Le XIXᵉ Siècle on October 8, 1887, below which an unsigned article insinuated that traitors were at work. The article pointed to army officers, government officials, and "cosmopolitan adventurers" who were conspiring in the lucrative sale of entry into France's Legion of Honor, and it demanded that official inquiries be made. This time there was no way to shut the press out. Within days General Caffarel confessed to participating in the corruption; he was handed a pistol by his superiors (a tradition allowing a doomed man the chance to commit suicide) and left his post. A parliamentary inquiry was launched. It found that Wilson sat atop a bureaucracy of corruption, which he ran from his perch at the presidential palace.

Wilson was clear-eyed about who was to blame for his impending demise. In a letter to Alice Wilson, he named Deputy Chief Goron as the "author of the leaks." Goron was doing everything he could to "favourably impress public opinion" after his implication in the skin affair.[89] President Grévy intervened to help his son-in-law, a misstep that brought him into the bad graces of the press. Pranzini's autopsist, Dr. Variot, recalled the firestorm several decades later: "At the time we viewed the *décorations* affair as a defensive action by the police, who pulled themselves out of a difficult position. I often heard it said that Monsieur Grévy had slipped on Pranzini's skin."[90]

Grévy was obliged to resign his beloved presidency. He died within a few years. Wilson was criminally charged and sentenced to prison (and later acquitted on appeal). The cabinet was entirely reshuffled. The police prefect Arthur Gragnon, being pushed out, officially resigned. Ernest Taylor was removed from his leadership role and relegated to bureaucratic work for the rest of his career. He did not speak publicly of the skin affair again; but in a cruel twist, when he died two decades later, the obituaries credited him for mounting the massive scandal.[91]

Rossignol retained his post, and Goron was promoted to chief of Security.[92] And the list went on. The editor Portalis surveyed the damages. Not only had the Rouvier government resigned, but the return of General Boulanger, who had been neutralized and kept at a remove from the action since July, suddenly seemed a foregone conclusion. Left behind to pick up the pieces was Sadi Carnot, "whom nobody, without the Wilson affair, would have imagined president of the Republic." Before too long, Boulanger would be back in Paris, well positioned for a coup d'état. "The things that shape the destinies of republics! No author of fairy tales would dare grant a talisman power equal to that of the card holders made from Pranzini's skin."[93]

RATHER UNEXPECTEDLY, the skin affair marked a turning point in the history of the death penalty in Paris, according to Goron. To illustrate the point, Goron told the story of Prado (aka Count Linska de Castillon), another rastaquouère whose case was "kind of complementary to the Pranzini affair." Prado was convicted of the 1886 murder of Marie Aguétant, a crime for which Pranzini had been briefly suspected. He was "like a bandit of the savannah who had found his way to the boulevard."[94]

Following his being sentenced to death in 1888, Prado made it clear that he had heard all about the card holders and, disquieted, he rose on the morning of his execution decrying the "butchery" that awaited him. Before Goron, Prado made a formal declaration: "I hereby demand that my body be buried in the ground and not subjected to the experiments of the medical faculty."[95] Nonetheless, when his headless corpse was delivered to the Ivry Cemetery that December morning, a medical school representative was there to recover it and bring it to the amphitheater for dissection. Perplexed, standing in the morning darkness and bereft of protocol, Goron ruled in favor of the deceased criminal and stood astride the gravesite to deny access to it. "Dispute over a cadaver," announced a Parisian newspaper, as more murky legal territory came into view. Like fellow "lords of crime" of foreign origin, Prado had no relatives in France to claim his body. Who should have the final say in the handling of his corpse in this case? "This is the first time—believe us—that an issue like this has taken place," commented a journalist. In his report Goron explained his reasoning thusly: "Even if the body was not claimed by the family, Prado claimed it for himself." The medical school dashed off a letter of protest but was overruled. Prado's remains "were placed in a pine coffin and buried in an unoccupied area bordering on the avenue du Sud."[96] It was subsequently ruled that the "obligatory dismemberment was an aggravation of the death penalty that was unforeseen by the law," and, Goron affirmed, the Medical School of Paris never again disputed an executed prisoner's request for proper burial.[97] Goron ensured that his tenure as chief, which lasted seven years, did not see another skin affair.[98]

Conclusion

On Imperial Insecurity

> Art thou not, fatal vision, sensible
> To feeling as to sight? or art thou but
> A dagger of the mind, a false creation,
> Proceeding from the heat-oppressed brain?
>
> —Shakespeare, *Macbeth*, Act 2, Scene 1

> His past is mysterious, must have already been thrown out of foreign stock exchanges. Doesn't speak of where he came from. We believe— or at least he says—that he was born in Alexandria. One senses in him the mix of Italian blood with Turkish blood. Very pleasing to women, vaguely kept by them.
>
> —Émile Zola, archived research notes for the character Sabatini, a Levantine migrant in the novel *Money*[1]

During the Pranzini case, the cultural imagination of the cosmopolitan co-lonial as criminal, like similar myths about Jews, freemasons, and socialists, took hold in a political environment that colonial expansionism itself had, in some measure, destabilized.

The right-wing nationalism that emerged in France in the late 1880s aimed to exclude or efface regional or composite identities, secure border integrity, and strictly define citizenship, often in the exclusive terms of race. Colonial empire was bound to complicate these issues, both abstractly and in the realm of policy, not least because empires are by nature ceaselessly reshaping their boundaries and posing new questions. Rather than resolving

security issues through an offensive engagement with the world, France's republican empire appeared to extend itself to the point of dissolving the security, if mostly symbolic, of fixed political borders.[2] To put it in the parlance
of the early Third Republic, the nationalists' policy of *recueillement*, meaning
a kind of contemplative pause, was invested in border security; and, as em-
braced by a range of politicians, including influential republicans, it sought
the consolidation of French strength for another war with Germany. The
movement fantasized about walling off the country from suspect forms of
immigration and foreign infiltration—a sort of locked-room nation. That
the modern French fixation on spies and enemies within began during this
period seems, in retrospect, a predetermined outcome of this fantasy.[3]

The political fallout of the Pranzini affair made manifest the costs of
trying to establish global dominion *and* securing the borders at the same
time. This was essentially the position that Léon Gambetta tried to stake
out: After years of advocating *recueillement*, he allied with Jules Ferry and
began to pretend that that policy could be integrated into a pro-colonialist
agenda.[4] Despite imperialism's obvious appeal to nationalist pride and its
supreme capacity to tap into popular anger and the bitterness that more
manifestly drove the revanchists, it could never overcome the essential con-
tradictions of Gambetta's course.

Ferry learned the hard way that, for all the security that colonial empire
promised, the policy did not keep its greatest proponents safe; soon enough,
Ferry was brought down by the colonial paranoia festering beneath the mar-
quee of national pride. In March 1885 news reports mistakenly overstated
the extent of a French military setback in Lang Son (modern northern Viet-
nam). Although the misinformation was rapidly corrected, the stock market
trembled and Ferry came under fierce attack in the Chamber of Deputies.
Could France's honor truly be at stake in Southeast Asia? With his reputation soiled by the specter of imperial failure, Ferry was ousted and never
governed again. Recall that his ally, Charles de Freycinet, had suffered a
similar fate after the loss of Egypt in 1882 (though he later staged a come-
back). Following Ferry's departure, critics latched onto a durable slogan:
l'affairisme colonial, with its suggestions of unpunished graft and lawlessness in the colonial empire.[5] It hung over Ferry and stained his legacy. By
happenstance, he was traveling in Algeria in the spring of 1887 when the
Pranzini case made news; back in Paris, Henri Rochefort, then a vocal an-
ticolonialist, hurled the epithet "Pranzini" at the disgraced Opportunist.[6]

I have tried to emphasize the links between the colonial and the criminal imaginaries. It was no mere coincidence that the republicans' debate over colonial policy in the first half of the 1880s ran concurrently with their debates over the criminal justice system, still less that these parliamentary clashes pitted two coalitions against each other. Georges Clémenceau and others on the left thrashed the Opportunists Ferry, Gambetta, and Pierre Waldeck-Rousseau, who sought to radically harshen criminal punishment by expanding France's penal colonies abroad. With popular fears in mind, Gambetta made "order" a watchword for the republicans in the 1870s and 1880s and inflated the "army of crime," a capacious category into which critics eagerly tossed Pranzini.[7] The simultaneous dialogues over colonial policy and anticrime measures naturally bled into each other.[8]

Even though recent research has chronicled the horrors of the French penal colonies overseas, historians of Paris lack a conceptual framework for capturing the early shocks felt in the metropole as a result of this intersection of the crime issue with that of colonialism. Imperial insecurity, an underexplored concept used occasionally and diffusely by literary historians of the British Empire, offers a means of historicizing this phenomenon in the Parisian context of the latter years of the nineteenth century, when *insécurité urbaine* became a motif in the press and in political discourse.

In the British case, imperial insecurity corresponds to the sense of fragility that came, paradoxically, with Britain's global hegemony in the 1880s. A rather amusing example of its usage can be found in London's response to the British seizure of Egypt from the French in 1882. As Britain, at last the putative winner of a long struggle, began its military occupation and governorship there, Prime Minister William Gladstone began to fret that "with a great Empire in each of the four corners of the world we may be territorially content, but less than ever at our ease."[9] Within the span of a lifetime, the British Empire was a dead elephant; so too was its French rival. Lest this observation be attributed to the relative clarity of hindsight, consider critics such as J. A. Hobson, a contemporary of Gladstone's who concluded that empire was a losing game for the British, save for the strident, hawkish investors among them.[10]

Even Gabriel Tarde, the robust supporter of empire who believed colonial warfare would help attenuate the alleged crime problem, came to regret that in his own era, admittedly rife with militarism, criminality would not likely diminish in proportion to France's buildup of weaponry, if it diminished at all.[11] Tarde's sunny optimism was checked by the Pranzini case, which, he acknowledged, had driven home the inevitable collapsing of space that came with globalizing empires; like barnacles on a steamer, colonial elements would return to the metropole. In Pranzini's case the implications were far-reaching.

In archived notes that Tarde took in October 1887, we find the criminologist's immediate reaction to the case of the murders in the rue Montaigne. Tarde looked on the migrant Pranzini as a symbol of imperial failure and collapse, that awful landscape of "lost colonies" around the world that loomed over every colonial rebirth.[12] Tarde's notes revisit past traumas of colonial violence that had reverberated back home. He likened the rue Montaigne case to the invasion of Napoleonic France by the Allied powers of Europe—a reverse colonization with a sexual dimension. Specifically, Tarde recalled the mass sexual violation of French women that followed Napoleon's defeat: "these Cossacks, these Prussians in great number who, in 1814, raped women and then slashed their throats in front of their husbands."[13] Like Pranzini, Allied soldiers had the markings of respectability: "More than one had surely, [like Pranzini], earned their military medal." The only substantive difference was that "Pranzini was alone."[14] Tarde indicated that these reflections on Pranzini were inspired by the work of the respected historian Henry Houssaye, especially an article in which Houssaye made reference to the continuing cycles of defeat that France had suffered (in 1709 and 1814), as though to identify the merciless course of empire, "these terrible futures that victories have, the sudden and ferocious reversals when good fortune runs out."[15] Tarde clearly understood that the *république coloniale* would suffer these unkind reversals too. Yet he did not come close to renouncing the imperial project.

In the meantime, imperial insecurity had serious ramifications in politics and legislation. The overlapping of the colonial and the criminal imaginaries proved a burden for French liberalism, which, like liberal currents elsewhere in Europe during the Age of Empire, entered a long period of crisis beginning in the late 1880s.[16] Rather than putting the public's mind at ease about security, the Opportunists, bafflingly, talked up the public crime epidemic *while in office*, thereby appearing to highlight their own insufficiencies, forcing themselves into regrettable legislative decisions, and gift wrapping a weapon that the New Right would turn against them.

One consequence of these decisions was on the issue of firearms, which brought together an international economic dimension, national security, and urban security. The left wing of the republican family, soon to turn Boulangist, found an angle to attack the Opportunists when Clémenceau's parliamentary colleague, Eugène Farcy, began pushing a program to boost the French arms industry in the global marketplace. Farcy wished for a total deregulation of the production and sale of guns in France in order to develop the domestic market. (Ferry, in principle a supporter of gun exportation, blanched at the idea of arming the citizenry.) On the floor of the Chamber of Deputies in the mid-1880s, Farcy charged that if there had been more armed marksmen at the French border, the Prussian army "would not have taken our defenseless big cities" so easily; in the same breath he complained that criminals "kill in broad daylight on the boulevards" with revolvers, while the "good citizens who follow the law have none to defend themselves." In Farcy's opinion the blame for urban crime belonged to Ferry's leadership: "I cannot understand how the government, incapable of enforcing existing laws when it comes to criminals, wants only to create restrictions for law-abiding people."[17] The Farcy law was adopted in August 1885, and guns flooded French cities, if government statistics are an accurate indication: In the thirty years between 1877 and 1907, the minister of justice recorded an 850% increase in gun-related crime.[18]

As a political cudgel, imperial insecurity also had lasting policy implications for the question of immigration. The 1880s saw a long and concerted attempt to establish tighter immigration controls. This took place within a years-long transformation in the bureaucratic and police treatment of migrants. Once again, the Pranzini affair provided the jolt, as evidenced by the infamous Pradon Report submitted to the Chamber of Deputies in February 1888. Named for its sponsor, republican deputy Christophe Pradon, the report strengthened the growing consensus that immigrants were getting away with crime and that the arrival of immigrant workers was best thought of as an "invasion."[19] In language that was bolder than its predecessors, the Pradon Report dramatically framed immigration as a "problem." The document has rightly been identified as a foundational text in the history of political xenophobia in France; it served as the basis for immigration control under the Third, Fourth, and Fifth Republics.[20] The Pradon Report connected immigration to empire, identification, and criminality. "All the great empires," it warned, needed to adjust to the flow of foreign populations across political boundaries.

Enrico Pranzini enters the French parliamentary record on the report's fifth page, in an allusion to the "pack of crimes" for which he was *incorrectly* suspected immediately after his arrest. In an ironic twist the report's oblique reference to the unsolved prostitute murders of Paris flows into the conclusion that greater surveillance of immigrants and proper identification procedures could have prevented unfounded suspicions of Pranzini. The text continues with phrases that could have been lifted from the progenitors—crime reporters, policemen, scientists, and authors—of the Levantine-rastaquouère, the original colonial criminal archetype.

> Paris receives the social dregs of two continents. An entire troublesome society of exotic adventurers of nondescript professions—the regular clientele of the criminal courts—convenes here. . . . The *fait-divers* columns of our newspapers are full of the tales of their sinister exploits and bloody frays. It's as though they popped out of the ground, suddenly, at the time and place of the crime and disappeared just as soon, having pulled off the act. Of their past, we know nothing. Their names, the first clue to identity and social labeling, are uncertain. They change them as needed.[21]

The Pradon Report's ratification some months later may have owed something to the intuition that, following Pranzini, future generations of colonial migrants might come from much farther afield. The report effectively criminalized these people in advance of their arrival on French shores.

As the archetype of the colonial migrant-criminal who impersonates the lifestyle of an honorable man, Pranzini resonated far beyond the halls of political power. French and British literature from the 1880s and after did not tire of this archetype. One thinks of the upper-class bearing and tastes of E. W. Hornung's stellar thief, Raffles, and of Pierre Souvestre and Marcel Allain's hugely successful *Fantômas* franchise. In both series, expertly criminal characters return from the colonial lands of Africa and Asia to outsmart metropolitan police.[22] The attributes that made Raffles and Fantômas so electrifying to contemporary readers—indifference to violence, a bottomless supply of aliases, upper-class appearances, use of modern technologies and transportation as a means of escape[23]—had, of course, distinguished the first generation of "lords of crime" in 1880s Paris.

The inability of the police ever to identify Fantômas made him the ideal literary foil for Alphonse Bertillon's "scientific" system of criminal identification in Paris, just as suspects like Pranzini were supposed to have demonstrated the clear need for *bertillonage*. When the *Fantômas* series begins, Souvestre and Allain's antihero is an accomplished seducer of women who has returned to France after some adventures in the colonial world, including service in the British imperial war effort in Africa. Like Raffles, Fantômas is a veteran of the Boer Wars. Thus these stories appear to suggest—and Goron certainly agreed—that colonial knowledge, particularly experience in colonial war, was a prerequisite for the modern sleuth at work in the metropole. In Arthur Conan Doyle's *A Study in Scarlet* (1886), the inaugural Sherlock Holmes story, Dr. Watson recalls the "misfortune and disaster" he personally suffered in the Second Anglo-Afghan War before his return to more beneficial work in London, "that great cesspool into which all the loungers and idlers of the Empire are irresistibly drained."[24]

None of this is to speculate, of course, that the Pranzini affair directly inspired these characters or plots. After all, it was not a *factual* mastery of disguises on Pranzini's part that made him so threatening; to the contrary, his petty thievery and minor brushes with the law are congruous with an utter lack of criminal talent. What the Levantine archetype, and the fictional criminals cited earlier, had the power to do was blend into metropolitan society *too well*. Antonin Proust's widely read contribution to *Les types de Paris*, a volume published in anticipation of the 1889 World's Fair (also the year of France's first nationality law), begins a long-winded discussion of foreigners in Paris with Enrico Pranzini. The "seductive Levantine," Proust writes, "is the foremost illustration of how easy it can be to remake oneself in Paris."[25]

In accordance with stereotypes, fictional Levantines encapsulated, in terms of social class, an array of criminal activity, including what the twentieth century would call white-collar crime. In the immediate wake of the Pranzini affair, Émile Zola linked the small-time colonial criminal and the colonial financial rogue in his stock market crime novel *Money*. Financial skulduggery and colonial migration are seamlessly blended in Sabatini, an erotically charged Levantine of "Italian and Oriental mix." In an effort to render the activities of the stock market as un-French as possible (Zola famously never purchased a stock), the author uses racist caricatures of Jews; his research notes show that he originally conceived Sabatini as the partner in crime of a Jewish crook.

Sabatini is depicted as a well-hung recidivist of uncertain origins whose underhanded dealings led him to different international stock exchanges before his arrival in Paris. His gauzy charm works like a cloaking device. He serves as Aristide Saccard's "strawman" stock manipulator, and the two facilitate sham investments in the Levant. The inevitable disintegration follows and with it the ruin of small-time investors across the nation. In contrast to Pranzini, however, the fictional fraudsters manage to escape punishment for their crimes; at the end of *Money* both Saccard and Sabatani have made it across the French border, free to start over.[26] Zola's novel proposes that Parisians, believing that they can profit from such colonial enterprises in the East *and* keep the likes of Saccard and Sabatini in check, are in over their heads.

Notes

Notes to Introduction

1. Archives de Paris, D2 U8 223. Unless otherwise noted, all translations are my own.

2. *Daily Telegraph*, 2 October 1888.

3. Like their Parisian counterparts, Londoners looked to crime fiction for clues: the tales of Poe and Stevenson and the "stealthy and cunning assassins" conjured up by the pioneering French crime novelist Émile Gaboriau and his acolyte, Fortuné du Boisgobey. *Lloyd's Weekly News*, 7 October 1888, quoted in Judith R. Walkowitz, "Jack the Ripper and the Myth of Male Violence," *Feminist Studies* 8, no. 3 (1982): 550. Robin Odell, *Ripperology: A Study of the World's First Serial Killer and Literary Phenomenon* (Kent, OH: Kent State University Press, 2006).

4. Dominique Kalifa, *L'encre et le sang: récits de crimes et société à la Belle Epoque* (Paris: Fayard, 1995). As it will become clear, Kalifa's vast and innovative historical analysis of the themes of crime, policing, the press, modern investigation, the social imaginary, and colonialism is crucial to this study.

5. Judith R. Walkowitz, *City of Dreadful Delight: Narratives of Sexual Danger in Late-Victorian London* (Chicago: University of Chicago Press, 1992), 25–26.

6. For a history of French citizenship, see Gérard Noiriel, *The French Melting Pot: Immigration, Citizenship, and National Identity*, trans. Geoffroy de Laforcade (Minneapolis: University of Minnesota Press, 1996); and Gérard Noiriel, *Immigration, antisémitisme et racisme en France (XIXe–XXe siècle): discours publics, humiliations privées* (Paris: Fayard, 2007).

7. *Le Gaulois*, 17 July 1887.

8. A number of works have explored Paris's reputation as a site of sexual deviance in the nineteenth century. See Hollis Clayson, *Painted Love: Prostitution in French Art of the Impressionist Era* (New Haven, CT: Yale University Press, 1991); Alain Corbin, *Women for Hire: Prostitution and Sexuality in France After 1850*, trans. Alan Sheridan (Cambridge, MA: Harvard University Press, 1990); Gert Hekma, "Same-Sex Relations Among Men in Europe, 1700–1900," in Franz X. Eder, Leslie Hall, and Gert Hekma, eds., *Sexual Cultures in Europe: Themes in Sexuality* (Manchester: Manchester University Press, 1999), 79–103; Lynn Hunt, ed., *The Invention of*

Pornography (New York: Zone Books, 1993); and Catherine van Casselaer, *Lot's Wife: Lesbian Paris, 1890–1914* (Liverpool: Janus Press, 1986).

9. Paul Gauguin, *Avant et après* (Paris: G. Crès, 1923), 177–78. For a more detailed version of this story, see Martin Gayford, *The Yellow House: Van Gogh, Gauguin, and Nine Turbulent Weeks in Arles* (New York: Fig Tree, 2006).

10. L. Curtis, *Jack the Ripper and the London Press* (New Haven, CT: Yale University Press, 2008), 79n64.

11. In English, nary a scholarly work has been published on Pranzini. The story has been told in different media in France, where it has also been fictionalized in a variety of ways. The Baron de Rothschild, a medical student in 1887, wrote a detailed firsthand account of the murders several decades after the fact; there have been popular histories and French TV reenactments and theater pieces, in addition to a recent historical novel. See Pierre Bouchardon, *L'affaire Pranzini* (Paris: Albin Michel, 1934); Alicia Croci, "Naissance de l'enquête journalistique: l'affaire Pranzini," Master's thesis, University of Paris I–Sorbonne, 2005; Paul Lorenz, *L'affaire Pranzini* (Paris: Rombaldi, 1974); André Mure, *La courtisane assassinée: affaire Pranzini* (Paris: Éditions de la Flamme d'Or, 1955); and Henri de Rothschild, *Pranzini: le crime de la rue Montaigne* (Paris: Émile-Paul Frères, 1933). The lone professional historian to write about the case has been Frédéric Chauvaud, "Le triple assassinat de la rue Montaigne: le sacre du fait divers," *Annales de Bretagne et des Pays de l'Ouest* 116, no. 1 (2009): 13–28.

12. I do not mean to imply that transnational criminality, or the investigation thereof, began in this period, though the scale of it changed. For a fascinating work linking smuggling, commerce, and law enforcement in eighteenth-century France, see Michael Kwass, *Contraband: Louis Mandrin and the Making of a Global Underground* (Cambridge, MA: Harvard University Press, 2014).

13. The term *Levantine* was, by the late nineteenth century, predominantly a racially charged exonym, as was the term *rastaquouère*. The fictions and realities of Enrico Pranzini's life injected a colonial element into the rich cultural history of the Parisian underworld, about which Dominique Kalifa has written extensively. See Dominique Kalifa, *Les bas-fonds: histoire d'un imaginaire* (Paris: Seuil, 2013). I use the term *glamour* in the sense of the visually pleasing and cosmopolitan elements conveyed by that word in the nineteenth century. See Stephen Gundle, *Glamour: A History* (Oxford: Oxford University Press, 2008).

14. On this process and its political ramifications, see Noiriel, *Immigration*.

15. Patricia Lorcin, *Imperial Identities: Stereotyping, Prejudice, and Race in Colonial Algeria* (London: I. B. Tauris, 1999), 202–4.

16. This theme is addressed in Louis Chevalier, *Classes laborieuses et classes dangereuses* (Paris: Plon, 1958). Any mention of Chevalier's flawed book must be complemented by a recommendation to see Barrie Ratcliffe, "Classes laborieuses et classes dangereuses à Paris pendant la première moitié du XIXᵉ siècle? The Chevalier Thesis Reexamined," *French Historical Studies* 17, no. 2 (1991): 542–74. For an overview of the later projection of frontier types such as "Mohicans" and "Apaches"

onto Parisian workers and criminals, see Dominique Kalifa, *Crime et culture au XIXe siècle* (Paris: Perrin, 2005), ch. 2.

17. Ann Laura Stoler, "Rethinking Colonial Categories," *Comparative Studies in Society and History* 31, no. 1 (1989): 137.

18. Ann Laura Stoler, "Preface to the 2010 Edition: Zones of the Intimate in Imperial Formations," in Ann Laura Stoler, *Carnal Knowledge and Imperial Power: Race and the Intimate in Colonial Rule* (Berkeley: University of California Press, 2010 [2002]), xiv–xv. Indeed, as social types and assemblages of stereotypes, the colonial racial categories of Levantine and rastaquouère can be viewed as "inappropriate colonial subjects," to borrow a concept from the influential critic Homi Bhabha, who has written extensively on hybridity, mimicry, and other unintended outcomes of the colonial relationship. See Homi Bhabha, *Location of Culture* (London: Routledge, 1995), 88.

19. Recent research on European imperialism has reconsidered the binary relationship between nation-state and colony, in which the former precedes the latter in a kind of logical progression. For an influential discussion of this, see Antoinette Burton, "Introduction: On the Inadequacy and the Indispensability of the Nation," in Antoinette Burton, ed., *After the Imperial Turn: Thinking With and Through the Nation* (Durham, NC: Duke University Press, 2003), 1–23.

20. *Le Figaro*, 10 July 1887.

21. Eugen Weber, *Peasants into Frenchmen: The Modernization of Rural France, 1870–1914* (Stanford, CA: Stanford University Press, 1976).

22. The expression *République coloniale* is borrowed from three French scholars who, in the footsteps of Benjamin Stora, have demanded a reassessment of the colonial past, countering nostalgia, the desire to promote the colonial past as beneficial, amnesia, and repression. See Nicolas Bancel, Pascal Blanchard, and Françoise Vergès, *La République coloniale: essair sur une utopie* (Paris: Albin Michel, 2003); and Benjaim Stora, *La gangrène et l'oubli: la mémoire de la guerre d'Algérie* (Paris: La Découverte, 1991).

23. For a review and bibliography, see Edward Berenson, "Making a Colonial Culture: Empire and the French Public, 1880–1940," *French Politics, Culture, and Society* 22, no. 2 (2004): 127–49. For another look at the cultural turn in colonial historiography, see Daniel J. Sherman, "The Arts and Sciences of Colonialism," *French Historical Studies* 23, no. 4 (2000): 707–29. Foundational scholarly texts that argue for the importance of imperialism in relation to culture are Edward Said, *Orientalism* (New York: Vintage, 1979); and Edward Said, *Culture and Imperialism* (New York: Vintage, 1993).

24. Edward Berenson, *Heroes of Empire: Five Charismatic Men and the Conquest of Africa* (Berkeley: University of California Press, 2010), 2. On colonial heroes and the role of the press in their construction, see also Beau Riffenburgh, *The Myth of the Explorer: The Press, Sensationalism, and Geographical Discovery* (New York: Oxford University Press, 1994); and Berny Sèbe, *Heroic Imperialists in Africa: The Promotion of British and French Colonial Heroes, 1870–1939* (Manchester: Manches-

ter University Press, 2013). For more on the heroes of the Third Republic, see Venita Datta, *Heroes and Legends of Fin-de-Siècle France: Gender, Politics, and National Identity* (Cambridge, UK: Cambridge University Press, 2011). Colonial "heroes" are important to the history of gender because their military service, colonial conquest, and exploration became enshrined as key components of virility in the latter part of the nineteenth century. See Odile Roynette, *Bons pour le service: l'expérience de la caserne en France à la fin du XIXe siècle* (Paris: Belin, 2000). Alain Corbin has identified some of the key components of virility in nineteenth-century France: "courage, even heroism, the willingness to die for the fatherland, the quest for glory, . . . the exploration and conquest of territories," and colonization. Alain Corbin, Jean-Jacques Courtine, and Georges Vigarello, eds., *L'histoire de la virilité*, vol. 2, *Le triomphe de la virilité: le XIXe siècle* (Paris: Seuil, 2011), 7, 9.

25. P. Larousse, *Grand dictionnaire universel du XIXe siècle*, suppl. 2 (Paris: Slatkine, 1982), vol. 17, pt. 3, 1735–36. This notion of the colonial adventurer gone rogue encompasses the ambivalence of the antiheroic literary type of Romantic and post-Romantic French literature pertaining to imperial conquest. For an analysis of the hero in relation to the attributes of the antihero, see Roger Fayolle, "Criticism and Theory," in Donald G. Charlton, ed., *The French Romantics* (Cambridge, UK: Cambridge University Press, 1984), 2: 213–16. One element that relegates the potentially heroic figure to antiheroism is his "lowly social condition."

26. Levantines or rastaquouères make appearances in Zola's *Money* and Maupassant's *Bel-Ami*. For a discussion of these types in work and specifically the anti-semitism of Huysmans, see Jean-Marie Seillan, "Huysmans, un antisémite fin-de-siècle," *Romantisme* 95 (1997): 113–26.

27. I revisit this issue in the Conclusion.

28. Ferry based his assertions on claims such as those made by Paul Leroy-Beaulieu in his *De la colonisation chez les peuples modernes* (Paris: Guillaumin, 1874). A classic historical debate has centered on the economic benefits and related motivations of the Third Republic's colonial empire. See Jacques Marseille, *Empire coloniale et capitalisme français: histoire d'un divorce* (Paris: Albin Michel, 1984). See also Henri Brunschwig, *Mythes et réalités de l'impérialisme colonial français (1871–1914)* (Paris: Colin, 1960). Brunschwig argued that economics were secondary to nationalist impulses in the renaissance of the French empire. For an example of an argument for empire's stabilizing force, see Berenson, *Heroes of Empire*, ch. 5.

29. This was true, Tarde believed, because individual criminal "impulsions" and collective ones operated analogically (this principle was borrowed from the "crowd theory" then in vogue). See Gabriel Tarde, *La criminalité comparée* (Paris: Alcan, 1886), 143. Tarde's conceptual link between criminality and empire therefore bore out his general claim that modern empires would act as "agents of pacification" within the European metropole. See Alberto Toscano, "Powers of Pacification: State and Empire in Gabriel Tarde," *Economy and Society* 36, no. 4 (2007): 599. As Emmanuelle Saada has observed, Tarde's most influential contribution to social thought, the "Laws of Imitation," explicitly endorses the colonial ordering of soci-

eties ("from superior to inferior"). See Emmanuelle Saada, "Entre 'assimilation' et 'décivilisation': l'imitation et le projet colonial républicain," *Terrain* 44 (2005): 21.

30. Gabriel Tarde, *La philosophie pénale* (Paris: Masson, 1892), 424–25.

31. This not the only dark parallel to colonial expansion as it pertained to penal policy in France. For a brilliant analysis of French penal colonies, see Dominique Kalifa, *Biribi: les bagnes coloniaux de l'armée française* (Paris: Perrin, 2009); and Miranda Frances Spieler, *Empire and Underworld: Captivity in French Guiana* (Cambridge, MA: Harvard University Press, 2012).

32. Kalifa, *L'encre et le sang*, 251. See also Dominique Kalifa, "Journalistes, policiers et magistrats à la fin du XIXe siècle: la question de l'insécurité urbaine," in Christian Delporte, ed., *Médias et villes (XVIIIe–XXe siècle)* (Tours: Presses universitaires François-Rabelais, 1999), 119–36. For an earlier period, see Arlette Farge, "L'insécurité à Paris, un thème familier au XVIII^{e}siècle," *Temps Libre* 10 (1984): 35–43.

33. See Michael B. Miller, *Shanghai on the Metro: Spies, Intrigue, and the French Between the Wars* (Berkeley: University of California Press, 1994).

34. The new republican building projects relied heavily on imported labor, and the entrenchment of global capitalism exacerbated economic instability and provoked the scapegoating of foreigners, who were often blamed for the rise in crime and the loss of jobs. Anti-immigrant flare-ups and violence were not uncommon. This tension was not limited to Paris. On the simmering anti-immigrant sentiment of southern France, see Gérard Noiriel, *Le massacre des italiens: Aigues-Mortes, 17 août 1893* (Paris: Fayard, 2010).

35. The conceptualization of imperial insecurity, discussed further in the Conclusion, is inspired more by Ann Laura Stoler's emphasis on the "precarious vulnerability" of European empires in the East than on the occasional usage that the term has seen in the context of the British Empire. Ann Laura Stoler, *Race and the Education of Desire* (Durham, NC: Duke University Press, 1995), 97. In French, the term *insécurité* has been conducive to the blurring of various levels of meaning—national, global, communal, and personal. Dominique Kalifa has found four principal applications for the term *insécurité* in nineteenth-century usage: (1) a subjective fear of crime, (2) a discursive-ideological expression of this fear, (3) the range of "practices" devised to address concerns about criminal repression, and (4) the pressures that criminality, particularly violent criminality, place on a community. See Dominique Kalifa, "Délinquance et insécurité urbaine en France (19e–20e siècles): un contrepoint," in Laurent Fouchard and Isaac Olawale Albert, eds., *Security, Crime, and Segregation in West African Cities Since the 19th Century* (Paris: Karthala, 2003), 73.

36. This is what Edward Said referred to as the "imagined geography" of European empires in the East. Said, *Orientalism*, 54–55. Indeed, it was this "crucial logic of difference that enabled the Empire to persist," observes Catherine Hall. Catherine Hall, "At Home with History: Macaulay and the *History of England*," in Catherine Hall and Sonya Rose, eds., *At Home with the Empire: Metropolitan*

Culture and the Imperial World (Cambridge, UK: Cambridge University Press, 2006), 26. For a general discussion of the logic of social segregation in the colonial context, see Frederick Cooper and Jane Burbank, *Empires in World History: Power and the Politics of Difference* (Princeton, NJ: Princeton University Press, 2010). On historiography that has debunked this fantasy, see Felix Driver and David Gilbert, "Imperial Cities: Overlapping Territories, Intertwined Histories," in Felix Driver and David Gilbert, eds., *Imperial Cities: Landscape, Display, and Identity* (Manchester: Manchester University Press, 2004), 1–17. In the case of French history, this urban-historical approach is situated within a broad historiographic move that highlights the "mutual reflexivity" between metropole and colony. See Herman Lebovics, *Bringing the Empire Back Home: France in the Global Age* (Durham, NC: Duke University Press, 2004), xv–xvi. For an approach that emphasizes religious questions and colonial and French identities in several contexts, see J. P. Daughton, *An Empire Divided: Religion, Republicanism, and the Making of French Colonialism, 1880–1914* (New York: Oxford University Press, 2006).

37. See Stephen D. Arata, "The Occidental Tourist: 'Dracula' and the Anxiety of Reverse Colonization," *Victorian Studies* 33, no. 4 (1990): 621–45. See also Yumna Siddiqi, *Anxieties of Empire and the Fiction of Intrigue* (New York: Columbia University Press, 2008).

38. Archives de Paris, D2 U8 223.

39. Noiriel, *Immigration*, 160.

40. Previously, a few hundred immigrants had come to France from Egypt in the aftermath of the Napoleonic retreat, although these individuals were heavily supervised by the state. As Ian Coller has shown in an important study, they struggled to negotiate composite identities and "visible difference" in the metropole. Ian Coller, *Arab France: Islam and the Making of Modern France* (Berkeley: University of California Press, 2010), 131.

41. Frantz Fanon, "Fureur raciste en France" (1959), reprinted in Frantz Fanon, *Pour la révolution africaine: écrits politiques* (Paris: La Découverte, 2001), 187.

42. On the "coercive force of external identifications," see Rogers Brubaker and Frederick Cooper, "Beyond 'Identity,'" *Theory and Society* 29, no. 1 (2000): 1–47. On colonial administrative policy and race, see Emmanuelle Saada, *Les enfants de la colonie: les métis de l'empire français entre sujétion et citoyenneté* (Paris: La Découverte, 2007).

43. As noted, Noiriel has studied the emergence of political xenophobia in connection with the advent of mass immigration to France in the latter part of the nineteenth century. More recently, as Catherine Raissiguier notes, historians have begun to lay bare the component parts of xenophobia within a broader analysis of how "interrelated processes of exclusion and domination" operated in contemporary France—in short, how exclusionary dynamics have been "*gendered* and *classed.*" Catherine Raissiguier, *Reinventing the Republic: Gender, Migration, and Citizenship in France* (Palo Alto, CA: Stanford University Press, 2010), 4–5; emphasis in original. For an overview of the historical relation between immigration and policing

in modern France, see Marie-Claude Blanc-Chaléard, C. Douki, N. Dyonet, and V. Milliot, *Police et migrants: France, 1667–1939* (Rennes: Presses universitaires de Rennes, 2001).

44. Presse judiciaire de Paris, *Le palais de justice de Paris: son monde et ses moeurs* (Paris: Librairies-Imprimeries Réunies, 1892), 346.

45. Campi was convicted of double homicide in 1884, Prado of homicide in 1888, Gruem of homicide in 1882, Rossel of homicide in 1887, and Eyraud of homicide in 1889. A noteworthy precursor of transnational criminal investigation, if not strictly colonial in nature, occurred in 1877, following a murder at the place Beauvau in Paris. Using telegraphic communications, police transmitted to French borders and port cities a suspect's description and were able to scan passenger lists of all the liners that had left France as well as the stopovers planned by these ships. The suspect was pursued to London, where the French police consulted with local authorities before heading to Liverpool. *Le Gaulois*, 9 October 1879.

46. *Encyclopedia Britannica* (1910), 7: 448. The verb "to globalize" is, of course, of mid-twentieth-century vintage.

Notes to Chapter One

1. *Le Matin*, 18 March 1887. Puy-de-Dôme, Conseil général, *Rapports du préfet, procès-verbaux des délibérations: conseil général du Puy-de-Dôme* (1874), 133. The Société hippique française kept its headquarters in the rue Montaigne. It was surrounded by a thriving aristocratic culture. During the 1880s the Baroness Decazes-Stackelberg, patron of the art and fashion worlds from a family of Russian ambassadors, was also a *salonnière* and a pillar of Parisian *mondanité*. "The success of her receptions—meetings of the high society of France and foreign countries— proves that the charm of a salon has nothing to do with its size," commented a journalist in *Gil Blas* (29 January 1884). The baroness's father was Tsar Alexander I's representative at the Congress of Vienna after Napoleon's fall, and her brother was Russia's ambassador to the court of Napoleon III. Among the regulars at her salon were the Princess Mentchikoff, the Duchess of Sesto, the Duc de Morny, the Marquise d'Aoust, the Vicomte de Kervéguen, the Vicomtesse de Croy, the Vicomtesse d'Argy, the Comtesse de la Ferronays, the Baron Calvet-Rogniat, and "almost all the members of the diplomatic corps" (*Gil Blas*, 29 January 1884). Others seen there were the minister of Italy in France, General Marquis de Menabrea; the Marquis de Noailles; the Count Léon de Béthune; the Baronne de Beyens; Mme. Borgès; the Baron and Baroness de Heckeren; the Prince de Hohenlohe; the Villar-Urratias; and Mme. Penlaver (*Gil Blas*, 4 March 1885). Achille de Colmont, *Historique de l'incendie du Ministère des finances (24–30 mai 1871)* (Paris: De Lapirot et Boullay, 1882), 95.

2. Georges Grison, *L'affaire de la rue Montaigne, notes prises au jour le jour par un reporter* (Paris: Librairie Illustrée, 1887), 1.

3. The petitioners' letter was reprinted in *L'Argus: Revue Théâtrale et Journal des Comédiens* (11 June 1850).

4. Antoine Claude, *Les mémoires de M. Claude, chef de la police sûreté sous le seconde Empire* (Paris: Rouff, 1881), 2: 52.

5. This anecdote is retold by Edward Shorter, *Written in the Flesh: A History of Desire* (Toronto: University of Toronto Press, 2005), 69.

6. Eric Hazan, *The Invention of Paris: A History in Footsteps*, trans. David Fernbach (New York: Verso, 2011), 118–19.

7. For a basic glossary of the street appellations and related anecdotes in the area around the Champs-Elysées, see Catherine Planel, *Mémoire des rues: Paris 8e arrondissement, 1900–1940* (Paris: Parigramme, 2015).

8. Félix Lazare, *Dictionnaire administratif et historique des rues de Paris et de ses monuments* (Paris: Lazare, 1849), 120.

9. Edmond Texier, *Tableau de Paris: ouvrage illustré de quinze gents gravures . . .* (Paris: Paulin, 1852), 1: 6–7.

10. Paul Féval, *La soeur des fantômes* (Brussels: Meline, 1852), 2: 5.

11. Colin Jones, *Paris: Biography of a City* (London: Penguin, 2004), 354.

12. See Jones, *Paris*, 348; and David P. Jordan, *Transforming Paris: The Life and Labors of Baron Haussmann* (New York: Simon & Schuster, 1995). For a classic exposition of the cultural reactions to the social and spatial transformation of Paris, see Marshall Berman, *All That Is Solid Melts into Air: The Experience of Modernity* (New York: Penguin, 1982), ch. 3; and T. J. Clarke, *The Painting of Modern Life: Paris in the Art of Manet and His Followers* (Princeton, NJ: Princeton University Press, 1984).

13. Hazan remarked on the moment when Paris began to attract serious artistic representation: "So Paris was until then a city without images—as distinct from Amsterdam and Delft, Venice or Rome. There were certainly Parisian *vedute*, often quite charming, but these were designed for the tourists and were not considered works of art. The 'view of Paris' did not fit into any of the styles that the Salon recognized: neither history, not landscape, nor 'genre'—the outdoor scenes of the latter being located in conventional frameworks. The only city whose representation was accepted in the category of landscape was precisely Rome, since it was considered the cradle of painting, and French artists, most commonly scholars at the Villa Medici, showed only picturesque ruins, timeless gardens, and an idealized countryside" (Hazan, *Invention of Paris*, 344).

14. Jordan, *Transforming Paris*, 348.

15. Gustave Claudin, *Mes souvenirs: les boulevards 1840–1870* (Paris: Calmann Lévy, 1884), 16–17. See also Jeanne Gaillard, *Paris la ville: 1852–1870* (Paris: Champion, 1976), 525–29.

16. The Île de la Cité, the ancient heart of Paris, lost two-thirds of its residents in the span of a few years. Jones, *Paris*, 356. Richard Sennett, *The Fall of Public Man* (New York: Norton, 1992), 136.

17. After one such meet-and-greet on the Champs-Elysées in the late 1880s, a high-society journalist judged the "nobles" pure because they were untainted even by "the champions of the demi-monde" (Septfontaines, *L'année mondaine 1889* [Paris: Firmin-Didot, 1890], 360).

18. Élie Frébault, *La vie de Paris: guide pittoresque et pratique du visiteur* (Paris: Dentu, 1878).

19. Paul Féval, "Les amours de Paris," *Musée Littéraire: Choix de Littérature Contemporaine Française et Étrangère*, ser. 7 (1852): 101.

20. Ariane Charton, *Lettres pour lire au lit* (Paris: Mercure de France, 2009). For the story of the doorman, see the letter dated 15 March 1833 (p. 48).

21. Quoted in Lauren M. E. Goodlad, "The Mad Men in the Attic: Seriality and Identity in the Modern Babylon," in Lauren M. E. Goodlad, Lilya Kaganovsky, and Robert A. Rushing, eds., *Mad Men, Mad World: Sex, Politics, Style, and the 1960s* (Durham, NC: Duke University Press, 2013), 342.

22. R. C. Le Clair, *Young Henry James, 1843–1870* (New York: Bookman, 1955), 262; and Fred Kaplan, *Henry James: The Imagination of Genius* (New York: Open Road, 2013), 1859–60.

23. Nancy L. Green, *The Other Americans in Paris: Businessmen, Countesses, Wayward Youth, 1880–1941* (Chicago: University of Chicago Press, 2014).

24. Police questioned an employee, a certain Morel, who worked in the Ministry of the Interior and whose bedroom window was situated 10 feet away.

25. Susan K. Goley and Charles Sowerwine, *A Political Romance: Léon Gambetta, Léonie Léon, and the Making of the French Republic, 1872–82* (New York: Palgrave Macmillan, 2012).

26. *Almanach national: annuaire officiel de la République française* (Paris: Berger-Levrault, 1875), 84. It is rarely mentioned that in May 1877 de Marcère's rue Montaigne apartment played a part in the Republic's survival. A hard-core group of republicans, known as the Committee of Eighteen and led by Ferry, Louis Blanc, and Charles de Freycinet, crowded into the apartment for tense after-hours strategy discussions that helped foil the monarchist president Patrice de Macmahon. On these meetings, see Charles de Freycinet, *Souvenirs*, vol. 2, *1878–1893* (Paris: Delgrave, 1913), ch. 1. See also Émile Louis Gustave Deshayes de Marcère, *Le seize mai et la fin du Septennat* (Paris: Plon-Nourrit, 1900).

27. Léon-Paul Fargue, *Banalité* (Paris: Gallimard, 2007 [1928]), 60.

28. The Palais des Beaux-Arts was built on the avenue Montaigne for the world's fair in 1855, definitively establishing the new revamped thoroughfare as a cultural site.

Notes to Chapter Two

1. Reprint of the song by F. Coppée, "La Petite blanchisseuse," *Le Gaulois*, 18 March 1887.

2. I use the simpler term Security (la Sûreté) to refer to the now defunct investigative arm of the Paris Police Prefecture, the full name of which was le Service de la police de sûreté.

3. These physical and character descriptions come from exhibited photographs at the Archives de la Préfecture de Police, numerous contemporary publications, and Goron's friend Émile Gautier, who wrote the introduction to the first volume

of Goron's memoirs. Émile Gautier, preface to François Goron, *Les mémoires de M. Goron*, vol. I, *De l'invasion à l'anarchie* (Paris: Flammarion, 1897), vii.

4. Alain Faure, *Paris carême-prenant: du carnival à Paris au XIXe siècle* (Paris: Hachette, 1978), 134. *Le Voleur Illustré*, 19 March 1887.

5. Faure, *Paris*, 29; *Le Gaulois*, 18 March 1887; *Le Petit Journal*, 10 March 1877.

6. *Le Gaulois*, 17 March 1887.

7. *Le Petit Parisien*, 19 March 1887.

8. *Le Petit Parisien*, 19 March 1887. Louis de Fourcauld, "Causerie," *Revue Illustrée* 3 (1887): 269–70.

9. Mary Donaldson-Evans, *Medical Examinations: Dissecting the Doctor in French Narrative Prose, 1857–1894* (Lincoln: University of Nebraska Press, 2000), 83–85. See also Jaimee Gruring, "Dirty Laundry: Public Hygiene and Public Space in Nineteenth-Century Paris," PhD diss., Arizona State University, 2011.

10. Gustave Guiches, *Le banquet* (Paris: Spes, 1926), 131. Georges Grison, *Paris horrible* (Paris: Dentu, 1882), 72.

11. *Le Figaro*, 14 and 16 March 1887.

12. *Le Figaro*, 7 March 1879. In his columns, in addition to advice on any range of practical matters, including the occasional touting of a household product, Grison did not shy away from an appeal to female readers. His advice for Catholic homemakers centered on holiday preparations, such as those for the Feast of the Epiphany, which involved the famed galette des rois. "The table must be superb for the Epiphany celebrations: tablecloth and napkins in grosse soie écrue, brodées d'or et de fleurs pâles à profusion," along with French mulled wine served in a bowl of Chinese porcelain (*Le Figaro*, 2 January 1886).

13. Faure, *Paris*, 127.

14. *Le Petit Journal*, 5 March 1875.

15. *Le Gaulois*, 17 March 1887. The most curious repudiation, however, issued from France's most widely read Catholic newspaper, *La Croix*, which suggested that the daylong bacchanalia was the fruit of a collusive union between the Municipal Council and the city's sausage-maker lobby (meat was proscribed during Lent with the exception of this one day, making it vital for revenues). *La Croix*, 19 March 1887.

16. *La Croix*, 18 and 19 March 1887.

17. *L'Estafette*, 19 March 1887.

18. *L'Estafette*, 19 March 1887.

19. *La Croix*, 18 and 19 March 1887.

20. The various reports that the various investigators filed are in the judiciary case file at the Archives de Paris, D2 U8 223. Many of the specific findings at the crime scene described here come from these reports. For a history of nineteenth-century experts in the field of crime and criminology, see Frédéric Chauvaud, *Les experts du crime: la médecine légale en France au XIXe siècle* (Paris: Aubier, 2000).

21. François Goron, *Les mémoires de M. Goron* (Paris: Flammarion, 1897), 2: 163. *Le Gaulois*, 18 March 1887.

22. Paul Brouardel, *Affaire Pranzini, triple assassinat: relation medico-legale* (Paris: J.-B. Baillière, 1887), 9.

23. Archives de Paris, D2 U8 223.

24. Alain Corbin, "Intimate Relations," in Michelle Perrot, ed., *A History of Private Life*, vol. 4, *From the Fires of Revolution to the Great War*, trans. Arthur Goldhammer (Cambridge, MA: Harvard University Press, 1990), 586–88.

25. *Le Matin*, 10 April 1887.

26. Georges Grison, *L'affaire de la rue Montaigne, notes prises au jour le jour par un reporter* (Paris: Librairie Illustrée, 1887), 12.

27. Goron, *Mémoires*, 2: 19.

28. Goron, *Mémoires*, 2: 17–18, 24, 36–37.

29. *Le Matin*, 18 March 1887.

30. Grison, *L'affaire*, 28.

31. Grison, *L'affaire*, 28.

32. Goron, *Mémoires*, 2: 27.

33. *Le Gaulois*, 20 January 1908.

34. Jean-Marc Berlière and René Lévy, *Histoire des polices en France de l'ancien régime à nos jours* (Paris: Nouveau Monde, 2011), 100, 102. By the turn of the century, the number of police reached 400. A part of this growth occurred after 1894, when the service was reorganized to pursue anarchist terrorists. Horace Valbel, *La police de sûreté en 1889* (Paris: Dentu, 1889), 11.

35. Berlière and Lévy, *Histoire des polices*, 101.

36. The *gardiens de la paix*, uniformed beat cops, were given formal training in civility to smooth their interactions with Parisian residents, to cite just one of the Prefecture's initiatives. On this and other cultural aspects to the process of professionalization, see Quentin Deluermoz, *Des policiers dans la ville: la construction d'un ordre public à Paris, 1854–1914* (Paris: Publications de la Sorbonne, 2012). See also Jean-Marc Berlière, *Le Préfet Lépine: vers la naissance de la police moderne* (Paris: Denoël, 1993). In using the term *professionalization*, historians of the French police have meant a variety of developments and have applied the term to changes in police work between the eighteenth and the twentieth century. For John Merriman, professionalization was manifest among French police in the eighteenth century in the form of self-regulation, organization, centralization, an objective of "efficiency" working against a reputation of corruption in the eighteenth century, "standardized training and assessment of professional competency within the context of a hierarchical structure of authority and a sense of collective identity." John Merriman, *Police Stories: Building the French State, 1815–1851* (Oxford: Oxford University Press, 2005), 6–7.

37. Antoine Claude, *Mémoires de Monsieur Claude* (Paris: J. Rouff, 1882), 8: 216.

38. *Le Gaulois*, 20 January 1908.

39. Hogier-Grison [F. Hogier and Georges Grison], *Les hommes de proie: ce qu'elle était, ce qu'elle est, ce qu'elle doit être* (Paris: Librairie illustrée, 1886–1887), 239–40.

40. Goron, *Mémoires*, 1: 163.

41. As a security measure, the Paris police had access to the registration rolls of the city's *garnis* (furnished hotel rooms).

42. Today Breslau is Wrocław, Poland.

43. Goron, *Mémoires*, 2: 22.

Notes to Chapter Three

1. Guy de Maupassant, *Bel-Ami* (Paris: Ollendorff, 1896), 196.

2. Pierre Giffard, *Souvenirs d'un reporter: le sieur de Va-Partout* (Paris: Dreyfous, 1880), 215.

3. François Goron, *Les mémoires de M. Goron* (Paris: Flammarion, 1897), 2: 31–32. This information was published in bits over several days, with a most complete inventory in *Le Petit Parisien*, 24 March 1887. The information also appeared in *Le Figaro* and in *L'Intransigeant*, *L'Estafette*, and *La Lanterne*.

4. Goron, *Mémoires*, 2: 39.

5. Goron, *Mémoires*, 2: 35–36.

6. Goron, *Mémoires*, 2: 31–32.

7. See Anne-Claude Ambroise-Rendu, *Petits récits des désordres ordinaires: les faits divers dans la presse française de la IIIe République à la Grande Guerre* (Paris: S. Arslan, 2004); Dominique Kalifa, *L'encre et le sang: récits de crimes et société à la Belle Époque* (Paris: Fayard, 1995); Marine M'Sili, *Le fait divers en République: histoire sociale de 1870 à nos jours* (Paris: CNRS, 2000); and Vanessa R. Schwartz, *Spectacular Realities: Early Mass Culture in Fin-de-Siècle Paris* (Berkeley: University of California Press, 1998). See also Peter Fritzsche, *Reading Berlin 1900* (Cambridge, MA: Harvard University Press, 2009).

8. Kalifa expounds on this in *L'encre et le sang*, passim.

9. Thomas Cragin, *Murder in Parisian Streets: Manufacturing Crime and Justice in the Popular Press, 1830–1900* (Lewisburg, PA: Bucknell University Press, 2006), 14, 25.

10. Dominique Kalifa, "Les tâcherons de l'information: petits reporters et faits divers à la Belle Époque," *Revue d'Histoire Moderne et Contemporaine* 40, no. 4 (1993): 580–81, 584.

11. Frédéric Chauvaud, "Le triple assassinat de la rue Montaigne: le sacre du fait divers," *Annales de Bretagne et des Pays de l'Ouest* 116, no. 1 (2009): 13–28. Chauvaud's claim, similar to my own, that the rue Montaigne case was an important event in the history of the *fait-divers* is sourced to Goron's stated opinion to this effect. Chauvaud does not mention Georges Grison, nor does he offer much evidence to show how this case was different from earlier ones—which is the only way for us to gauge how it fitted into a broader context of change. In addition, a few years into my research for this book, I was alerted to the existence of an unpublished master's thesis in Paris that also argues for the importance of the rue Montaigne case in the development of investigative reporting, taking the Troppmann case as a point of reference. Alicia Croci, "Naissance de l'enquête journalistique: l'affaire Pranzini," Master's thesis, University of Paris I–Sorbonne, 2005.

12. Michelle Perrot, "L'affaire Troppmann (1869)," *L'Histoire* 30 (1981): 28–37.

Olivier Isaac, "Les enquêtes balbutiantes des journalistes durant l'affaire Troppmann," in Jean-Claude Farcy, Dominique Kalifa, and Jean-Noël Luc, eds., *L'enquête judiciaire en Europe au XIXe siècle* (Paris: Créaphis, 2007): 231–39.

13. Goron, *Mémoires*, 2: 35; Georges Grison, *L'affaire de la rue Montaigne, notes prises au jour le jour par un reporter* (Paris: Librairie Illustrée, 1887), 26.

14. *Le Figaro*, 21 March 1887. Grison, *L'affaire*, 27.

15. *Le Figaro*, 21 March 1887. Grison, *L'affaire*, 27.

16. In the aftermath of the 1881 law guaranteeing press liberties, a series of legal cases in the 1880s aimed at defining the rights and responsibilities that would be open to journalists. In 1887 the principal associations of the French press formed the Comité general des associations de la presse française. Its function was to safeguard freedoms of speech guaranteed by the 1881 law, even as the state continued its pursuit of articles and journalistic practices deemed harmful to the Republic. Christian Delporte, *Les journalistes en France, 1880–1950: naissance et construction d'une profession* (Paris: Seuil, 1999), 40.

17. *Gil Blas*, 23 February 1884.

18. Edmond de Goncourt, *Journal des Goncourts: mémoires de la vie littéraire* (Paris: Bibliothèque Charpentier, 1892), entry for 11 May 1880, 6: 115.

19. *Le Figaro*, 6 May 1886.

20. Grison, letter dated 26 August 1900. Archives Nationales, Georges Grison, 454AP/192.

21. Gustave Guiches, *Le banquet* (Paris: Spes, 1926), 131.

22. Kalifa, "Les tâcherons," 600. Guillaume Pinson, "Le Reporter fictif," *Autour de Vallès* 40 (2010):88.

23. Kalifa, "Les tâcherons," 601.

24. "Sociétaires décédés," *Bulletin de l'Association des Journalistes Parisiens*, no. 43 (1928): 50–51.

25. With the exception of his highly quotable *Paris horrible*, the only one of his books that was ever reissued, Grison's writings have never attracted attention.

26. *Le Journal Amusant*, 4 October 1932. *Le Monde Illustré*, 26 January 1884. Grison's "Les violateurs des sépultres" is cited in *La Revue des Journaux et des Livres*, 25 October 1885. His "Les découpeurs de cadavres" appeared in *Le Figaro*, 2 July 1884. On street slang, see *Le Figaro*, 23 November 1881. Grison boasted of never having missed an occasion to watch a convict "kiss the widow," as it was said in contemporary slang, that is, walk to the guillotine; his accounts of public executions earned him comparisons with a contemporary drama critic. When World War I sparked a cultural interest in mass death, orphans, and vampires, Grison tried to keep up with the cutting edge of morbid literature, taking up the themes of vampires and orphans in two books: Georges Grison, *Margot la vampire, roman inédit* (Paris: Ferenczi, 1918); and Georges Grison, *Fille Martyre, roman inédit* (Paris: Ferenczi, 1919).

27. "Sociétaires décédés," 50–51 Grison's superiors at *Le Figaro*, such as the *chroniqueur* Albert Bataille and the editor Francis Magnard, became members of the organization, which was founded in 1885, years before Grison did.

28. Archives Nationales, Georges Grison, 454AP/192. *Le Temps*, 13 December 1897; *Le Radical*, 19 December 1905; *Le Temps*, 22 December 1921; *Le Matin*, 17 December 1895.

29. Kalifa, "Les tâcherons," 584–85.

30. Aurélien Scholl, *Mémoires du trottoir* (Paris: E. Dentu, 1882), 180, 228.

31. Kalifa, *L'encre et le sang*, 9. Delporte, *Les journalistes*, 133–34.

32. Pinson makes this useful distinction. Guillaume Pinson, "Le Reporter fictif," *Autour de Vallès* 40 (2010): 90.

33. Fortuné du Boisgobey, *Cornaline la dompteuse* (Paris: Plon, 1887). The novel went to press during the first half of 1887 and was registered with the government in May of that year. Kalifa, "Les tâcherons," 600–601. Pinson,"Le Reporter fictif," 94. Only in the waning years of the nineteenth century did a fictional reporter attain the status of a protagonist around which an entire novel could be built.

34. Du Boisgobey, *Cornaline*, 254–55, 278.

35. Du Boisgobey, *Cornaline*, 254–55.

36. Grison wrote for *Le Figaro*, mostly as Jean de Paris but also under his own name on certain stories, from the early 1870s until 1923. He also contributed to *Le Moniteur, Le Petit Bleu, Le Soir, L'Evénement*, and *La Liberté*.

37. Grison co-authored a theater piece at the height of the Dreyfus affair, in 1898. Georges Grison and Albert Dupuy, *France, armée, honneur, patrie: Fergus, drame patriotique en 5 actes et 6 tableaux* (Paris: Bouffes-parisiens, 29 June 1898). The play was finished in April 1898 but was at first censored by Alfred Nicolas Rambaud, Ministre de l'instruction publique, and permitted to run only after a two-month delay.

38. *Le Temps*, 30 March 1914. *Le Journal*, 29 March 1914.

39. For example, Grison gave testimony during the Port-Breton affair of 1883, a *calomnie* (calumny) case involving allegations of adultery and fornication on the part of the wife of the poet and journalist Clovis Hugues. This story is recounted in detail in *La Lanterne*, 30 November 1883. Grison also testified in the case of the estate of the Baron Seillière, a matter involving a battle over the last will and testament of a man who was perhaps coerced before his death. *Revue des Grands Procès Contemporains* 13 (1895): 23.

40. *Le Temps*, 5 September 1917; *Le Journal*, 4 September 1917.

41. *Le Temps*, 15 May 1892; *Le Radical*, 15 May 1892. Grison's seconds were Henri Chabrillat and Charles Chincholle.

42. E. Charton, *Dictionnaire des professions*, 3rd ed. (1880), quoted in Theodore Zeldin, *A History of French Passions*, vol. 1, *Ambition, Love, and Politics* (Oxford: Oxford University Press, 1993), 91.

43. *La Justice*, 15 October 1880.

44. Kathleen Kete, "Stendhal and the Trials of Ambition in Postrevolutionary France," *French Historical Studies* 28, no. 3 (2005): 468. On Stendhal's *The Red and the Black*, Kete writes, "To see Julien as embodying generally feared ambition—and not simply opposition to a class—is to step out of the binary opposition of rebel intel-

lectual and complacent bourgeois society that has been institutionalized in the right- and left-wing interpretations of the novel. It is also to see postrevolutionary France in broader cultural terms, as caught between a traditional resistance to individualism and the appeal of modernity, with no easy options in sight" (Kete, "Stendhal," 478–79).

45. Zeldin, *History of French Passions*, 1: 91.

46. Zeldin, *History of French Passions*, 1: 91.

47. Zeldin, *History of French Passions*, 1: 92.

48. David Bell, "A Grub Street Hack Goes to War," in Charles Walton, ed., *Into Print: Limits and Legacies of the Enlightenment; Essays in Honor of Robert Darnton* (University Park: Penn State University Press, 2011), 131–45. At the same time, Bell observes, the French Revolution created a society of individuals and encouraged great achievements in the military, thereby opening the door to a respectable, Romantic form of ambition commonly associated with Bonaparte (Bell, "Grub Street Hack," 141).

49. Zeldin, *History of French Passions*, 1: 97.

50. Maupassant, *Bel-Ami*.

51. Adrien Peladan, commentary in *La France littéraire, artistique, scientifique* (14 July 1860): 664. Grison's essay on the dunes of the Grande Côte was entered in the journal's spring contest that spring, 5 May 1860.

52. Roger Bonniot, *Émile Gaboriau ou la naissance du roman policier* (Paris: Vrin, 1985), 499.

53. Marc Martin, *Médias et journalistes de la république* (Paris: Odile Jacob, 1997), 122. Christophe Charle, *Le siècle de la presse (1830–1939)* (Paris: Seuil, 2004), 144, 147–49.

54. Kalifa, "Les tâcherons," 602.

55. Georges Grison, *Paris horrible* (Paris: E. Dentu, 1882), 11.

56. Kalifa, "Les tâcherons," 583.

57. Christian Delporte, *Histoire du journalisme et des journalistes en France* (Paris: Presses universitaires de France, 1985), 31.

58. Guillaume Pinson and Marie-Eve Thérenty, "L'invention du reportage," *Autour de Vallès* 40 (2010): 6, 8.

59. Delporte, *Les journalistes*, 65–66. Kalifa, *L'encre et le sang*, 9. Pinson and Thérenty, "L'invention du reportage," 5–22; Guillaume Pinson and Marie-Eve Thérenty, "Les microrécits médiatiques: Les formes brèves du journal, entre médiations et fiction," *Études Françaises* 44, no. 3 (2008): 5–12.

60. Dalloz ran *Le Moniteur* and *Le Monde Illustré*. The penny press eschewed lengthy political analysis, and in its early days *La Petite Presse* avoided political topics and focused on diverse daily news stories, though it later ran afoul of the Communards, along with Dalloz's other papers, which were viewed as aiding the national government's cause. Ernest Alfred Vizetelly, *My Adventures in the Commune, 1871* (Paris: Duffield, 1914), 190, 261.

61. Perhaps just one of Grison's early pieces merits mention. Published in 1872, it tells the story behind Gustave Courbet's scandalous *Retour des conférences* (1863),

which the great master had painted near Grison's hometown (the Salon rejected the work, which features a biting representation of the priesthood as fat and drunken). The article displays Grison's raw storytelling gifts and permits him to impersonate the sort of in-the-know critic with an eye for detail that graced the highbrow press. The article also announces his republican conservatism, notably in a swipe at Courbet's participation in the Paris Commune, which seemed so out of character of the man Grison had met all those years before: "How did the man I knew there—so gay, so quick to laugh, and such a good attitude—become the ally of Raoul Rigault and company? How did the artist who truly admired our old basilicas of the Middle Ages come to approve the savage devastation of Paris?" (*Journal pour Tous*, 9 March 1872). Courbet spent two productive summers (in 1862 and 1863) in the Charente valley with Corot and other friends. Grison's anecdote may be of interest to art historians: "What twist of fate had brought him there? I can't say. All I know is that he had gone to Port-Berteau to meet another landscape painter, Auguin, an artist of conscience and merit whose exaggerated modesty does him wrong." According to Grison, the donkey portrayed in the painting as overwhelmed by the weight of his priestly masters had been a difficult model for Courbet to procure. At that time of year the Saintonge donkeys passing along Courbet's route were all heavily loaded with work. And because their owners were not given to sparing them as muses, the painter struggled to find an animal and needed to make haste when he finally found someone willing to lend him one.

62. Bonniot, *Émile Gaboriau*, 478.

63. Marie-Eve Thérenty, *La littérature au quotidien: poétiques journalistiques au XIXᵉ siècle* (Paris: Seuil, 2007), 284; Kalifa, *L'encre et le sang*, 253.

64. Auguste Lepage, *Les dîners artistiques et littéraires de Paris*, 2nd ed. (Paris: Frinzine, Klein, 1884), 13. A contemporary history observes that the Société des gens de lettres was a "complex and influential body that protects and orders the literary world of France." Samuel Squire Sprigge, *The Society of French Authors (Société des gens de lettres): Its Foundation and Its History* (London: Incorporated Society of Authors, 1889), 12.

65. The writer whom du Boisgobey blocked was Jules-Hippolyte Percher, who wrote under the pen name Harry Alis. *Grand dictionnaire universel du XIXᵉ siècle: français, historique, géographique, mythologique, bibliographique, littéraire, artistique, scientifique, etc., etc.* (Paris: Administration du Grand dictionnaire universel, 1866–1890), 17: 1368. Charles Simond, ed., *La vie parisienne à travers le XIXᵉ siècle: Paris de 1800 à 1900 d'après les estampes et les mémoires du temps* (Paris: Plon, 1900–1901), 2: 656. Other members of the Société des gens de lettres included G. de la Landelle, Eugène Muller, Alexandre de Lavergne, Camille Doucet, Clément Caraguel, Jules Claretie, Charles Canivet, Torrès Caicedo (the plenipotentiary minister of the Republic of San Salvador), Henri Martin, and Ferdinand de Lesseps.

66. Archives Nationales, Georges Grison, 454AP/192.

67. Olga Flinch, *Paris of To-day*, trans. Richard Kaufmann (New York: Cassell, 1891), 175.

68. Lepage, *Les dîners artistiques*, 19. *Grand dictionnaire universel du XIXᵉ siècle*, 17: 1098, 1060.

69. Jules Claretie, *La vie à Paris: 1880–1885* (Paris: V. Havard, 1882), 2(1881): 36.

70. Henri d'Alermas, "Entre éditeurs et auteurs," *La Revue Mondiale* 64 (1907): 467.

71. There were several connections between the Taylor Dinner and *Le Figaro*; it could very well have been someone else at the dinner who introduced Grison to Dentu.

72. Quoted in Colin Jones, *Paris: Biography of a City* (London: Penguin, 2004), 368. Simone Delattre has discussed this issue. See Simone Delattre, *Les douze heures noires: la nuit à Paris au XIXᵉ siècle* (Paris: Albin Michel, 2000), 794.

73. The tradition of the "social investigation" goes back to Etienne de Jouy and the *Tableaux de Paris*. Croci, "Naissance," 15–16.

74. In fact, fidelity to what Dominique Kalifa calls Sue's "topographic imaginary of crime" remained strong until the 1920s. Dominique Kalifa, "Crime Scenes: Criminal Topography and Social Imaginary in Nineteenth-Century Paris," *French Historical Studies* 27, no. 1 (2004): 187.

75. Pierre Zaccone, *Les nuits du boulevard: grand roman parisien très dramatique* (Paris: Fayard, 1879 [1876]), 220.

76. Kalifa analyzes this "decentering" of imagined criminality from the razed quarters of central Paris outward, toward the north and west, in relation to Haussmannization. Kalifa, "Crime Scenes," 181–82.

77. Kalifa, "Crime Scenes," 184. Delattre, *Les douzes heures*, 794.

78. Auguste Lepage, *Les boutiques d'esprit* (Paris: Olmer, 1879), 63.

79. *Le Figaro*, 6 March 1879.

80. Grison, in *Le Figaro*, 7 March 1879.

81. The cultivation of this popular taste dovetailed nicely with a nascent paradigm of "clues" that swept the Western investigative imagination in the late nineteenth century; clues shifted primacy from what seemed immediately evident or obvious to that which appeared marginal or small and ostensibly meaningless. (This epistemological model is now commonly associated with the likes of Sigmund Freud and the crime writer Arthur Conan Doyle, both of whom, beginning in the 1880s, made art of the clues hidden in plain sight.) Carlo Ginzburg makes this claim in a celebrated article published in 1978. See Carlo Ginzburg, "Clues: Roots of a Scientific Paradigm," *Theory and Society* 7, no. 3 (1979): 273–88.

82. *Le Figaro*, 5 April 1879; *Le Temps*, 6 April 1879.

83. *Le Figaro*, 6 March 1879.

84. Grison reported that Guillot had asked Dr. Bergeron, the forensics expert, if the blood spurts of the victim would necessarily have landed on the murderer. "We stated our opinion on this point in the Monday morning edition, and the answer is negative," Grison alerted readers, adding with characteristic modesty, "We are happy to see our opinion confirmed by a practitioner as able as Monsieur Bergeron." Grison, *Le Figaro*, 6 March 1879.

85. *Gil Blas*, 24 July 1885.

86. Alain Bauer and Christophe Soullez, *Une histoire criminelle de la France* (Paris: Odile Jacob, 2012), 92. Louis Andrieux, *Souvenirs d'un préfet de police* (Paris: Rouff, 1885), 1: 117.

87. This generalization is derived from a Gallica search of "assassin de filles publiques" in a host of newspapers: *La Presse*, *Le Temps*, *Gil Blas*, and *Le XIXᵉ Siècle*. The prostitute murderer became a recognized urban type in Paris, known for his "sinister pleasure," according to a guide to Parisian vice. Charles Virmaitre, *Paris-impur* (Paris, 1891), 157.

88. Grison's title, *Paris horrible and Paris original*, alluded to Alexandre Privat d'Anglemont's *Paris anecdote and Paris inconnu* and fell within a burgeoning category of post-Sue authors who promised revelations of the strange and hidden parts of Paris. Two other books in this genre were Alfred Delvau's *Les dessous de Paris* (1860) and Alexandre de Lamothe's *Les métiers infames* (1873). Jean-Didier Wagneur, "Portrait de privat en 'reporter,'" *Autour de Vallès* 40 (2010): 26–28.

89. Grison, *Paris horrible*, 1–2.

90. Grison, *Paris horrible*, 4.

91. *Le Figaro*, 3 December 1884; this article, signed by Georges Grison, was later quoted in Alfred Duplessin's reactionary book, *Au pays de la revanche*. Dr. Rommel [Alfred Duplessin], *Au pays de la revanche*, 3rd ed. (Geneva: Stapelmohr, 1886), 162–63.

92. Hogier-Grison [F. Hogier and Georges Grison], *Les hommes de proie: ce qu'elle était, ce qu'elle est, ce qu'elle doit être* (Paris: Librairie Illustrée, 1886–1887), 245.

93. Grison, *Paris horrible*, 307.

94. Grison, *Paris horrible*, 300.

95. Grison, *Paris horrible*, 302.

96. Grison, *Paris horrible*, 4.

97. *Le Tintamarre*, 27 November 1881.

98. *La Justice*, 1 July 1882.

99. *La Nouvelle Revue* (1882): 712. Grison revisited the taxonomies of crime, a staple of the genre, detailing the "36 ways to steal." He included the *vol à la pelote*, the theft of little girls' earrings as they leave school. Grison, *Paris horrible*, 44.

100. Grison, *Paris horrible*, 24.

101. *Le Figaro*, 13 July 1883.

102. *Gil Blas*, 14 and 15 July 1883.

103. *Gil Blas*, 14 July 1883.

104. *Le Figaro*, 13 July 1883.

105. *La Justice*, 14 July 1883.

106. *Journal des Débats*, 15 July 1883.

107. *La Justice*, 30 August 1883.

108. *Gil Blas*, 24 July 1885.

109. *Gil Blas*, 5 August 1883; *Le Radical*, 27 July 1883.

110. *La Justice*, 5 August 1885.

111. Grison, *Le Figaro*, 9 August 1883.

112. *La Justice*, 15 October 1880. *Le Radical*, 2 October 1885.

113. Kalifa, "Les tâcherons," 584.

114. Grison later became a member of the Société des auteurs dramatiques and led the Association générale des nouvellistes parisiens. *Le Matin*, 22 February 1896. On the importance of the Association des journalistes parisiens during this period, see Marc Martin, "La grande famille: l'Association des journalistes parisiens (1885–1939)," *Revue Historique* 275, no. 1 (557) (1986): 129–57.

115. *Gil Blas*, 19 April 1886.

116. *Gil Blas*, 19 April 1886.

117. *Le Gaulois*, 27 September 1888.

118. *Le Gaulois*, 18 April 1895.

119. Léo enjoyed highly successful runs at the Folies-Bergère and the Chatelet. *Gil Blas*, 26 October 1910.

120. Georges Montorgueil, *Les déshabillés au théâtre* (Paris: Floury, 1896), 22.

121. *Le Gaulois*, 1 December 1886.

122. Léo appeared in Grison's *A nous la dernière* (1890) at the Alhambra, which earned praise for its originality. Grison's productions also contained a heavy component of the criminal life of Paris and the police who pursued the culprits (*Muselez-les*, at the Gaite Rouchechouart, 1893). In the 1890s Léo suffered an unspecified illness that kept her from the stage for most of the rest of her life, although she starred in the aforementioned 1898 play that showcased the sentiments of the anti-Dreyfus crowd. With her disappearance from the stage, Grison's theater projects diminished. *Le Radical*, 31 January 1890; *Le Radical*, 11 January 1893; *Le Figaro*, 1 December 1884; *Le Figaro*, 25 October 1910. Two documents establish that Grison and Léo were likely never married. One is Grison's personal file at the Société des gens de lettres, which lists extensive family information; and the other is an official document of 1908 which uses the honorific "mademoiselle" before Lucy Léo's name. *Journal Officiel de la République Française*, 8 March 1908, 1689. Nonetheless, when Léo died, press tributes referred to her as the reporter's wife.

123. *Le Voleur Illustré*, 22 January 1885.

124. Cavailhon, *Les haras de France*, lxiv.

125. *Le Figaro*, 7 May 1886. Giffard, *Souvenirs*, 214.

126. Adolphe Guillot, *Les prisons de Paris et les prisonniers: Paris qui souffre* (Paris: Dentu, 1889), 416; Adolphe Guillot, *Paris qui souffre: la basse geôle du Grand-Châtelet et les morgues modernes* (Paris: Rouquette, 1887), 69. With time, Grison's reporting began to feed into a new current of right-wing nationalism, earning mention from such popular nationalists as Édouard Drumont, who read and quoted Grison approvingly and at length. Édouard Drumont, *La fin d'un monde: étude psychologique et sociale* (Paris: Savine, 1889), 458–60.

127. Thérenty, *La littérature au quotidien*, 90.

128. Grison, *L'affaire*, iii.

129. Goron, *Mémoires*, 2: 207.

130. *Polybiblion: Revue bibliographique universelle* (1887), 267–68.

Notes to Chapter Four

1. *Le Figaro*, 23 March 1887. Georges Grison, *L'affaire de la rue Montaigne, notes prises au jour le jour par un reporter* (Paris: Librairie Illustrée, 1887), 16, 19–20.

2. François Goron, *Les mémoires de M. Goron* (Paris: Flammarion, 1897), 2: 47.

3. *Le XIXᵉ Siècle*, 19 March 1889.

4. For a brilliant history of courtesans in the Old Regime, see Nina Kushner, *Erotic Exchanges: The World of Elite Prostitution in Eighteenth-Century Paris* (Ithaca, NY: Cornell University Press, 2014).

5. Julie Kavanagh, *The Girl Who Loved Camellias: The Life and Legend of Marie Duplessis* (New York: Knopf, 2013), 226.

6. Edmond Roland, writing in *Le Radical*, 25 July 1885.

7. Grison reported that Stein's funeral, at the Église de Saint-Eugène, and burial cost 300 francs; the sum was covered by a close friend, Adèle X., and Stein's unnamed *amant en titre*. *Le Figaro*, 27 July 1885.

8. *Gil Blas*, 30 August 1885.

9. *Le Figaro*, 22 July 1885.

10. *Le Figaro*, 31 July 1885 and 2 August 1885. "We have not wanted to record all manner of rumors that have circulated in the past two days. . . . Bien nous en a pris. The leads followed were not serious ones and the killer remains at large—unless he is at ease, that is, which is more likely" (*Le Figaro*, 26 July 1885).

11. *Le Figaro*, 22 July 1885.

12. *Le XIXᵉ Siècle*, 24 July 1885.

13. *Le Radical*, 25 July 1885.

14. These photograph copies are in the file on the case at the Archives de la Préfecture de Police, BA 83

15. Archives de Paris, D2 U8 223.

16. Brouardel is quoted at length on the Pranzini case in Alexandre Lacassagne, ed., *Précis de médecine légale* (Paris: Masson, 1906), 32, 360.

17. *Le Figaro*, 22 March 1887.

18. *Le Figaro*, 22 March 1887.

19. Archives de Paris, D2 U8 223.

20. *Le Figaro*, 22 March 1887.

21. Grison, *L'affaire*, 3.

22. Goron, *Mémoires*, 2: 45.

23. Archives de Paris, D2 U8 223.

24. Archives de Paris, D2 U8 223.

25. *Le Figaro*, 24 July 1885.

26. Information on Marie Regnault's early life can be found in the investigative report signed by Chief Taylor and in newspaper reporting. Archives de Paris, D2 U8 223; *Le Matin*, 10 April 1887.

27. For decades the Second Empire was remembered as the halcyon days of the demimonde. Frédéric Loliée, *The Gilded Beauties of the Second Empire* (New York: Brentano's, 1909).

28. A number of historians have worked on these themes. See, for example, Jann Matlock, *Scenes of Seduction: Prostitution, Hysteria, and Reading Difference in Nineteenth-Century France* (New York: Columbia University Press, 1994). Corbin's classic study remains a reference work on prostitution in France during this period. Alain Corbin, *Women for Hire: Prostitution and Sexuality in France after 1850*, trans. Alan Sheridan (Cambridge, MA: Harvard University Press, 1996).

29. Donald Reid, *Paris Sewers and Sewermen: Realities and Representations* (Cambridge, MA: Harvard University Press, 1991), 23.

30. Gabrielle Houbre, ed., *Le livre des courtisanes: archives secrètes de la police des moeurs (1861–1876)* (Paris: Tallandier, 2006), 36. Jean-Marc Berlière, *La police des moeurs sous la IIIᵉ republique* (Paris: Seuil, 1992), 56–58.

31. Houbre, *Le livre des courtisanes*, 14.

32. Houbre, *Le livre des courtisanes*, 19–20.

33. *Le Figaro*, 22 July 1885.

34. Houbre, *Le livre des courtisanes*, 9–10.

35. Houbre, *Le livre des courtisanes*, 28.

36. Matlock, *Scenes of Seduction*, 107.

37. Paul Gerbod, "A propos du Loisir parisien au XIXᵉ siècle," *Ethnologie Française* 23, no. 4 (1993): 619.

38. Houbre, *Le livre des courtisanes*, 29, 14.

39. Archives de Paris, D2 U8 223.

40. *Le Matin*, 10 April 1887.

41. Houbre, *Le livre des courtisanes*, 32.

42. Houbre, *Le livre des courtisanes*, 206.

43. Houbre, *Le livre des courtisanes*, 201, 169, 250.

44. Calderon pushed the limits far enough to run afoul of the police during the Mathey affair, which saw his arrest and brief jailing in June 1873 (technically, the case was a closed-door legal matter in that the names of society men were kept off the public record). Houbre, *Le livre des courtisanes*, 250, 277.

45. Police report of January 1873; Houbre, *Le livre des courtisanes*, 278.

46. Houbre, *Le livre des courtisanes*, 30.

47. Houbre, *Le livre des courtisanes*, 530, 535.

48. Houbre, *Le livre des courtisanes*, 30.

49. Houbre, *Le livre des courtisanes*, 171, 475, 578n.

50. Hogier-Grison [F. Hogier and Georges Grison], *Les hommes de proie: ce qu'elle était, ce qu'elle est, ce qu'elle doit être* (Paris: Librairie Illustrée, 1886–1887), 245. Here Grison was reiterating a point he had made in *Paris horrible*, 294–99.

51. Houbre, *Le livre des courtisanes*, 166.

52. Goron, *Mémoires*, 2: 110.

53. Cora Pearl, *The Memoirs of Cora Pearl: The English Beauty of the French Empire* (London: George Vickers, 1886), 103, 131.

54. *The Pretty Women of Paris: Their Names and Addresses, Qualities and Faults,*

Being a Complete Directory; or, Guide to Pleasure for Visitors to the Gay City (Paris: 1883), 155, 157, 3, 63.

55. Corbin, *Women for Hire*, 70; Houbre, *Le livre des courtisanes*, 44.

56. Police report of 16 October 1874; Houbre, *Le livre des courtisanes*, 277–78.

57. Houbre, *Le livre des courtisanes*, 413.

58. Benoit Lecoq, "Les cercles parisiens au debut de la troisième république: de l'apogée au declin," *Revue d'Histoire Moderne et Contemporaine* 4 (1985): 616, 595, 598, 603. Houbre, *Le livre des courtisanes*, 577, 413.

59. This contemporary is quoted in Gaston Jollivet, *Souvenirs de la vie de plaisir sous le second empire* (Paris: Tallandier, 1927), 29–30.

60. Archives de Paris, D2 U8 223.

61. Houbre, *Le livre des courtisanes*, 460.

62. *Le Matin*, 10 April 1887.

63. *Le Matin*, 10 April 1887.

64. *Le Matin*, 10 April 1887.

65. *Le Matin*, 10 April 1887.

66. *New York Times*, 11 April 1887.

67. *Le Matin*, 10 April 1887.

68. *Le Matin*, 10 April 1887.

69. Christophe Charle, *A Social History of France in the 19th Century*, trans. Miriam Kochan (Oxford: Berg, 1994 [1991]), 265. Small business managers and small landowners, midlevel public officials, teachers, and officers earned between 2,500 and 5,000 francs per year.

70. Carol A. Mossman, *Writing with a Vengeance: The Countess de Chabrillan's Rise from Prostitution* (Toronto: University of Toronto Press, 2009), 4.

71. Houbre, *Le livre des courtisanes*, 55–57.

72. Nicholas Green, "Dealing in Temperaments: Economic Transformations of the Artistic Field in France During the Second Half of the Nineteenth Century," in Mary Tompkins Lewis, ed., *Critical Readings in Impressionism and Post-Impressionism: An Anthology* (Berkeley: University of California Press, 2007), 35–37.

73. Paul Eudel, *L'Hôtel Drouot et la curiosité en 1883* (Paris: Charpentier, 1884), 83.

74. Paul Eudel, *L'Hôtel Drouot et la curiosité en 1881* (Paris: Charpentier, 1882), 246.

75. Reports of forgeries trafficked through the Hôtel Drouot were common in the 1880s. *The Art Union* 1, no. 2 (February 1884), 38–40.

76. Robert Jensen, *Marketing Modernism in Fin-de-Siècle Europe* (Princeton, NJ: Princeton University Press, 1994), 50–51.

77. Vincent van Gogh, letter to Theo van Gogh, Paris, 29 June 1875, quoted in Jennifer Helvey, *Irises: Vincent van Gogh in the Garden* (Los Angeles: J. Paul Getty Museum, 2009), 134.

78. The dealer was Paul Durand-Ruel, who had a gallery nearby, in the rue Laffitte. Durand-Ruel worked as an expert for the Hôtel Drouot. The money he made from selling the work of Millet and other Barbizon painters led him to speculate in the work of the Impressionists. Zola skewers Parisian art dealers, portraying

Durand-Ruel and other gallerists in his 1886 novel *L'Oeuvre* as having learned their techniques for inflating the prices of artworks from the Bourse, the subject of a subsequent novel, *Money.* Jensen, *Marketing Modernism*, 53, 60, 61.

79. Peter H. Feist, *Pierre-Auguste Renoir, 1841–1919: A Dream of Harmony* (Cologne: Taschen, 1987), 93. Jensen, *Marketing Modernism*, 50–51.

80. Paul Eudel, *L'Hôtel Drouot et la curiosite en 1882* (Paris: Charpentier, 1883), 87.

81. *New York Times*, 18 October 1886.

82. Eudel, *L'Hôtel Drouot en 1881*, III.

83. Alexandre Dumas *fils*, foreword to *Le Demimonde, comédie en cinq actes, en prose*, in Alexandre Dumas, *Théâtre complet de Al. Dumas* (Paris: Michel Lévy, 1868), 10. Dumas *fils* believed that courtesans should be distinguished from demimondaines.

84. Eudel, *L'Hôtel Drouot et la curiosité en 1884–1885* (Paris: Charpentier, 1886), 22.

85. Eudel, *L'Hôtel Drouot en 1882*, 217, 221.

86. Janell Watson, *Literature and Material Culture from Balzac to Proust: The Collection and Consumption of Curiosities* (Cambridge, UK: Cambridge University Press, 2004), 15.

87. Robert A. Nye, "The Medical Origins of Sexual Fetishism," in Emily Apter and William Pietz, eds., *Fetishism as Cultural Discourse* (Ithaca, NY: Cornell University Press, 1993), 13–30.

88. Eudel, *L'Hôtel Drouot en 1882*, 217.

89. Watson, *Literature and Material Culture*, 10.

90. Timothy Brown, "The Gendering of Cultural Consumption in the Public Sphere of the French Second Empire and the Early Third Republic," *Proceedings of the Annual Meeting of the Western Society for French History* 23 (1996):449.

91. A production of Théodore Barrière's *Les filles de marbre* in the summer of 1887 was alleged to have used the salon furnishings of the "horizontale célèbre" Marie Regnault's apartment in its staging—a false rumor put out for publicity's sake, and the intervening months had only stoked curiosity. *Gil Blas*, July 1887.

92. Paul Eudel, *L'Hôtel Drouot et la curiosité en 1887–1888* (Paris: Charpentier, 1889), 130.

93. Eudel, *L'Hôtel Drouot en 1887–1888*, 141–42.

94. *The Bookmart* 5 (1888): 488.

95. Eudel, *L'Hôtel Drouot en 1887–1888*, 146.

96. Edmond About, *Le décaméron du salon de peinture pour l'année 1881* (Paris: Librairie des bibliophiles, 1881), 32.

97. *The Bookmart* 5, (1888): 488; and Eudel, *L'Hôtel Drouot en 1887–1888*, 143.

98. Eudel, *L'Hôtel Drouot en 1887–1888*, 146.

99. Eudel, *L'Hôtel Drouot en 1887–1888*, 143, 146.

Notes to Chapter Five

1. *Le Bosphore Égyptien*, 17 April 1887.

2. Archives de Paris, D2 U8 223.

3. For a historical overview of modern Egypt, see Afaf Lutfi Al-Sayyid Marsot, *A History of Egypt: From the Arab Conquest to the Present*, 2nd ed. (Cambridge, UK: Cambridge University Press, 2007).

4. *L'Année Politique*, 23 February 1883, 69.

5. *L'Année Politique*, 23 February 1883, 69. For an idea of the saddened response to the events of 1882, see Pierre Giffard, *Les Français en Égypte* (Paris: Havard, 1883).

6. Olivier Jens Schmitt, *Les Levantins: cadres de vie et identités d'un group ethno-confessionnel de l'empire ottoman au "long" 19ᵉ siècle*, trans. Jean-François de Andria (Istanbul: Isis, 2007).

7. Claude Liauzu, "Éloge du Levantin," *Confluences Méditerranée* 24 (winter 1997–1998): 61–62, 65. See also G. Z. Hochberg, "'Permanent Immigration': Jacqueline Kahanoff, Ronit Matalon, and the Impetus of Levantinism," *Boundary* 31, no. 2 (2004): 221; and G. Z. Hochberg, *In Spite of Partition: Jews, Arabs, and the Limits of Separatist Imagination* (Princeton, NJ: Princeton University Press, 2010), 47.

8. Hala Halim, *Alexandrian Cosmopolitanism: An Archive* (New York: Fordham University Press, 2013), 2–3.

9. Olympe Audouard, *Les mystères de l'Egypt dévoilés*, 2nd ed. (Paris: E. Dentu, 1866), 461, 469–70.

10. Audouard, *Les mystères*, 469.

11. Schmitt, *Les Levantins*.

12. Martin Staum, "Nature and Nurture in French Ethnography and Anthropology, 1859–1914," *Journal of the History of Ideas* 65, no. 3 (2004): 475–95.

13. Arthur de Gobineau, *The Inequality of Human Races*, trans. Adrian Collins (New York: Putnam, 1915 [1855]), 150.

14. E. Baring Cromer, *Modern Egypt* (New York: Macmillan, 1908), 2: 248–50.

15. *L'Illustration*, 16 July 1887.

16. Robert Ilbert, *Alexandrie, 1830–1930: histoire d'une communauté citadine* (Cairo: Institut Français d'Archeologie Orientale, 1996), 73. Michael J. Reimer, "Colonial Bridgehead: Social and Spatial Change in Alexandria, 1850–1882," *International Journal of Middle East Studies* 20 (1988): 531. Mercedes Volait, "La communauté italienne et ses édiles," *Revue de l'Occident Musulman et de la Méditerranée* 46 (1987): 138, 140.

17. Ilbert, *Alexandrie*, 36, 38.

18. David G. LoRomer, *Merchants and Reform in Livorno, 1814–1868* (Berkeley: University of California Press, 1987), 217, 243. Marie-Christine Engels, *Merchants, Interlopers, Seamen, and Corsairs: The "Flemish" Community in Livorno and Genoa* (Amsterdam: Uitgeverij Verloren, 1997), 45.

19. Volait, "La communauté italienne," 141.

20. For a vivid episode illustrating the realities and dangers of cosmopolitanism, see Maya Jasanoff, "Cosmopolitan: A Tale of Identity from Ottoman Alexandria," *Common Knowledge* 11, no. 3 (2005): 393–409.

21. On the role of finance and commerce in Europe's seizure of Egypt's governmental powers, the classic study is David S. Landes, *Bankers and Pashas: Inter-*

national Finance and Economic Imperialism in Egypt (New York: Harper & Row, 1969).

22. Marsot, *History of Egypt*, 79. Robert Ilbert, "L'exclusion du voisin: pouvoirs et relations intercommunautaires, 1870–1900," *Revue de l'Occident Musulman et de la Méditerranée* 46, no. 1 (1987): 177–86.

23. Reimer, "Colonial Bridgehead," 545; Volait, "La communauté italienne," 138, 140.

24. Robert Ilbert, "Bombardement et incendie juillet 1882: Un Témoignage," *Revue de l'Occident Musulman et de la Méditerranée* 46, no. 1 (1987): 157–67.

25. Mathew Burrows, "'Mission Civilisatrice': French Cultural Police in the Middle East, 1860–1914," *The Historical Journal* 29, no. 1 (1986): 111.

26. Ilbert, *Alexandrie*, 95–96.

27. Volait, "La communauté italienne," 140–41.

28. Owen White and J. P. Daughton, eds., *In God's Empire: French Missionaries in the Modern World* (Oxford: Oxford University Press, 2012), 5–6. The Catholics' duels with other Christian denominations amounted to what one historian has called a "conversion war" in Ottoman cities of the Ottoman Empire, where impoverished European Christians sometimes also found advantages in converting to Islam. (Conversely, Ottoman administrators took a harsh, if not entirely consistent, stance against Muslims who converted to Christianity.) Sarah A. Curtis, "Charity Begins Abroad: The Filles de la Charité in the Ottoman Empire," in Owen White and J. P. Daughton, eds., *In God's Empire: French Missionaries in the Modern World* (Oxford: Oxford University Press, 2012), 99.

29. Jean-Jacques Luthi, *Vie quotidienne en Egypte au temps de khédives* (Paris: L'Harmattan, 1999), 139–40.

30. Maṣlaḥat al-Barīd, *All About Postal Matters in Egypt* (Florence: Landi Press, 1898), 23.

31. Archives de Paris, D2 U8 223.

32. *Journal des Débats*, 28 March 1887.

33. Archives de Paris, D2 U8 223.

34. Archives de Paris, D2 U8 223.

35. For geographically diverse studies of middlemen and interlopers who worked as go-betweens within the structures of the British and French empires at this time, see Andrew Arsan, *Interlopers of Empire: The Lebanese Diaspora in Colonial French West Africa* (New York: Oxford University Press, 2014); and Nara Dillon and Jean C. Oi, eds., *At the Crossroads of Empires: Middlemen, Social Networks, and State-Building in Republican Shanghai* (Stanford, CA: Stanford University Press, 2007).

36. Cromer, *Modern Egypt*, 2: 248–50.

37. Halim has noted this commonplace about interpreters. Halim, *Alexandrian Cosmopolitanism*, 202.

38. "Allowances to R.N. Officers for Passing in Oriental Languages and Acting as Interpreters," 1873, British Archives, L/MIL/7/1583: Royal Navy Squadron in Indian Waters.

39. Letter dated 1 June 1866, British Archives, L/MIL/7/1582.

40. Letter from Lord Cromer to the Secretary Admiralty from the India Office, Simla, 20 July 1883, British Archives, Li/MIL/7/1584.

41. Records of Pranzini's military service were furnished by the British at the request of the French consulate. Archives de Paris, D2 U8 223. I have found documentation of Pranzini's tour in Sudan. Entry for Enrico Pranzini, "UK, Military Campaign Medal and Award Rolls, 1793–1949," consulted at the National Archives, London.

42. Quoted in Saloni Mathur, *India By Design: Colonial History and Cultural Display* (Berkeley: University of California Press, 2007), 87.

Notes to Chapter Six

1. François Goron, *Les mémoires de M. Goron* (Paris: Flammarion, 1897), 1: 29.

2. Goron, *Mémoires*, 2: 53.

3. Both reports appeared in *La Croix*, 19 April 1887.

4. Archives de Paris, D2 U8 223.

5. The capture of Michel Eyraud in Spanish Cuba a couple of years later, a coup masterminded by Goron himself, stands out among these.

6. Quotes in the previous paragraphs are from Goron, *Mémoires*, 1: 1, 5, 7, 9, 11.

7. J. P. Daughton, "When Argentina Was 'French': Rethinking Cultural Politics and European Imperialism in Belle-Epoque Buenos Aires," *Journal of Modern History* 80, no. 4 (2008): 836, 843. Daughton cites François Weil, "French Migration to the Americas in the 19th and 20th Centuries as a Historical Problem," *Studi Emigrazione* 33 (1996): 443–60. Daughton includes a useful discussion of French cultural influence in Argentina and the historiography on this and related themes. His observation that historians are only beginning to see informal colonization—that is, unofficial forms of French imperial influence during this period—in relation to officially established French colonies is a starting point for this chapter. However, whereas Daughton, following other historians of colonialism, expresses some misgivings about the vagueness of "informal empire," I side with those who use that term as the basis of a distinction—though by no means the only one—between territories and peoples on whom an imperial regime makes manifest formal claims and those on whom a state does not make such claims.

8. Goron, *Mémoires*, 1: 29.

9. Goron, *Mémoires*, 1: 29, 30, 32.

10. Horace Valbel, *La police de la sûreté en 1889* (Paris: Dentu, 1889), 19, 101.

11. In his memoirs, Louis Andrieux, police prefect from 1879 to 1881, tells of receiving a tip regarding a certain Georges de Carmona, a "rich Mexican" who had served in the French imperial campaigns in Mexico and was well-known in the *colonie étrangère* in Paris since his arrival in 1875. Carmona had ingratiated himself with Parisian aristocrats by donating large sums of money to their charitable works and throwing lavish soirées at his residence in the avenue Hoche, just off the Champs-Elysées. In April 1881 he was denounced for disloyalty to the European im-

perial forces under the Archduke Maximilian in Mexico twenty years before and for having murdered a man in Mexico City. Did Carmona's "unbelievable adventures," as the denunciation letter put it, pose a public danger to Paris? Andrieux contacted the Mexican Foreign Ministry and was informed that Carmona had participated in an expedition that left Mazatlan at the end of 1864 but had not betrayed the expedition. To the contrary, he was wounded and decorated with the Ordre Imperialiste de Guadeloupe and left the army only after the empire's collapse. Andrieux found no evidence of involvement in a murder. Louis Andrieux, *Souvenirs d'un préfet de police* (Paris: Rouff, 1885), 1: 316.

12. Clive Emsley, "A Typology of Nineteenth-Century Police," *Crime, Histoire et Sociétés/Crime, History, and Societies* 3, no. 1 (1999): 29–44. Jean Vidalenc, "Armée et police en France, 1814–1914," in Jacques Aubert, ed., *L'état et sa police en France, 1789–1914* (Geneva: Librairie Droz, 1979), 135.

13. Jean-Marc Berlière, *Le Prefet Lépine: vers la naissance de la police moderne* (Paris: Denoël, 1993), 130–38.

14. Clive Emsley, *Gendarmes and the State in Nineteenth-Century Europe* (Oxford: Oxford University Press, 1999), 140, 143. Napoleon called the gendarmerie "moitié civile, moitié militaire." Georges Carrot, *Histoire de la police francaise des origines à nos jours* (Paris: Tallandier, 1992), 203. In 1903 the gendarmerie's status was clarified with respect to the civil authorities and military authorities, essentially confirming that it was an institution whose glory was behind it. Beginning in 1880, we see a "normalisation du métier" of the police, writes Quentin Deluermoz in his wonderful recent history. As a modern professional identity took root, the question was how the military background, practices, training, and self-representation would fit into the prefecture's new public effort to portray the police as civil servants: "The distance that separated an institution that was still very military from civilian service faded," as in other areas of public service. The *gardiens de la paix*, uniformed beat cops, were given formal training in civility to smooth their interactions with Parisian residents, to cite just one of the prefecture's initiatives. Quentin Deluermoz, *Des policiers dans la ville* (Paris: Publications de la Sorbonne, 2012), 22, 227.

15. Another means was the creation of a memorial to policemen "killed in the line of duty" (*victimes du devoir*), in the manner that nations commemorate military victories and losses, thus recasting policemen as quasi-military heroes. When this monument was erected to policemen in the mid-1880s, another friend of Goron's, Viguier, was the first man buried beneath it, "like so many others in the Parisian police, where heroism is a tradition and everyone is a soldier." Goron, *Mémoires*, 1: 50. Deluermoz cites several other examples of the Paris police borrowing military aesthetics, as in the police's new public "marches" and the rigorous annual military training that the police prefect Louis Lépine made a requirement for policemen in the mid-1890s. In terms of the number of men this affected, the statistics tell a story. Whereas only 10% of the French male population performed military service under the Restoration monarchy, by the late 1880s that figure stood at 60%. The spillover of military veterans into police work was virtually preordained by

a law promulgated in 1872. Crafted to entice young men into prolonging their military service, the law promised state employment to soldiers who did so; in practice, these jobs often took the form of police work. Odile Roynette, *"Bons pour le service": l'expérience de la caserne en France à la fin du XIXe siècle en France* (Paris: Belin, 2000). A similar law followed in 1889. Berlière, *Le Préfet Lépine*, 130–38.

16. The question of the relation between colonial empire and metropolitan policing began to receive attention in the context of twentieth-century Britain and France. See Georgina Sinclair, *At the End of the Line: Colonial Police Forces and the Imperial Endgame, 1945–1980* (Manchester: Manchester University Press, 2006). See also Emmanuel Blanchard, *La police parisienne et les Algériens* (Paris: Editions du Nouveau monde, 2011).

17. *Histoire et dictionnaire de la police*, s.v. "Police coloniale" (Paris: Laffont, 2005).

18. On police memoirs, see Dominique Kalifa, *Crime et culture au XIXe siècle* (Paris: Perrin, 2005), ch. 3.

19. Several prominent future members of Security were quickly redeployed to Algeria. There was Bleuze, who, like Gustave Rossignol, joined the so-called elite, who were nominated to Security's *brigade spéciale*. Bleuze spent 14 years in the army, including a stint as a sous-officier in the Zouaves, with whom he fought in the campaigns of Algeria from 1864 to 1870. The sous-brigadier Clairet served in Kabylie, Algeria, where Rossignol had served, in the 1860s. The son of peasants, Clairet left home at age 17 to join the third regiment of the chasseurs d'Afrique in Constantine. He participated in several *colonnes expeditionnaires* and was posted on the Tunisian border, where several times he pursued the Kroumirs and other tribes who raided the French-controlled tribes in the area. Clairet crossed the Sahara on a walk that lasted three months, living on biscuits, before returning in 1870. He was wounded and captured and then sent back to Kabylie the following year.

20. Valbel, *La police*, 157.

21. Goron, *Mémoires*, 1: 54.

22. Claude actively worked for the Versailles government and was imprisoned by the Communards. Valbel, *La police*, 283–84.

23. Théodore Laborieu, *Mémoires de M. Claude, chef de la police de sûreté*, (Paris: J. Rouff, 1881–1883), 8: 8, 10.

24. Archimbaud, following his service against Prussia, sided against the Communards, was taken hostage, condemned to death, held as hostage, escaped, and saw combat. He was sent to spy on the Communards by the government at Versailles. Captured and imprisoned, he was twice condemned to die but managed to escape and took fire. Valbel, *La police*, 235–37.

25. Gaillarde joined the police before the war against Prussia, when he put his "incroyable audace" on display. Valbel, *La police*, 62.

26. Macé also counted freemasons and ne'er-do-wells among the Security officers, along with agitators and undisciplined schemers. G. Macé, *Le service de la sureté* (Paris: Charpentier, 1884), 301–2, 306.

27. Quoted in Charles Virmaitre, *Paris Police* (Paris: Dentu, 1886), 284–85.

28. Valbel, *La police*, 19, 101.

29. Rossignol was stabbed several times in his arrest of the anarchist Clément Duval. For this, the president of the Republic awarded the inspector a "first-class gold medal." It was one of more than 700 arrests that Rossignol recorded in his career at Security. Valbel, *La police*, 159.

30. *Histoire et dictionnaire de la police*, s.v. "Rossignol," 849.

31. Rossignol and his colleague Fortuné Jaume, who was perhaps the most famous of all Parisian detectives at the turn of the century, were given a 100-franc salary raise for one noted capture. Valbel, *La police*, 164–65, 177, 180.

32. Goron, *Mémoires*, 1: 191–92.

33. Goron, *Mémoires*, 1: 193–94.

34. Goron, *Mémoires*, 1: 149.

35. Goron, *Mémoires*, 2: 54, 55, 76, 77, 80, 92, 252.

36. Charles-V. Aubrun, "Rastaquouère et rasta," *Bulletin Hispanique* 57, no. 4 (1955): 430–39.

37. René Maizeroy (Baron René-Jean Toussaint), *La fin de Paris* (Paris: Victor-Havard, 1886), 56.

38. Gaston Jollivet, *Souvenirs de la vie de plaisir sous le second empire* (Paris: Tallandier, 1927), 79–80. By the 1920s, when Jollivet published his memoirs, the word *rastaquouère* had been shortened to simply *rasta* and lost some of its pejorative bite, which was in turn subsumed by the term *apache*, which carried connotations of harder edged criminality. The slur *métèque*, a favorite of the right-wing novelist Maurice Barrès, took on the geographic designation of Latin America.

39. Aurélien Scholl, *Paris aux cent coups* (Paris: Librairie Illustrée, 1887), 157–59, 215.

40. Scholl, *Paris aux cent coups*, 215.

41. Hugues Le Roux, *L'enfer parisien* (Paris: Victor-Havard, 1888), 110, 105–6.

42. Bachaumont, preface to Jules Guérin and Paul Ginisty, *Les rastaquouères* (Paris: Rouveyre et Blond, 1883), v, viii, ix. Gérard Noiriel, *Immigration, antisémitisme et racisme en France* (Paris: Fayard, 2007), 210.

43. Édouard Drumont, *La France juive* (Paris: Flammarion, 1886), 2: 176–77.

44. Paul Belon and Georges Price, *Paris qui passe* (Paris: Savine, 1888), 278, 280.

45. *L'Illustration*, 16 July 1887.

46. Albert Bataille, writing in *Le Figaro*, 10 July 1887.

47. Archives de la Préfecture de Police, BA83.

48. *L'Illustration*, 16 July 1887.

49. Goron, *Mémoires*, 2: 54–56, 65. One could continue in this vein with Pranzini's other characteristics: His hair, for example, was described alternately as brown, blond, reddish, or deep black.

50. Stories from abroad were rarely reported in the *faits-divers* columns during this period. Dominique Kalifa, "Les tâcherons de l'information: petits reporters et faits divers à la Belle Époque," *Revue d'Histoire Moderne et Contemporaine* 40, no. 4 (1993): 586. Perrot observes that the *fait-divers* served as a basis for everyday conversation. Michelle Perrot, "Fait divers et histoire au XIXe siècle," *Annales: Économies,*

Sociétés, Civilisations 38, no. 4 (1983): 912. On the emergence of the grand reporter from the tradition of the *journaliste voyageur*, see Marie-Eve Thérenty, "Les 'vagabonds du télégraphe': représentations et poétiques du grand reportage avant 1914," *Sociétés et Représentations* 21 (2006): 101–15.

51. *Journal des Débats*, 28 March 1887; *Le Matin*, 27 March 1887.

52. Archives de la Préfecture de Police, BA83.

53. Once more, Georges Grison's fictional alter ego, Saintonge, served as a timely model. Picking up on the xenophobic overtones of the demimonde murder investigations, du Boisgobey's novel follows Saintonge as he tries to uncover the dealings of a rastaquouère, the glamorous Marquis de Simancas, a Cuban-Spanish "satyr from overseas" who is obsessed with sex and money. Befitting the stereotype, Simancas is described as a "superb sample of that race of transatlantic adventurers" who arrive decked out in rings, chains, and shirts with diamond buttons. The epitome of corrupt cosmopolitanism and border-crossing fakery, he is the natural enemy of the "true *peuple*" of France. "Where do they come from, these rich foreigners, decked out in sonorous titles, who arrive in numbers every year in Paris like locusts on the harvests of our colonials in Algeria? . . . Have they escaped from some overseas penal colony, having donned the skin of someone else, like the old convict Coignard, who was received at the court of King Louis XVIII as the Count de Saint-Hélène?" What is Simancas up to? We learn that he has come to Paris to "debauch the young women of the *peuple*" and to buy up the city's elite prostitutes, whom he exploits as though they were "locked up in a harem in Constantinople." The implication is clear enough: Simancas is a trader of white slaves. Fortuné du Boisgobey, *Cornaline la dompteuse* (Paris: Plon, 1887), 103, 107, 164.

54. Alain Corbin, *Women for Hire: Prostitution and Sexuality in France After 1850*, trans. Alan Sheridan (Cambridge, MA: Harvard University Press, 1990), 275.

55. Corbin, *Women for Hire*, 280.

56. Corbin, *Women for Hire*, 239, 283, 287–88.

57. *The Pretty Women of Paris: Their Names and Addresses, Qualities and Faults, Being a Complete Directory; or, Guide to Pleasure for Visitors to the Gay City* (Paris, 1883), 8–9.

58. Cora Pearl, *The Memoirs of Cora Pearl: The English Beauty of the French Empire* (London: Vickers, 1886), 107–8.

59. Robert Nye, "Heredity or Milieu: The Foundations of European Criminological Theory," *Isis* 67, no. 238 (1976): 335–55; and Martin J. Weiner, *Reconstructing the Criminal: Culture, Law, and Policy in England, 1830–1914* (New York: Cambridge University Press, 1990).

60. Gabriel Tarde, *La philosophie pénale* (Paris: Masson, 1890), 157, 165.

61. Henri Joly, *Le crime: étude sociale* (Paris: Cerf, 1888), 290.

62. Alphonse Bertillon's file lists the color of Pranzini's iris as follows: a pupillary zone of dark orange, a ciliary zone of light greenish-slate. "Une visite à la préfecture de police, au bureau des signalements anthropométriques de M. Alphonse Bertillon," *Revue d'Anthropologie*, ser. 3, 16 (1887): 579.

63. Gerard Noiriel, "Les pratiques policières d'identification des migrants et leurs enjeux pour l'histoire des relations de pouvoir," in Marie-Claude Blanc-Chaléard, Caroline Douki, Nicole Dyonet, and Vincent Milliot, eds., *Police et migrants: France, 1667–1939* (Rennes: Presses universitaires de Rennes, 2001), 128.

64. Alphonse Bertillon, *Ethnographie moderne: les races sauvages* (Paris: G. Masson, 1883). Alphonse Bertillon, *L'identité des récidivistes et la loi de la relégation* (Paris: G. Masson, 1883). Timothy Mitchell observed that the history of the systematization of paper identification and controls began in the East; these measures were subsequently implemented in the metropole. Timothy Mitchell, *Colonising Egypt* (Berkeley: University of California Press, 1991), 34–35. For an overview of the bureaucratic stages of Bertillon's rise and contribution to the modernization of identification techniques, see Ilsen About, "Les fondations d'un systeme national d'identification policière en France (1893–1914)," *Genèses* 54 (March 2004): 28–52.

65. *Journal des Débats*, 1 April 1887.

66. Paul Brouardel, *Affaire Pranzini: triple assassinat; relation medico-legale* (Paris: J.-B. Baillière, 1887), 30.

67. These are the papers now housed at the Archives de Paris, D2 U8 223.

68. Press clipping, "Affaire Pranzini," *La Vie Judiciaire*, Archives de la Préfecture de Police, BA83.

69. Quotes in this paragraph and the preceding paragraph from Archives de Paris, D2 U8 223.

70. Presse judiciaire de Paris, *Le palais de justice de Paris: son monde et ses moeurs* (Paris: Librairies-Imprimeries Réunies, 1892), 346.

71. Adolphe Guillot, *Les prisons de Paris et les prisonniers: Paris qui souffre* (Paris: Dentu, 1889), 166.

72. Jean-Claude Farcy, "L'enquête pénale dans la France du XIXᵉ siècle," in Jean-Claude Farcy, Dominique Kalifa, and Jean-Noël Luc, eds., *L'enquête judiciaire en Europe au XIXᵉ siècle: acteurs, imaginaires, pratiques* (Paris: Créaphis, 2007), 27–28.

73. For more on this, see Chapter 8.

74. Farcy, "L'enquête pénale," 39.

75. Emphasis added.

76. All quotes in the preceding paragraphs are from Archives de Paris, D2 U8 223.

77. Goron, *Mémoires*, 2: 53.

78. Goron, *Mémoires*, 2: 82.

79. Goron, *Mémoires*, 1: 94.

80. Goron, *Mémoires*, 2: 102, 121.

81. Goron, *Mémoires*, 2: 123.

82. Marc Martin, *Les grands reporters: les débuts du journalisme moderne* (Paris: Éditions Audibert, 2005).

83. Goron, *Mémoires*, 2: 127. Félix Dubois, "La vie noire: un voyage d'exploration au Soudan français," *L'Illustration*, 8 October 1892, 285–92. Félix Dubois, *La vie au continent noir* (Paris: J. Hetzel, 1895).

84. Goron, *Mémoires*, 2: 124.
85. Goron, *Mémoires*, 2: 116.
86. Goron, *Mémoires*, 2: 125.
87. Goron, *Mémoires*, 2: 126.
88. Dana Simmons, *Vital Minimum: Need, Science, and Politics in Modern France* (Chicago: University of Chicago Press, 2015), 45.
89. *Gil Blas*, 23 April 1887.
90. *Requisitoire définitif*, Archives de Paris, D2 U8 223.
91. *Le Matin*, 5 May 1887.

Notes to Chapter Seven

1. A. Remy, "La semaine des amours," in Charles Gille, V. Rabineau, Ch. Colmance et al., eds., *La chanson de tout le monde: chansonnier nouveau* (Paris: Durand, 1861), n.p.
2. *Le Gaulois*, 25 June 1887 and 26 March 1896.
3. Georges Grison, *Le procès Pranzini: compte rendu complet des débats* (Paris: La Librairie Illustré), 5–6.
4. *L'Illustration*, 16 July 1887.
5. On the classic, but not the consensus, argument on the rise of the New Right in France, see Zeev Sternhell, *La droite révolutionnaire: les origines françaises du Fascisme, 1885–1914* (Paris: Seuil, 1978). On the anticosmopolitanism of the nationalist right, see Michel Winock, *Histoire de l'extrême droite en France* (Paris: Seuil, 1998). A great many works have examined the history of laughter and its functions in different contexts. I cite two that have informed and inspired my use of this angle in the Pranzini trial: Antoine de Baecque, *Les éclats du rire: la culture des rieurs au XVIIIe siècle* (Paris: Calmann-Lévy, 2000); and Mary Beard, *Laughter in Ancient Rome: On Joking, Tickling, and Cracking Up* (Oakland: University of California Press, 2014).
6. Quoted in Andrew Hussey, *Paris: The Secret History* (New York: Penguin, 2007), 305. For a deep historical reading of the Eiffel Tower and the subsequent turn away from its aesthetic principles, see Deborah L. Silverman, *Art Nouveau in Fin-de-Siècle France: Politics, Psychology, and Style* (Berkeley: University of California Press, 1989).
7. The contemporary historian Édouard Hervé, a monarchist, was likely accurate when he observed that Boulanger "did not create Boulangism, rather it was Boulangism that created him" (*Le Gaulois*, 11 October 1889). In fact, few observers knew where Boulanger stood ideologically, perhaps not even Boulanger himself. Historians have taken turns highlighting the origins of Boulangism in the Jacobin nationalism of the left and the subsequent transfer of this nationalist political strain to the right. At the same time, we know that the old monarchists provided financial support to Boulanger in the hope that he could be used politically; at the ballot box the general appealed to frustrated socialists, artisans, and workers; and Boulanger fit the patently Bonapartist mold of a tough-talking general who, having

made his name in colonial warfare overseas, attempts to parlay his fame into a run on a vulnerable political regime. See Frederic Seager, *The Boulanger Affair: Political Crossroad of France, 1886–1889* (Ithaca, NY: Cornell University Press, 1969). Seager treats the Boulanger phenomenon as the result mainly of "chronic discontent" with the Third Republic's institutions. Seager, *Boulanger Affair*, 3. See also William D. Irvine, *The Boulanger Affair Reconsidered: Royalism, Boulangism, and the Origins of the Radical Right in France* (New York: Oxford University Press, 1989).

8. Gérard Noiriel, *The French Melting Pot: Immigration, Citizenship, and National Identity*, trans. Geoffroy De Laforcade (Minneapolis: University of Minnesota Press, 1996), 215. Alan Mitchell, "The Xenophobic Style: French Counterespionage and the Emergence of the Dreyfus Affair," *Journal of Modern History* 52, no. 3 (1980): 419–21.

9. Grégoire Kauffmann, *Édouard Drumont* (Paris: Perrin, 2008), 138–39.

10. Édouard Drumont, *La fin d'un monde: étude psychologique et sociale* (Paris: Albert Savine, 1889), 472. Drumont remained a committed Boulangist, whereas Georges Clémenceau abandoned the cause when he saw the threat that the general represented to the Third Republic. Boulangism shifted rightward, and the two men became enemies; Drumont later accused Clémenceau of shielding a favored courtesan from a subpoena to testify in the Pranzini trial. Drumont, *La fin d'un monde*, 268–69. On the common ground that brought Drumont toward Boulangism, if slowly at first, see Kauffmann, *Édouard Drumont*, 151–52.

11. Georges Grison, *Le Général Boulanger jugé par ses partisans et ses adversaires* (Paris: Librairie Illustrée, 1888), 461.

12. Grison, *Général Boulanger*, 464.

13. Patrick Hutton, "Popular Boulangism and the Advent of Mass Politics in France, 1886–90," *Journal of Contemporary History* 11, no. 1 (1976): 90.

14. *L'Estafette*, 10 July 1887.

15. Grison, *Général Boulanger*, 500.

16. Edmond Biré, "Chroniques," *Revue de la Révolution*, 28 April 1887.

17. Grison, *Le procès Pranzini*, 183.

18. *Le Figaro*, 19 June 1887.

19. The choreography was so tight and the Gare de Lyon crowd so large and relentless that Boulanger's departure drained some energy from the tired Boulangist crowd, according to *Le Journal des Débats*, 10 July 1887.

20. *Morning Post* (London), 17 October 1887.

21. *New York Times*, 11 April 1887.

22. Bréville came from one of Normandy's oldest families, with roots in the tenth century. His was the sort of conservative Catholic milieu that the French revolutionaries had tried hard to eradicate near the end of the eighteenth century. Bréville's grandfather was financially ruined by the revolution, held hostage in Nantes, and rescued by the turnabout known as the Thermidorian Reaction. The family supported the regime of Napoleon I—education and government service would offer a path back to prestige—and rallied to the fallen emperor's aid after his prison break on the island of Elba. The family's affinity with Bonapartism persisted until the bitter

end of the Second Empire in 1870. By then, Camille Onfroy de Bréville (1799–1889), the judge's father and a civil engineer, had contributed to the design of France's Northern Railway. An anti-Semitic tract published in 1846 approvingly cited the elder Bréville for having "formally refused," in the name of public safety, to sign the bill of sale turning over control of the Northern Railway to Baron James Rothschild, a prominent Jew; the judge's father was later named director of the École des ponts-et-chaussees during the Second Empire. *Le Figaro*, 15 November 1867 and 24 February 1895; M. de Lagrené, "Notice sur M. Onfroy de Bréville," *Annales des ponts et chaussées: partie technique; mémoires et documents* (Paris: Dunod, 1890), 258–65; Georges Dairnvaell, *Histoire édifiante et curieuse de Rotschild Ier, roi des juifs, par Satan* (Paris, published anonymously, 1846), 35. The judge's son was Jacques Marie Gaston Onfroy de Bréville, a militarist artist and illustrator who signed his works "JOB."

23. Bréville was present when Troppmann was confronted with the bodies of his victims, five members of the Kink family, whose bodies were found on the eastern outskirts of Paris. *Le Rappel*, 28 September 1869.

24. Grison, *Le procès Pranzini*, 7, 61. Katherine Fischer Taylor, *In the Theater of Criminal Justice: The Palais de Justice in Second Empire Paris* (Princeton, NJ: Princeton University Press, 1993).

25. *Le Gaulois*, 8 July 1887.

26. Archives de Paris, D2 U8 223.

27. *La Lanterne*, 11 July 1887.

28. *Le Figaro*, 9 July 1887.

29. Grison, *Le procès Pranzini*, 183.

30. *New York Times*, 8 April 1887.

31. Grison, *Le procès Pranzini*, 63.

32. Robert A. Nye, *Masculinity and Male Codes of Honor in Modern France* (Berkeley: University of California Press, 1998), 151. A nineteenth-century observer asserted that France had kept these values alive in its "national character" better than the other nations of Europe (Nye, *Masculinity*, 274n43).

33. Of the list of thirty-six jury candidates for this trial, all were men and none were workers. Cour d'Appel de Paris, Tirage des jurés, Archives de Paris, DU U8 223.

34. Albert Bataille, *Causes criminelles et mondaines de 1887–1888* (Paris: Dentu, 1888), 431.

35. On the distinctions between a pimp and an *amant de coeur*, see Alain Corbin, *Women for Hire: Prostitution and Sexuality in France After 1850*, trans. Alan Sheridan (Cambridge, MA: Harvard University Press, 1990), 155.

36. "All these *avocats* are arch blarneyers," sneered London's *Cornhill Magazine*. "Their fantastic arguments and hysteric declamations make judges to moan [*sic*], but they cause juries to weep, and all the gain is for the prisoners." "A French Assize," *Cornhill Magazine*, reprinted in *The Eclectic Magazine of Foreign Literature, Science, and Art* (New York: Leavitt, Trow, 1882), 215.

37. Demange was the first attorney to step forward as a legal advocate for Drey-

fus. He stuck with the case for more than a decade, aiding Dreyfus and his family through two trials—both of which were lost—and years of subsequent litigation that ultimately cleared Dreyfus's name. The definitive history of the case is Jean-Denis Bredin, *The Affair: The Case of Alfred Dreyfus*, trans. Jeffrey Mehlman (New York: Braziller, 1986).

38. Joseph Reinach, *Histoire de l'affaire Dreyfus: le procès de 1894* (Paris: Éditions de la Revue blanche, 1901), 324.

39. C. Léandre, "Maitre Demange," *Le Figaro*, supplément littéraire, 14ᵉ année, no. 31 (4 August 1888).

40. Reinach, *Histoire de l'affaire Dreyfus*, 324.

41. Léandre, "Maitre Demange."

42. Archives de Paris, D2 U8 223.

43. *Le Gaulois*, 14 July 1887.

44. Cited in a professional tribute to Georges Reynaud following his death. Cour de cassation, "Les audiences solonelles de début d'année judiciaire," October 1918. www.courdecassation.fr/cour_cassation_1/occasion_audiences_59/debut_annee_60/annees_1910_3270/octobre_1918_11143.html (accessed February 21, 2014).

45. Archives de Paris, D2 U8 223.

46. Grison, *Le procès Pranzini*, 20.

47. Grison, *Le procès Pranzini*, 11.

48. Grison, *Le procès Pranzini*, 12.

49. Grison, *Le procès Pranzini*, 7.

50. *Le Gaulois*, 14 July 1887.

51. *Le Figaro*, 10 July 1887.

52. Alain Corbin, *Histoire de la virilité*, vol. 2, *Le triomphe de la virilité: le XIXᵉ siècle* (Paris: Seuil, 2011), 8.

53. Factum to *Le triple assassinat de la rue Montaigne: compte rendu complet du procès* (Paris: Louis Gabillaud, 1887).

54. Grison, *Le procès Pranzini*, 150–51. Here was the genesis of an infamous theory of disguised handwriting that would later be known as autoforgery, which prosecutors used to fabricate proof of Alfred Dreyfus's correspondence with the Germans.

55. *Gil Blas*, 11 July 1890.

56. Just because the term did not exist before the nineteenth century does not mean that such arrangements did not exist. Rather, they were unspeakable. For an example of the gigolo in the ancient world, see Pierre Boyancé, "Une exégèse stoïcienne chez Lucrèce," *Publications de l'École Francaise de Rome* 11, no. 1 (1972): 213. The eighteenth-century culture of aristocratic masked balls in France, to cite another example, allowed women of means to select younger men for relationships, provided that discretion was maintained. Elisabeth Detis, "Le bal masqué: espace de liberté . . . surveillée," *Bulletin de la Société d'Études Anglo-Américaines des XVIIᵉ et XVIIIᵉ Siècles* 30, no. 30 (1990): 97. In eighteenth-century European fiction, a precursor to the gigolo stood for untamed sexual adventurism. The popular

pornographic novel *Le petit-fils d'Hercule* (The Grandson of Hercules; Paris, 1781) gives voice to the gigolo prototype as a hero and narrator of a life based on the motto "Pleasure—pleasure above all" (166). After getting his start as a gigolo in Paris, the title character moves eastward beyond France's borders, travels through Europe, and enjoys invigorating sex with women of every social strata and nationality; Catherine the Great appoints him a viceroy in provincial Russia, where he is free to procreate and populate the outer reaches of her empire. The historian of sexuality Pamela Cheek has argued that *Le petit-fils d'Hercule* offers an example of how eighteenth-century stories showcased male sexual desire as an object and necessary tool of state power. See Pamela Cheek, *Sexual Antipodes: Enlightenment, Globalization, and the Placing of Sex* (Stanford, CA: Stanford University Press, 2003), 115–16. In the British novel *The History of Tom Jones, a Foundling*, by Henry Fielding, published in 1749 to massive popular success (the novel's racy sequences probably helped), the title character, like that in *Le petit-fils d'Hercule*, is a figure of uncertain origins whose mobility is key to his sexual conquests; he settles only when he is imprisoned or housed by an older lover, Lady Bellaston, a figure of London society.

57. Judith Surkis, *Sexing the Citizen: Morality and Masculinity in France, 1870–1920* (Ithaca, NY: Cornell University Press, 2006), 14, 114, 182.

58. Alfred Delvau, *Dictionnaire de la langue verte: argots parisiens comparés* (Paris: Dentu, 1866), 182.

59. Delvau, *Dictionnaire de la langue verte*, 11.

60. Robert opened the Folies-Robert in the mid-1850s. His background and tastes exemplified the midcentury gigolo as an urban type, particularly his gender play, which may have confirmed Delvau's impression that the Folies-Robert was a hotbed for gigolos. Robert had been a working-class drifter for much of his life. He got his start in dance by giving secret lessons in train cars to fellow workers who built the Northern Railway. Later he worked on a steamship routing to and from Constantinople, learned to make mechanical dolls, and dreamed of launching his own dance club. He wanted to teach dance, but lacking funds and proper training, he contrived to gain free entry to the Bal de l'Opéra by disguising himself as a woman—every evening for a decade. His break came when he met an English army major who supposedly believed that he was a member of the opera's ballet troupe. The two men went out to sup and the ruse continued, the story goes, until Robert betrayed his biological gender by shucking the oysters. The English major was delighted and appointed Robert his personal *maître de danse*, which came with extravagant pay. Robert netted the 1,000 pounds sterling required to embellish a 700-square-meter dance space in Moorish style. The annual Carnaval festival was the club's high point, with 2,000 people streaming in to partake in pleasures that lay outside the mainstream. Antonio Watripon, *Paris qui danse: études, types et moeurs* (Paris: Chez tous les libraires, 1861), 14, 40. Later, at a similar establishment, the Concert de l'Horloge in the Faubourg Montmartre, an offbeat crowd—pimps, gigolettes, and bourgeois—gathered for light songs and cheap entertainments. *Paris intimes et mystérieux: guide des plaisirs mondains et des plaisirs secrets à Paris* (Paris: André Hall, 1904), 113.

61. Alfred Delvau, *Les cythères parisiennes: histoire anecdotique des bals de Paris* (Paris: Dentu, 1864), 83–85.

62. Proust would evoke the gigolo's fluid sexuality—the gigolo is a man for "whom there might be need in a brothel"—in *À la recherche du temps perdu*, a novel that revisits the link between homosexuality and dance culture of a more highbrow sort. Marcel Proust, *À la recherche du temps perdu*, ed. Jean-Yves Tadié (Paris: Gallimard, 1987–89), 3: 668–69, quoted in Marion Schmid, "Proust at the Ballet: Literature and Dance in Dialogue," *French Studies: A Quarterly Review* 67, no. 2 (April 2013): 187.

63. Sexual taboos encouraged lexical and legal lacunae. During the nineteenth century, homosexual male prostitution remained unspoken because it was regarded as falling beneath the criminal rubric of homosexuality. On this history, see John Scott, "A Prostitute's Progress: Male Prostitution in Scientific Discourse," *Social Semiotics* 13, no. 2 (2003): 179–201.

64. *L'Estaffette*, 11 July 1887.

65. Alfred Delvau, *Dictionnaire érotique moderne, par un professeur de langue verte* (Basel: Karl Schmidt, 1850), 206.

66. *L'Estafette*, 13 July 1887.

67. *L'Estafette*, 13 July 1887.

68. Philip G. Nord, *The Politics of Resentment: Shopkeeper Protest in Nineteenth-Century Paris* (New Brunswick, NJ: Transaction, 1986), 279, 453.

69. Recently, scholarship on the gigolo in the developing world has preferred terms such as *romance entrepreneur*, which diminishes the cultural baggage of *gigolo* even as it evokes sexual-economic ties between Western female tourists and male sex workers in the developing world. See Joan van Wijk, "Romance Tourism on Ambergris Caye, Belize: The Entanglement of Love and Prostitution," *Etnofoor* 19, no. 1 (2006): 71–89. For a discussion of the transnational, postcolonial gigolo drawn toward France by sexual ties, see the discussion of Simon Njami's *African Gigolo* in Bennetta Jules-Rosette, "Identity Discourses and Diasporic Aesthetics in Black Paris: Community Formation and the Translation of Culture," *Diaspora* 9, no. 1 (2000): 39–58.

70. *Gil Blas*, 25 April 1900.

71. It is telling in this regard that this usage of *draguer* dates only to the 1960s. See Jean Claude Bologne, *L'invention de la drague: une histoire de la conquete amoureuse* (Paris: Seuil, 2007), 8–10.

72. *La Lanterne*, 5 April 1887.

73. Grison, *Le procès Pranzini*, 18.

74. Grison, *Le procès Pranzini*, 18.

75. Fabienne Costas-Rosaz, *Histoire du flirt: les jeux de l'innocence et de la perversité, 1870–1968* (Paris: Bernard Grasset, 2000), 24, 100.

76. *Le Correspondant*, 108 (1887: 364.

77. *Le Gaulois*, 17 July 1887.

78. Corbin, *L'histoire de la virilité*, 8.

79. *Le Figaro*, 5 September 1887. Edward Said analyzed this stereotypical vision

of Oriental men. See Edward Said, *Orientalism* (New York: Random House, 1978), 138, 182.

80. Archives de Paris, D2 U8 223.

81. Bataille, *Causes criminelles*, 136. *Le Gaulois*, 17 July 1887.

82. Delvau, *Dictionnaire érotique moderne*, 18–19.

83. Paul Brouardel, *Affaire Pranzini: triple assassinat* (Paris: Baillière, 1887), 6.

84. *L'Illustration*, 16 July 1887.

85. Grison, *Le procès Pranzini*, 184.

86. Archives de Paris, D2 U8 223.

87. *Le Petit Parisien*, 24 March 1887.

88. Archives de Paris, D2 U8 223. *Le Matin*, 10 April 1887. *Le Petit Parisien*, 4 April 1887.

89. Archives de Paris, D2 U8 223.

90. *Journal des Débats*, 10 July 1887.

91. One journalist spanned these extremes, estimating Sabatier's age at about 50, adding that she looked more like 40. *La Justice*, 13 July 1887.

92. Listening to Sabatier at trial, Grison, who was otherwise eager to call attention to an accent, called her "articulate."

93. *Le Figaro*, 19 July 1887.

94. *Le Figaro*, 13 July 1887.

95. *La Lanterne*, 5 April 1887.

96. *Le Radical*, 24 March 1887.

97. *Le Petit Parisien*, 4 April 1887 and 9 July 1887. The sources disagree on this point. It seems that Percheron may have given Sabatier a leave of absence of indefinite duration. Later in the summer, Percheron came to Sabatier's aid, so it would seem that they remained on good terms. Sabatier later said that Percheron's "kindness . . . was always precious to me" (*L'Oued-Sahel: Journal Politique, Littéraire, Commercial et Agricole*, 21 August 1887).

98. Joan W. Scott, "Gender as a Useful Category of Analysis," *American Historical Review* 91, no. 5 (1986): 1054.

99. On the New Woman and the controversies she provoked, see Mary Louise Roberts, *Disruptive Acts: The New Woman in Fin-de-Siècle France* (Chicago: University of Chicago Press, 2002).

100. *Gil Blas*, 11 July 1890.

101. Much has been said about the crisis of masculinity during this period. The theme of manhood in jeopardy is a leitmotif in the period's politics and literature, says Gerald Izenberg in his illuminating discussion of the relevant scholarship. See Gerald Izenberg, *Modernism and Masculinity: Mann, Wedekind, Kandinsky Through World War I* (Chicago: University of Chicago Press, 2000), 2.

102. *Le Figaro*, 15 March 1887.

103. Robert A. Nye, "Sexuality, Sex Difference, and the Cult of Modern Love in the French Third Republic," *Historical Reflections/Réflexions Historiques* 20, no. 1 (1994): 68.

104. *Le Figaro*, 13 July 1887.

105. *La Lanterne*, 5 April 1887. This baseless rumor was likely a twist on the police discovery that Pranzini had purchased a bearded disguise for a masked ball on Mid-Lent.

106. This description is based on an artist's sketch, published in *La Lanterne*, 15 July 1887.

107. Grison, *Le procès Pranzini*, 187.

108. Grison, *Le procès Pranzini*, 187.

109. Grison, *Le procès Pranzini*, 188.

110. Grison, *Le procès Pranzini*, 189–90.

111. Quotes in the preceding paragraphs are from Grison, *Le procès Pranzini*, 190–92.

112. *Le Figaro*, 13 July 1887.

113. Grison, *Le procès Pranzini*, 193.

114. Grison, *Le procès Pranzini*, 198.

115. Grison, *Le procès Pranzini*, 202.

116. Grison, *Le procès Pranzini*, 209.

117. Grison, *Le procès Pranzini*, 210.

118. C.-E. Curinier, ed., *Dictionnaire national des contemporains* (Paris: Office général d'édition, 1899–1919), 4: 22.

119. "Ceux qui s'en vont: me demange," *Les Annales Politiques et Littéraires: Revue Populaire Paraissat le Dimanche* (22 February 1925).

120. Grison, *Le procès Pranzini*, 276.

121. Grison, *Le procès Pranzini*, 276.

122. Grison, *Le procès Pranzini*, 277.

123. Grison, *Le procès Pranzini*, 280.

124. The decadent writer Jean Lorrain was the first to fictionalize this woman in a novella, *The Unknown Lady* (1891), a story that describes Pranzini's unknown upper-class lover as "a nymphomaniac with a lesion of the brain, with complicated and bizarre appetites." Jean Lorrain, *The Unknown Lady*, in Asti Hustvedt, trans. and ed., *The Decadent Reader* (New York: Zone, 1998), 906.

125. Grison, *Le procès Pranzini*, 281.

126. Grison, *Le procès Pranzini*, 282.

127. *Le Gaulois*, 25 March 1887.

128. Grison, *Le procès Pranzini*, 298.

129. L. Mariage, *Manuel du président d'assises* (Paris: Marchal, Billard, 1884), 69.

130. *Le Figaro*, 14 July 1887.

131. Paul Mougeolle, *Le règne des vieux* (Paris: Albert Savine, 1890), 239–40; emphasis in original.

132. *La Revue Britannique*, 63rd année, 4: 266.

133. *The Standard*, 14 July 1887.

134. *New York Times*, 8 August 1887.

135. Grison, *Le procès Pranzini*, 299–301.

Notes to Chapter Eight

1. Quoted in François Goron, *Les mémoires de M. Goron* (Paris: Flammarion, 1897), 2: 178.

2. Goron, *Mémoires*, 2: 130.

3. *Le Petit Parisien*, 14 August 1887.

4. *Le Petit Parisien*, 14 August 1887.

5. Gabrielle Houbre, *Le livre des courtisanes: archives secrètes de la police des moeurs (1861–1876)* (Paris: Tallandier, 2006), 171, 475, 578n. Historians have judged Wilson harshly, seeing him as a symbol of the graft that pervaded the halls of government during these years. Jean-Yves Mollier, *Le scandale de Panama* (Paris: Fayard, 1991), 260. *Contemporary Review* (London), 53 (February 1888): 307.

6. *Le Petit Parisien*, 14 August 1887.

7. *Le Gaulois*, 26 August 1887.

8. *Le Petit Parisien*, 14 August 1887.

9. *L'Oued-Sahel: Journal Politique, Littéraire, Commercial et Agricole*, 21 August 1887.

10. *Le Petit Parisien*, 14 August 1887.

11. *Le Petit Parisien*, 14 August 1887.

12. *Gil Blas*, 28 August 1887.

13. *Le Gaulois*, 13 August 1887.

14. Michel Foucault, *Discipline and Punish: The Birth of the Prison*, trans. Alan Sheridan (New York: Vintage, 1995), 13–14.

15. *Journal Officiel de la République Française*, Chambre des députés, annexe 1265, séance du 20 mars 1879, published 3 April 1879, p. 2868. Lepère (Edme-Charles-Philippe), Le Royer (Philippe-Elie), *Projet de loi sur les exécutions capitales, présenté, au nom de M. Jules Grévy (20 mars 1879)* (Versailles: Cerf et fils, 1883). Grévy made it clear that he was not proposing clandestine executions. Rather, he wanted to admit about twenty "delegates" from the press to transmit the news across France. It was an absurdly low figure, given the long-standing popularity of the public execution as a moment of public celebration. In Paris, where the number of registered newspapers, magazines, and other periodicals came to about 700, Grévy's bill had no chance, and it fizzled accordingly.

16. *Gil Blas*, 18 July 1887.

17. Jean-Marie Lazare Caubet, *Souvenirs, 1860–1889* (Paris: L. Cerf, 1893), 204. Caubet was the director of the Municipal Police from about 1879 until his retirement in 1889.

18. In the middle of the night, police encircled several hundred individuals who were shouting from the prison walls for Pranzini's head. Of the 127 arrested, only 8 were released in the ensuing 48 hours. *The Standard*, 29 August 1887. Caubet, *Souvenirs*, 208.

19. Caubet, *Souvenirs*, 206.

20. *The Standard*, 27 August 1887.

21. Fernand Xau, writing in *Gil Blas*, 26 August 1887.

22. On this story's unfolding, see *La Lanterne*, 2 August 1887; and *Le Temps*, 29 and 30 July 1887.

23. Caubet, *Souvenirs*, 209.

24. *Gil Blas*, 1 November 1887.

25. The police put Romanoff in a cell with two "sheep," whose job it was to establish trust and get Romanoff talking. *La Nation*, 31 January 1888. Romanoff had been held in Mazas Prison for four months by this time. He had been arrested when a letter signed in his name was found at the residence of a man accused of being a member of a criminal gang.

26. Archives de la Préfecture de Police de Paris, BA 83.

27. G. Macé, *Mon musée criminel* (Paris: Charpentier, 1890), 210.

28. Fernand Xau, writing in *Gil Blas*, 26 August 1887. *Le Petit Parisien*, 2 September 1887.

29. Goron, *Mémoires*, 1: 168. Georges Grison, *Souvenirs de la place de la Roquette* (Paris: Dentu, 1883), 2.

30. *Le correspondant: revue mensuelle—religion, philosophie, politique* (Paris: Waille, 1887), 949.

31. *Gil Blas*, 28 August 1887; *The Standard*, 29 August 1887.

32. *The Standard*, 29 August 1887.

33. L'Abbé Faure, *Au pied de l'échafaud: souvenirs de la Roquette* (Paris: Maurice Dreyfous, 1896), 137.

34. "Pranzini: Execution . . . ," *Le Petit Parisien*, 2 September 1887.

35. *Le Petit Parisien*, 2 September 1887.

36. *Le Petit Parisien*, 2 September 1887.

37. Grison, *Souvenirs*, 316.

38. For the Deibler family history, see Anatole Deibler, *Carnets d'exécutions, 1885–1939*, ed. Gérard A. Jaeger (Montréal: L'Archipel, 2004).

39. *Le Petit Parisien*, 2 September 1887.

40. Archives de la Préfecture de la Police de Paris, BA 887. *Le Petit Parisien*, 2 September 1887.

41. On the origins and importance of Dr. Paul Broca's organization for the study of physical anthropology and its role in the development of racial science, see Alice L. Conklin, *In the Museum of Man: Race, Anthropology, and Empire in France, 1850–1950* (Ithaca, NY: Cornell University Press, 2013), ch. 1.

42. Sir Francis Bond Head, *A Faggot of French Sticks* (London: Murray, 1852), 1: 130.

43. The collection of specimens—human and animal anatomy as well as ancient art and architecture—was a crucial element of French imperial culture beginning in the 1790s. André Thouin, a contemporary horticulturist and denizen of the Jardin des Plantes, hoped that the "magnificent spectacle of the power of nature" would be democratically accessible to "all citizens of this grand Empire." At the same time, the "art of collecting" objects from around the world was, as cultural historian Paula Young Lee has argued, "transformed into an act of war." The backstory of colonial

conquest was integral to the crowds' appreciation of the objects that were set out for viewing in public exhibitions; the objects were always also material evidence "of military dominance and, by extension, of national superiority." Paula Young Lee, "The Musaeum of Alexandria and the Formation of the Muséum in Eighteenth-Century France," *Art Bulletin* 79, no. 3 (1997): 408, 410. For a longer, more geographically and chronologically expansive exploration of this argument, see Maya Jasanoff, *Edge of Empire: Lives, Culture, and Conquest in the East, 1750–1850* (New York: Vintage, 2005).

44. Historians are beginning to explore the possibilities of this kind of research on remains unearthed in archaeological digs. See Robin Fleming, "Writing Biography at the Edge of History," *American Historical Review* 114, no. 3 (2009): 606–14.

45. The May 2014 sale at auction of the skull of John Parker, a robber hanged in Gloucester in 1813 whose remains were used for anatomical study, prompted a researcher in Britain to object that such a sale—bidding for the skull reached £2,000—was "disturbing for a number of reasons, and it should raise ethical concerns among those who sell, buy, and curate the body parts of people who have been executed." Shane McCorristine, "The Dark Value of Criminal Bodies: Context, Consent, and the Disturbing Sale of John Parker's Skull," *Journal of Conservation and Museum Studies* 13, no. 1 (2015): 1.

46. Susanne Regener has discussed the trophyization of objects in contemporary criminological museums. See Susanne Regener, "Criminological Museums and the Visualization of Evil," *Crime, Histoire et Sociétés/Crime, History, and Societies* 7, no. 1 (2003): 43–56.

47. See Myra Giesen and Liz White, "International Perspectives Towards Human Remains Curation," in Myra Giesen, ed., *Curating Human Remains: Caring for the Dead in the United Kingdom* (Woodbridge, UK: Boydell Press, 2013), 13–24.

48. Debarati Sanyal, *The Violence of Modernity: Baudelaire, Irony, and the Politics of Form* (Baltimore: Johns Hopkins University Press, 2006), 118. See also Sander L. Gilman, *Difference and Pathology: Stereotypes of Sexuality, Race, and Madness* (Ithaca, NY: Cornell University Press, 1985), 214–15.

49. A diplomatic controversy began when South African president Nelson Mandela formally requested the removal of Baartman's remains from the Museum of Man and their repatriation. In the ensuing debate, Mennecier took a public position against their relinquishment. An assistant curator at the Museum of Man at the time, he argued that science may yet find an interest in Baartman's anatomy, telling a London newspaper that "for us she remains a very important treasure." In response, the historian Sadiah Qureshi criticized Mennecier and reminded readers that Baartman was but one example of the African women whose bodies were used as "taxidermic material, their skins stripped and stuffed to preserve them as specimens of the anomalous." Keeping Baartman in the Museum of Man, Qureshi argued, was tantamount to "continuing to legitimate her putative value as an artefact." Sadiah Qureshi, "Displaying Sara Baartman, the 'Hottentot Venus,'" *History of Science* 42 (2004): 246, 247.

50. *La Justice*, 1 September 1887.

51. *Le Figaro*, 17 September 1887.

52. *Le Figaro*, 14 September 1887.

53. *Gazette Anecdotique, Littéraire, Artistique et Bibliographique* 18 (30 September 1887): 186–87.

54. Léon Millot, "La peau de Pranzini," *La Justice*, 22 September 1887.

55. *Le Gaulois*, 25 September 1887; emphasis in original.

56. Alphonse Daudet, *The Support of the Family*, in Alphonse Daudet, *The Works of Alphonse Daudet*, trans. G. B. Ives (New York: Little, Brown, 1900), 159.

57. Max Nordau, *Dégénérescence*, trans. Auguste Dietrich (Paris: Alcan, 1896), 1: 8.

58. This was the society journalist Henry Fouquier's opinion. *Le XIXe Siècle*, 24 September 1887.

59. Foucault, *Discipline and Punish*, 13.

60. David Garland, "The Problem of the Body in Modern State Punishment," *Social Research* 78, no. 3 (2011): 768.

61. *Le Petit Parisien*, 2 September 1887.

62. Margaret M. Lock and Judith Farquhar, "Colonized Bodies, or Analyzing the Materiality of Domination," in Margaret M. Lock and Judith Farquhar, eds., *Beyond the Body Proper: Reading the Anthropology of Material Life* (Durham, NC: Duke University Press, 2007), 307.

63. *Le Petit Parisien*, 2 September 1887.

64. *La Lanterne*, 2 September 1887.

65. *Le Petit Parisien*, 2 September 1887.

66. Hugues Le Roux, *L'enfer parisien* (Paris: Victor-Havard, 1888), 378.

67. Gustave Variot, "Constatations faites sur le cadavre d'un supplicié," *Bulletin Médical* 1, no. 54 (1887): 856.

68. Eugène Demolder, "Le surmâle," *L'Art Moderne* 22, no. 8 (13 July 1902): 235–36.

69. Pranzini's skull, along with a plaster cast of his severed head, was originally preserved in the Musée de la Société d'Anthropologie in Paris. Numerous scientific studies were published on Pranzini's remains, some of which were exhibited at the 1889 Exposition universelle; the plaster cast is today displayed in the Musée de la Préfecture de Police in Paris. Most of Pranzini's skeletal remains (including leg bones and spine) are still available for scholarly consultation at the Collections d'anthropologie of the Musée de l'Homme.

70. *La Croix*, 23 and 25 September 1887.

71. Albert Wolff, "Solution," *Le Figaro*, 24 September 1887.

72. Gustave Rossignol, *Mémoires de Rossignol, ex-inspecteur principal de la sûreté*, 6th ed. (Paris: Société d'éditeurs littéraires et artistiques, 1900), 263.

73. Goron, *Mémoires*, 244.

74. *Le Siècle*, 24 September 1887.

75. *Le Figaro*, 23 September 1887.

76. *La Croix*, 23 and 25 September 1887.

77. Laurence Guignard has asked whether scientific research in this period was not, to some extent, also a respectable reworking of "popular practices, [and] of the taste for relics." Laurence Guignard, "Les suppliciés au XIXe siecle," in Michel Porret, ed., *Le Corps violenté: du geste à la parole* (Geneva: Droz, 1998), 175–76.

78. A fair amount of research has been conducted on these topics in the French context. See, for example, Régis Bertrand and Anne Carol, eds., *L'exécution capitale: une mort donnée en spectacle, XVIe–XXe siècles* (Aix-en-Provence: Publications de l'Université de Provence, 2003); and Sylvie Châles-Courtine, "La place du corps dans la médiatisation des affaires criminelles," *Sociétés et Représentations* 18 (2004): 171–90.

79. The skin of executed criminals was occasionally removed during the medical examination and used in the binding of books. Régis Bertrand, "Que faire des restes des exécutés?" in Régis Bertrand and Anne Carol, *L'exécution capitale: une mort donnée en spectacle, XVIe–XXe siècles* (Aix-en-Provence: Publications de l'Université de Provence, 2003), 51.

80. Troppmann's blood was collected upon his death in 1870. Michelle Perrot, "Fait divers et histoire au XIXe siècle," *Annales: Histoire, Sciences Sociales* 38, no. 4 (1983): 916. There was probably also a good deal more chicanery on the part of the medical students and researchers charged with criminal cadavers. Following the skin affair, Paul Belon and Georges Price interviewed one of the medical staff and found that, "like old soldiers who recall their campaigns," they spoke of this kind of mischief as a commonplace. Paul Belon and Georges Price, *Paris qui passe* (Paris: Savine, 1888), 278, 280.

81. This is how the matter came to the attention of Adolphe Guillot. Adolphe Guillot, *Les prisons de Paris et les prisonniers: Paris qui souffre* (Paris: Dentu, 1889), 63.

82. *Le XIXe Siècle*, 23 September 1887.

83. *Le XIXe Siècle*, 23 September 1887. Rossignol left the military in 1875, according to the article, and was said to have participated in 1,200 arrests in his 12 years on the force before the skin affair.

84. Maurice Barrès, *L'appel au soldat* (Paris: E. Fasquelle, 1900), 97.

85. Adrien Dansette, *L'affaire Wilson et la chute du président Grévy* (Paris: Perrin, 1936). In his otherwise informative article on the Wilson affair, Michael Palmer seems unsure as to whether the skinning in fact occurred. "The silly season continued, however, with reports that the deputy chief of the Sûreté had made a card holder out of the skin of the murdered [sic] Pranzini," writes Palmer, who also refers to Goron's "alleged penchant for card holders made of human skin." Michael Palmer, "Daniel Wilson and the Decorations Scandal of 1887," *Modern and Contemporary France* 1, no. 2 (1993): 145. Other historians do not mention the skin affair at all in connection with the Wilson affair.

86. Goron, *Mémoires*, 1: 287.

87. A. Édouard Portalis, *Guet-apens judiciaire, mémoire d'un condamné par défaut, à l'opinion, à la presse, à ses juges* (Paris: Savine, 1896), 197.

88. There is consensus among historians that the exposés in *Le XIXe Siècle* were the catalyst for the criminal proceedings against Wilson.

89. Letter from Daniel Wilson to Alice Wilson, 11 October 1887, translated and quoted in Palmer, "Daniel Wilson," 146.

90. Gustave Variot, "Remarques sur l'autopsie et la conformation organique du supplicié Pranzini et sur le tannage de la peau humaine: séance du 2 mai 1929," *Bulletin et Mémoires de la Société d'Anthropologie de Paris*, ser. 7, 10 (1929): 44.

91. The skin affair was, according to one newspaper, Taylor's "first" stroke of genius. *Le Gaulois*, 20 January 1908.

92. Detective Rossignol professed to be "very upset" about Taylor's departure and acknowledged that the skin affair was the reason for it. Rossignol, *Mémoires*, 263.

93. Portalis, *Guet-apens judiciaire*, 197.

94. Goron, *Mémoires*, 2: 185, 245.

95. "La Dispute du cadavre," *Le Petit Parisien*, 2 January 1889.

96. François Goron, "Prado," report of 28 December 1888, Archives de la Préfecture de Police, BA 82; *Gil Blas*, 30 December 1888.

97. Goron, *Mémoires*, 2: 244–45.

98. This did not keep artists from exploring the gory aesthetics of the death penalty, as they always had. Goron did not attend Pranzini's execution, but he made sure to see Prado's. Had he heard the rumor of Pranzini's skull being transformed into a punch bowl? Paul Gauguin's *Jug in the Form of a Head, Self-Portrait* (1889), now in the collections of the Danish Museum of Art and Design, is a glazed ceramic piece with streaks of blood bearing Gauguin's own likeness.

Notes to Conclusion

1. "Personnages," *L'Argent*, 378–79, Archives Nationales, Fonds Zola, NAF 10346.

2. For more on this point, see Marc Silberman, Karen E. Till, and Janet Ward, "Introduction: Walls, Borders, Boundaries," in Marc Silberman, Karen E. Till, and Janet Ward, eds., *Walls, Borders, Boundaries: Spatial and Cultural Practices in Europe* (New York: Berghahn, 2012): 1–22.

3. Michael B. Miller, *Shanghai on the Metro: Spies, Intrigue, and the French Between the Wars* (Berkeley: University of California Press, 1994).

4. Wolfgang Schivelbusch, *The Culture of Defeat: On National Trauma, Mourning, and Recovery*, trans. Jefferson Chase (New York: Metropolitan Books, 2003), 180–82.

5. Jean-Pierre Biondi, *Les anticolonialistes (1881–1962)* (Paris: Laffont, 1992), 26.

6. Joseph Reinach, *Pages républicaines* (Paris: Altan, 1894), 17. For a pithy analysis of the relationship between the colonial debate and the pursuit of revanche in Alsace-Lorraine, see Schivelbusch, *Culture of Defeat*, 180–82.

7. Félix Platel, *L'armée du crime* (Paris: Victor-Havard, 1890), 162.

8. Robert A. Nye, *Crime, Madness, and Politics in Modern France: The Medical Concept of National Decline* (Princeton, NJ: Princeton University Press, 1984), 83.

9. Philip Darby, *The Fiction of Imperialism* (London: A & C Black, 1998), 56.

10. J. A. Hobson, *Imperialism: A Study* (New York: James Pott, 1902).

11. Gabriel Tarde, *La philosophie pénale* (Paris: Masson, 1890), 424–25. Rival crime theorist Armand Corre's major research work can be read either as a rebuke to Tarde's arguments about crime and empire or as an affirmation of them. Corre, a colleague of Alexandre Lacassagne's at Lyon and a hard-liner on criminal punishment, went on to observe how the civilizing mission had affected crime rates in the French colonies. His "criminal ethnography" was based on crime records and anecdotes from a "group of very diverse races." Rather than lowering crime rates, though, Corre found that the presence of the French had been a blight on them. France's foreign conquests were a *cause* of rising crime rates in its colonies, according to Corre's research. The situation was so bleak that it led Corre to a rather severe judgment of colonialism in general: "The history of all conquests and colonizations [is the] occupation by brutal force or aided by hypocritical and cowardly ruse; immoral work, it is criminal from the view of human law [*droit humain*]." By posing as "the colonizer, the civilizer, and the protector," he continued, an imperial occupier such as France is "nothing other than a parasite." *Every colonial history was a crime story.* Empire was bad penal policy. Armand Corre, *L'ethnographie criminelle d'après les observations et les statistiques judiciaires recueillies dans les colonies françaises* (Paris: C. Reinwald, 1894), vi, 2, 3.

12. Kate Marsh, "Introduction: Territorial Loss and the Construction of French Colonial Identities," in Kate Marsh and Nicola Firth, eds., *France's Lost Empires: Fragmentation, Nostalgia, and la Fracture Coloniale* (Lanham, MD: Lexington, 2010), 4.

13. Archives Gabriel Tarde, GTA 12.

14. An edited version of these reflections appeared later in Tarde, *La philosophie pénale*, 224.

15. Henry Houssaye, "La France en 1814," *Revue des Deux Mondes* 57 (15 October 1887): 788–820.

16. A great many books have dealt with this crisis in European culture and politics, arguably none better than Carl E. Schorske, *Fin-de-Siècle Vienna* (New York: Random House, 1979).

17. *Journal Officiel de la République Française*, Débats parlementaires, Chambre, 18 June 1885.

18. L. Améline, *Le port d'armes et le droit pénal* (Paris: Laval, 1919), 24.

19. Gérard Noiriel, *Immigration, antisémitisme et racisme en France* (Paris: Fayard, 2007), 162.

20. Gérard Noiriel, *The French Melting Pot: Immigration, Citizenship, and National Identity*, trans. Geoffroy De Laforcade (Minneapolis: University of Minnesota Press, 1996), 58–59. The *décret* was confirmed by the Law of 8 August 1893, "relative to the right of foreigners to stay in France, and to the protection of French labor" [*relative au séjour des étrangers en France et à la protection du travail national*]. On the creation of modern immigration control in the twentieth century, see Clifford Rosenberg, *Policing Paris: The Origins of Modern Immigration Control Between the Wars* (Ithaca, NY: Cornell University Press, 2006).

21. "Chambre des députés, quatrième législature, session de 1888: Annexe au procès-verbal de la séance du 2 février 1888," p. 5, Archives Nationales, F7 12839, no. 2, "Étrangers en France."

22. E. W. Hornung, *The Collected Raffles Stories* (Oxford: Oxford University Press, 1996); Pierre Souvestre and Marcel Allain, *Fantômas: édition intégrale*, ed. Loïc Artiaga and Matthieu Letourneux (Paris: Laffont, 2013).

23. I rely here on Robin Walz's discussion of *Fantômas* in Robin Walz, *Pulp Surrealism: Insolent Popular Culture in Early Twentieth-Century Paris* (Berkeley: University of California Press, 2000), 43–67.

24. Arthur Conan Doyle, *The New Annotated Sherlock Holmes*, ed. Leslie Klinger (New York: Norton, 2005). My analysis here is indebted to Joseph McLaughlin and Yumna Siddiqi for their work on British literature and empire in the late nineteenth century. See Joseph McLaughlin, *Writing the Urban Jungle: Reading Empire in London from Doyle to Eliot* (Charlottesville: University of Virginia Press, 2000); and Yumna Siddiqi, "The Cesspool of Empire: Sherlock Holmes and the Return of the Repressed," *Victorian Literature and Culture* 34, no. 1 (2006): 233–47.

25. Antonin Proust, "Paris et les étrangers," in *Les types de Paris* (Paris: Plon, 1889), 41.

26. Émile Zola, *L'argent* (serialized in 1890, published in volume form in 1891) (Paris: Flammarion, 2009).

Acknowledgments

It is a pleasure to acknowledge the help of individuals and institutions without whom this book would not have been possible. Research funding was provided by grants and fellowships from the Institute of European Studies at the University of California, Berkeley, Princeton University's Council of the Humanities, and the City University of New York (CUNY). CUNY's Faculty Fellowship Publication Program also provided time and a forum in which to discuss my writing with colleagues.

In writing their stories, historians rely a lot on archivists and librarians, who make sources easier to find and readily available. I wish to recognize the professionals and research assistants at the New York Public Library, the City University of New York's library system, Firestone Library at Princeton University, Bobst Library at New York University, Butler Library at Columbia University, the Bibliothèque Nationale de France, the Bibliothèque historique de la ville de Paris, the Archives de la Préfecture de Police de Paris, the Archives Nationales, the Archives de Paris, the British Library, and the British Archives at Kew. Thanks also to Nicolas L'Hermitte for helping me find regional issues of contemporary French newspapers.

For their feedback on the manuscript, I thank the anonymous peer reviewers at Stanford University Press. I have been fortunate to have responsive editors at Stanford. I am indebted to Kate Wahl, Nora Spiegel, and Anne Fuzellier and to my copyeditor, Mimi Braverman.

I am grateful to friends, mentors, and colleagues who read various portions of the manuscript over the past several years: Tyler Stovall, Stéphane Bouquet, John Merriman, Peter Connolly-Smith, Virginia Sanchez Korrol, and the members of my cohort in the FFPP program at CUNY.

Dominique Kalifa has been generous with his knowledge on an array of topics that are central to this book. Just as his published work serves as a foundation for the study of the cultural history of nineteenth-century France, so have his seminars been a welcoming and stimulating forum for expat graduate students. Dominique co-edited, with Jann Matlock, an issue of the journal *Sociétés et Représentations* that allowed me to introduce some of this book's claims to a French audience; Jann's attentive readings during that period were truly invaluable. The journal issue itself was dedicated to the memory of Susanna Barrows, my beloved thesis adviser at Berkeley. I also received early counsel from Allan Pred, a much missed urban geographer at Berkeley.

Here in New York, Peter Vellon has been a great interlocutor on matters pertaining to race and Italian migration. Frank Warren, Joel Allen, and Elena Frangakis-Syrett have guided me through the publication process, among other things. Special thanks to Matt Corcoran for being a supportive friend and reader at all hours, and to Raf Allison for his encouragement during our Friday lunches. Alex Kadrie has provided advice, dazzling meals, and brilliant conversation for years now; he is family *and* friend.

My deepest gratitude goes to Cécile, Amara, and Sienna. This book is dedicated to them.

Index